GW00836599

Yours faithfully
John A. Macdonald,

Ex-Captain 43rd Battalion (Ottawa and Carleton Rifles).

TROUBLOUS TIMES IN CANADA

A HISTORY OF

THE FENIAN RAIDS

OF 1866 AND 1870

BY

CAPT. JOHN A. MACDONALD

(A Veteran of 1866 and 1870)

The Naval & Military Press Ltd

Published by

The Naval & Military Press Ltd
Unit 10 Ridgewood Industrial Park,
Uckfield, East Sussex,
TN22 5QE England

Tel: +44 (0) 1825 749494
Fax: +44 (0) 1825 765701

www.naval–military-press.com
www.military-genealogy.com
www.militarymaproom.com

To my Old Comrades of 1866 and 1870.
this Book is respectfully Dedicated.

Printed and bound by CPI Group (UK) Ltd, Croydon, CR0 4YY

*In reprinting in facsimile from the original, any imperfections are inevitably reproduced
and the quality may fall short of modern type and cartographic standards.*

Troublous Times in Canada.

TABLE OF CONTENTS.

Fenian Raid of 1870

Appendix

PREFACE.

One of the most dangerous and critical periods in the history of Canada was that which closely followed the termination of the Civil War between the Northern and Southern States of America in the year 1865. It is a strange fact that Canadian authors and historians do not seem to have fully realized the gravity of the situation that then existed, as the event has been passed over by them with the barest possible mention. Thus the people of the present generation know very little of the Fenian troubles of 1866 and 1870, and the great mass of the young Canadian boys and girls who are being educated in our Public Schools and Colleges are in total ignorance of the grave danger which cast dark shadows over this fair and prosperous Dominion in those stormy days. It was a period of great peril to this rising young Nation of the North, which might possibly have ended in the severance of Canada from British dominion. But happily this was prevented by the prompt measures that were taken to defend our soil, and the quick response that was made by the resolute Canadian Volunteers when the bugles sounded the call to assemble for active service on our frontiers.

The fierce conflict which had been waged in the United States of America for four long years between the North and the South was terminated by the subjugation of the latter in the spring of 1865, and the tattered battle flags of the Confederate forces were furled forever. Over a million of men, veteran soldiers of both armies, were still in the field when the Civil War ended, and when these mighty forces were disbanded, hundreds of thousands of trained warriors were thrown upon their own resources, without occupation or employment. While the majority of these soldiers quickly resumed their old business or farming pursuits, yet there remained idle a vast number of turbulent and restless spirits who were ready and willing to embark in any fillibustering expedition that might present itself. These men were all trained and seasoned veterans of both the Union and Confederate armies—soldiers who were inured to the hardships and rigors of many campaigns and fierce battles, and thousands of them readily enrolled themselves under the Fenian banners in anticipation of a war being inaugurated against the British nation, with the invasion of Canada as the first step.

The defence of our extensive Canadian frontier depended mainly upon the volunteer militia force of the scattered Provinces, and to their patriotism and gallantry in springing to arms when their services were needed to defend their native land, may be ascribed the glory of frustrating the attempts of the Fenian invaders to establish themselves on Canadian soil. True, there were some British regular troops on duty in Canada in 1866 around which to rally, and they did their duty nobly, but in the operations on the Niagara frontier especially, it was the Canadian volunteers who bore the brunt of battle, and by their devotion to duty, courage and bravery under hostile fire, succeeded in causing the hasty retirement of the Fenian invaders from our shores, and again, as in days of yore, preserved Canada to the Empire, as one of the brightest jewels in the British Crown.

Having personally seen active service on the Niagara frontier during both of the Fenian Raids of 1866 and 1870, and retaining vivid recollections of the situation of affairs at the front during these two campaigns, I will endeavor in the succeeding chapters of this book to give the reader a faithful account of what occurred on these stirring occasions. I have not relied on memory alone to present these facts, but have corroborated my personal knowledge by reference to official records, and reports of officers, which may be found in the archives of the Militia Department at Ottawa, and the Ontario Bureau of Archives at Toronto.

I have endeavored to fully cover the subject, and put on record the splendid service which our gallant volunteers rendered to their country in 1866 and 1870. Hoping that the reader will find these pages interesting, and at all times be ready to emulate their example,

I am yours faithfully,

JOHN A. MACDONALD.

41 Macdonell Ave., Toronto, May, 1910.

CHAPTER I.

Unhappy Ireland Seething in Sedition—The Fenian Brotherhood—Hatching the Plot—The Movement of '65—
A Split in the Fenian Camp.

Every student of history is aware that for centuries the
condition of affairs in Ireland has not been altogether happy,
owing largely to the revolutionary schemes which have from
time to time been hatched by so-called "patriots" to "free
Ireland from the yoke of the oppressor," as they termed it in
their appeals to the people to incite rebellion, but more properly speaking to bring about a repeal of the union between
Great Britain and Ireland and establish an Irish nation on Irish
soil. Many brave but misguided men have been led to their
death by joining in such rebellious conspiracies against con-
stitutional government in years gone by, and still the spirit of
discontent and hatred of British rule is kept smouldering, with
occasional outbursts of revolt as succeeding leaders appear on
the scene to inflame the passions of the people.

Of the Irish troubles of earlier years it is not the purpose
of the writer to speak, but rather to deal with events which
occurred immediately prior to and during the period involving
the Fenian invasions of Canada.

For some time previous to the year 1865 the leader of the
revolutionary movement in Ireland was James Stephens. He
was a man of considerable influence among his compatriots,
possessed of good executive ability, and had great capacity for
organization along revolutionary lines. Being an energetic
worker and a forcible speaker, he quickly enlisted the co-
operation of other "patriots" in promoting the establishment
of the Fenian Brotherhood, of which he was chosen the "Head
Centre" for Ireland. This organization spread with such
rapidity throughout Ireland and America that it soon became
one of the most dangerous and formidable revolutionary forces
ever known in the history of any country. Its members were
oath-bound to use every means to bring about the emancipa-

tion of Ireland from the rule of Great Britain, and to encompass the downfall of "the bloody Sassenachs" on every hand. After thoroughly planting the seeds of sedition in Ireland, Head Centre Stephens and his coadjutor General John O'Mahony visited America for the purpose of invoking the aid of their compatriots on this side of the Atlantic. Their idea was to make an attempt to emancipate Ireland by striking a blow for freedom on the soil of the Emerald Isle itself, and if successful to establish their cherished Republic firmly, become recognized as a nation by the different nations of the earth, and thereafter govern their own affairs. On their arrival in the United States the Irish envoys received a most enthusiastic welcome from their countrymen, and receptions were arranged in their honor on their visits to all of the principal cities in the Union. The speeches delivered at these gatherings were of the most fervid and enthusiastic nature, and the hopes of the Irish people rose high in the belief that an Irish Parliament would soon hold a session in Dublin. Money and men were asked for from America by Head Centre Stephens, both of which were freely promised "for the sake of the cause." In due course of time the Irish-Americans contributed over $200,000 in cash, besides an immense quantity of war material, towards making the proposed insurrection a success. Volunteers for active service on Irish soil were numerous, and everything looked rosy for Head Centre Stephens when he left America for Ireland to direct "The Movement of '65." But, alas, his high hopes were doomed to be shattered. The initial steps in the campaign had barely been taken when "dark clouds in the horizon" began to loom up. A small vessel, called the "Erin's Hope," had been dispatched from America with a cargo of rifles, ammunition and other war supplies for the use of the Fenians in Ireland. A company of adventurous patriots were on board to assist their brethren in "the rising," and all were brave and confident of success. They had hoped to run into a secluded bay on the coast of Ireland during the favored hours of night, and land their expedition and supplies. But on arrival at the chosen point the ship was hailed by a British man-of-war and captured without resistance. The officers and crew were consigned to a British dungeon, and the ship and cargo confiscated. A British spy had kept the authorities informed, and the war vessel was at the designated point of landing to gather in the "forlorn hope" of the invaders. Other Irish-Americans who were constantly arriving as passengers by the ocean steamships to take part in the conflict were promptly arrested as they landed on the quays, and the rebellion of 1865 was nipped in the bud. Much dissension and dissatisfaction then arose within the Fenian Councils. A great deal of money had been spent and the attempt had proved a failure. The vigilance of the British authorities was so keen, and arrests so numerous, that the available prisons were soon filled, and the hopeful warriors who so valiantly boasted that they would quickly unfurl the "Sunburst of Erin" on the walls of Dublin Castle were obliged to retire into strict seclusion until an opportunity occurred to be smuggled out of Ireland by their friends and stowed away on ships bound back for America.

The failure of the rising in 1865 caused a serious division among the adherents of the cause in both America and Ireland, and the Fenian Brotherhood was split into two hostile camps thereby. It was considered that Stephens' policy of carrying on the rebellious operations in Ireland was an impossible and suicidal one to the success of the cause. Many Irish-Americans were languishing behind the bars of British prisons, with an uncertain fate awaiting them when they were arraigned for trial, and their comrades in the United States bitterly blamed Stephens and O'Mahony for the fiasco. Consequently the majority in America revolted, and seceded from the Stephens faction, claiming that he had woefully misrepresented the state of affairs that existed in Ireland, both as regarded preparations for a successful issue, and also the enthusiasm that was said to sufficiently dominate the people there to induce them to take up arms when the American contingent arrived.

Col. Wm. R. Roberts, of New York, was the leader of the American secessionists, who declared their belief that "No direct invasion or armed insurrection in Ireland would ever be successful in establishing an Irish Republic upon Irish soil, and placing her once more in her proper place as a nation among the nations of the earth." The forces of Col. Roberts gathered strength daily, and soon usurped control of the Fenian forces in America, much to the chagrin of Stephens and his followers.

Gen. O'Mahony, who Head Centre Stephens had placed in supreme charge of the affairs of the Fenian Brotherhood in America, was charged by Colonel Roberts and his colleagues with having dipped too deep into the treasury and by extravagance and other questionable methods dissipated the funds of the Brotherhood. This widened the breach, and Roberts became the popular idol with the majority of the American Fenians. Yet O'Mahony held on to office with a ragged remnant of his old retainers to support him, until finally Roberts triumphed and became the star around which all of the other Fenian "planets" revolved.

CHAPTER II.

THE FENIAN CONVENTION AT CINCINNATI—THE BIRTH OF THE
IRISH REPUBLIC—"ON TO CANADA!"—GEN. SWEENY'S
PROGRAMME.

The seceders from the Stephens faction met in Convention
in Cincinnati, Ohio, in September, 1865, a very large number
of delegates being present from all of the States in the Union.
After the usual preliminary oratory and the adoption of
several resolutions, the delegates formed themselves into a
body which they termed "the Senate Wing of the Fenian
Brotherhood." They ridiculed the idea of invading Ireland
successfully, and changed their base of operations. "On to
Canada" became their slogan, and the idea was so popular
that they quickly secured the allegiance of thousands of disappointed Irishmen who were anxious and ready to strike a
blow at England in any quarter. In order that there should
be some recognized source from which all orders, proclamations
and edicts could be officially promulgated, it was resolved to
form an Irish Republic (on paper), as the Fenians were without territory until they captured it. This was accomplished by
the adoption of a constitution framed on the model of that
used by the United States. Its provisions included the usual
regulations (both civil and military) for a Republican form
of government, and its unanimous acceptance by the delegates
was received with glad acclaim. Col. Wm. R. Roberts was
chosen as President of the new Republic, and Gen. T. W.
Sweeny (who was then commanding officer of the 16th United
States Infantry) as Secretary of War. The other Cabinet
port-folios were handed out to "lesser lights" in the Fenian
fold.

As even Republican governments cannot be maintained, or
military campaigns conducted without the expenditure of
money, the Irish Republic could prove no exception to the
rule, and therefore the work of collecting funds and gathering
munitions of war for the invasion of Canada was immediately

commenced. Fenian "circles," or lodges, were organized in every possible corner of the United States for the purpose of stirring up the enthusiasm of the Irish people and securing money to purchase arms and ammunition. Military companies and regiments were formed wherever practicable, and drilling and parading was pursued openly during the fall of 1865 and winter of 1866, getting ready for the coming fray.

Funds were raised in various ways—by voluntary subscriptions, by holding picnics, excursions, fairs, bazaars and other methods. But the largest source of revenue was derived by imposing upon the credulity of the sons and daughters of Erin by the sale to them of bonds of the Irish Republic, a chimerical dream which was painted in such glowing colors and presented with such stirring appeals to their patriotism that hard-earned dollars were pulled out from every nook and cranny in many Irish homes to invest in these "securities" and thus help along the cause. The following is a copy of the bond, which will serve to show its wording:—

No........   No........

It is Hereby Certified that

The Irish Republic

is indebted to.........................or bearer in the sum of TEN DOLLARS, redeemable six months after the acknowledgment of THE IRISH NATION, with interest from the date hereof inclusive, at six per cent. per annum, payable on presentation of this Bond at the Treasury of the Irish Republic.

Date.................

[Stamp, Office   JOHN O'NEILL,
of the Treasury.]   Agent for the Irish Republic.

In the light of subsequent events, when the dreams of the visionary enthusiasts have been so rudely dispelled, the sight of one of these bonds must present as much sadness and pathos to the beholder as the vision of an old Confederate bank note does to the erstwhile defenders of the "Lost Cause" of the Southern States.

As the coffers of the Irish Republic began to fill rapidly, the Fenian leaders became more hopeful and bombastic, while enthusiasm among the rank and file continued to be worked up to fever pitch. President Roberts gathered a select coterie about him at his headquarters in New York to assist in upholding his dignity, and incidentally help to boost the cause. Plots and plans of all kinds were hatched against Great Britain, and loud-mouthed orators were kept busy for several months fanning the embers of Irish patriotism into flame.

General Sweeny was very active during the winter of 1865 and 1866 in getting his "War Department" fully organized and his field forces ready for the spring campaign against Canada. His staff was composed of the following officers, all of whom had seen active service in the Civil War:—

Chief of Staff—Brigadier-General C. Carroll Tavish.
Chief of Engineer Corps—Col. John Meehan.
Chief of Ordnance—Col. C. H. Rundell.
Engineer Corps—Lieut.-Col. C. H. Tresiliar.
Assistant Adjutant-General—Major E. J. Courtney.
Ordnance Department—Major M. O'Reilly.
Quartermaster—Major M. H. Van Brunt.
Aide-de-Camps—Capt. D. W. Greely and Capt. Daniel O'Connell.

This galaxy of officers strutted majestically around Headquarters garbed in the gorgeous green and gold uniforms of the Fenian Army, looked wise, and promised all enquirers that important movements would be made in the spring. Secret meetings were held almost daily at Headquarters, when the plan of campaign would be discussed over and over again, and amendments made wherever necessary. Finally the following plan of operations was given out in March, 1866, as the gist of one evolved by the Council, which is said to have embodied Gen. Sweeny's whole strategic programme:—

"Expeditions for the invasion of Canada will rendezvous at Detroit and Rochester, and at Ogdensburg and Plattsburg, and at Portland. The forces assembled at the two first-named points are to operate conjointly against Toronto, Hamilton, and the west of Upper Canada. From Ogdensburg and Plattsburg demonstrations will be made against Montreal, and ultimately Quebec; Kingston will be approached by Cape Vincent, while Portland will be the general place of embarkation for expeditions against the capitals of New Brunswick and Nova Scotia.

THE BASES OF OPERATIONS.

"The Canadian and provincial borders once crossed, bases of operations will be established in the enemy's country, so that international quarrels with the Washington Government may be evaded. There are to be lands chosen at the head of Passamaquoddy Bay, Saint John's, on the Chambly,·close to the foot of Lake Champlain; Prescott, on the Saint Lawrence; Wolfe Island, at the foot of Lake Ontario; Hamilton, Cobourg Goderich, and Windsor, in Upper Canada. These places are all within convenient distances of the United States, and afford by water an easy retreat, as well as cunning receptacles for fresh American levies.

THE FORCES AT THE DISPOSAL OF THE FENIANS.

"The Irish Republic calculates to have, by the first of April, fifteen millions of dollars at its disposal in ready cash. This will give transportation and maintenance for one month to thirty thousand men, a greater number than were ever before mustered to the conquest of the Canadian possessions. Of this force, eight thousand will carry the line of the Grand Trunk road west of Hamilton; five thousand, crossing from Rochester to Cobourg, will be prepared to move either east, in time to act jointly with three thousand men from Wolfe Island, upon Kingston, or to take part with the western detachment in the capture of Toronto. All this, it is believed, will be the work of two weeks. Thus intrenched securely in Upper Canada, holding all the routes of the Grand Trunk, sufficient rolling stock secured to control the main line, the Fenians hope to attract to their colors fifty thousand American Irishmen, and equip a navy on Lakes Huron, Erie and Ontario. The avenues to return so being secured, thirty thousand men, under General Sweeny, will move down the Saint Lawrence, upon Kingston, simultaneously with ten thousand men by the lines of the Chambly, and these will converge upon Montreal; in the meantime isolated expeditions from the rendezvous at Saint Andrews will reduce Saint John and Halifax, these furnishing depots for privateers and ocean men-of-war to intercept British transports and effectually close the Saint Lawrence. Quebec will thus fall by the slow conquest of time; or, if the resources of the garrison should be greater than the patience of the invaders, the same heights which two Irishmen have scaled before, will again give foothold to the columns of the brotherhood.

THE PLAN OF INVASION IN DETAIL.

"At Chicago the Fenians already possess five sailing vessels, a tug. and two steam transports; at Buffalo they are negotiating for vessels; at Bay City, Michigan, and at Cleveland they have other craft in process of refitting; these will simultaneously raise the green flag and stand ready to succor the land forces. Goderich, Sarnia and Windsor will be simultaneously occupied; all the available rolling stock seized, and the main line of the Grand Trunk cut at Grand River, to prevent the passage of cars and locomotives to Hamilton. The geographical configuration of the western half of Upper Canada will permit of a few thousand men holding the entire section of the country between Cobourg and the Georgian Bay. These are connected by a chain of lakes and water courses, and the country affords subsistence for a vast army. Horses sufficient to mount as many cavalry as the Brotherhood can muster, quartermasters' teams in quantity, and a vast amount of lake shipping, will at once be reduced to a grand military department, with Hamilton for the capital, and a loan advertised for. While this is being negotiated, Gen. Sweeny will push rapidly forward on the line of the Grand Trunk, in time to superintend the fall of Montreal, where ocean shipping will be found in great quantity. With the reduction of Montreal a demand will be made upon the United States for a formal recognition of Canada, whose name is to be changed at once to New Ireland. While this is being urged, the green flag will scour all the bays and gulfs in Canada; a Fenian fleet from San Francisco will carry Vancouver and the Fraser River country, to give security to the Pacific squadron, rendezvousing at San Juan, and the rights of belligerents will be enforced from the British Government by prompt retaliation for the cruelties of British courtmartials.

ABILITY OF THE FENIANS TO HOLD CANADA.

"The population of the British provinces is little above two and a half millions, and the military resources of the united provinces fall short of sixty thousand men. Of these nearly ten thousand are of Irish birth or descent. The States will furnish for the subjugation of these, eighty thousand veteran troops. With the single exception of Quebec, it is believed the whole of the British provinces will fall in a single campaign. During the ensuing winter diversions will be put in motion in Ireland, and while it is believed the Brotherhood can defy the Queen's war transports to land an army in the west, arrangements will be developed to equip a powerful navy for aggressive operations on the sea. Before the 1st of June, it is thought, fifty commissioned vessels of war and privateers, carrying three hundred guns, will be afloat, and to maintain these a tremendous moral influence will be exerted upon every Irish-American citizen to contribute the utmost to the general fund for the support of the war.

"By the tempting offer of a surrender of Canada to the United States, Mr. Seward, it is hoped, will wink at connivance between American citizens and the Fenian conquerors, and by another summer it is thought the dominion of the Brotherhood north of the St. Lawrence will be formally acknowledged by the United States, Russia, and each of the American republics. The third year of Irish tenure in Canada will, it is believed, array two of the great powers against Great Britain. John Mitchell, at Paris, will organize the bureau of foreign agents; and Ireland, maintaining a position of perpetual revolt, will engage for her own suppression a considerable part of the regular British levies.

EUROPEAN OPERATIONS.

"At the present time a bureau of operations is being quietly organized in Paris, where the opposition press has already proclaimed for Irish nationality. It is Mr. Mitchell who sees that the funds of the Brotherhood are distributed in Ireland; he also is in correspondence with liberal statesmen in Great Britain, and conducts the disintegration of the British army by touching the loyalty of the Irish troops, who constitute one-third of the Queen's service.

THE CUNARD STEAMERS TO BE SEIZED.

"Among the earliest aggressive operations will be the overhauling of a Cunard steamer between New York and Cape Race, with her usual allotment of specie. In like manner the British lines of steamers proceeding from England to Quebec, Portland, Boston and Halifax, will be arrested and their funds secured.

THE WAR IN IRELAND.

"Military operations in Ireland must, of necessity, be confined to the interior. Three military departments will be organized—the Shannon, the Liffey, and the Foyle—and the campaign will be entirely predatory or guerilla in its conduct. The British Coast Guard stations will fall easy conquests, their number and isolation contributing to their ruin; while from the Wicklow Mountains, through all the rocky fastnesses of Ireland, the cottagers will descend upon the British garrisons, maintaining perpetual and bloody rebellion till the better news comes across the sea or the patience of England is quite worn out."

This was a mighty and stupendous programme truly, but oh how visionary! It embraced the extreme aspirations of the boldest and most sanguinary Fenians, and its publication no doubt served to bring more money into their treasury. But, alas for human hopes, its execution never happened. Yet it fired the hearts of the soldiers of the Irish Republican Army, and they eagerly awaited the summons to march "On to Canada." All through that winter drilling and preparation continued, and the enthusiasm of the men was kept warm by fervid oratory appealing to their patriotism, while they boldly chanted their song :—

> "We are a Fenian Brotherhood, skilled in the arts of war,
> And we're going to fight for Ireland, the land that we adore.
> Many battles we have won, along with the boys in blue,
> And we'll go and capture Canada, for we've nothing else to do."

Meanwhile the Canadian Government deemed it prudent to place troops at some of the exposed points along the border, and on the 15th of November, 1865, the following volunteer corps were called out for Frontier Service, and were stationed at the following places, the whole force being under the command of the Lieutenant-General commanding Her Majesty's Forces in North America :—

At Prescott—The Ottawa Garrison Battery of Artillery; Capt. A. G. Forrest, First Lieutenant W. Duck, and Second Lieutenant Albert Parson.

The Morrisburg Garrison Battery of Artillery; Capt. T. S. Rubidge, First Lieutenant Peter A. Eagleson, and Second Lieutenant G. S. L. Stoddart.

At Niagara—Quebec Rifle Company; Capt. D. Gagnier, Lieut Elzear Garneau, and Ensign Thos. H. A. Roy.

Montreal Rifle Company; Capt. P. J. M. Cinqmars, Lieut. J. O. Labranche, and Ensign G. d'O. d'Orsonnens.

At Sarnia—Toronto Rifle Company; Capt. Wm. D. Jarvis, Lieut. Farquhar Morrison, and Ensign W. C. Campbell.

Woodstock Rifle Company; Capt. Henry B. Beard, Lieut. John Matthewson, and Ensign James Coad.

At Windsor—Hamilton Infantry Company; Capt. Henry E. Irving, Lieut. Robert Grant, and Ensign J. J. Hebden.

London Infantry Company; Capt. Arch. Macpherson, Lieut. Edward W. Griffith, and Ensign George Ellis.

At Sandwich—Port Hope Infantry Company; Capt. A. T. H. Williams, Lieut. James F. McLeod, and Ensign Francis E. Johnson.

Major C. F. Hill, of the First Prince of Wales Regiment (Montreal), was in command of the forces stationed at Sandwich, Windsor and Sarnia. These troops were kept on service for several months, and their presence at the points named and the constant vigilance maintained, had an effect in warning the Fenians that Canada's sons were alive to the duty of the hour, and were resolved to guard and protect their homes and firesides from desecration by invading foes or sacrifice their lives if necessary in performing that sacred duty.

THE BROCKVILLE RIFLES.

While the above detachments were on service at the points named, the danger was equally great at other places, especially along the St. Lawrence frontier. The town of Brockville was particularly exposed to attack, as during the winter months the river is usually frozen over, which would afford the Fenians an easy way of crossing on a solid bridge of ice. At this time the town was exceptionally fortunate in having a most excellent volunteer military corps as one of its most popular local institutions, which was known as the Brockville Rifle Company. This command figured so prominently in the service of the Volunteer Militia Force of Canada in the early days that it deserves special mention in the records of the country.

The Brockville Rifles was one of the first companies organized under the Volunteer Militia Act, being promoted in the spring of 1855 by Capt. Smythe (who was afterward captain of a company in H. M. 100th Regiment, which was raised in Canada in 1857 and 1858 for service in the British Army, and who subsequently became commanding officer of that regiment).

As Brockville and vicinity was first settled in 1783 and 1784 by the U. E. Loyalists (all of whom had borne arms in defence of the British Crown), their descendants have always been noted for their unswerving loyalty and fealty to the Mother Country. Therefore when the opportunity was offered to its citizens to exemplify their patriotism by serving their Queen and country, they promptly obeyed the call, and in a short time the ranks of the Brockville Rifles were filled up, and drilling commenced. The muster roll was sent in to Militia Headquarters, and the Company was formally gazetted on September 5th, 1855. Among the names that appear on the first roll of this Company are those of William H. Jackson and Wilmot H. Cole, both of whom are still living at this date, and are supposed to be the only two survivors of the old corps. Each of these gentlemen took a great interest in military affairs, and after duly qualifying themselves, were gradually promoted in the service until they attained high commands—the former being appointed one of the first Brigade Majors under the Militia Act of 1862 (and subsequently becoming a Deputy Adjutant-General, who discharged important duties at Brockville, London, Winnipeg and Ottawa), while Wilmot H. Cole, after serving through all the grades, rose to the rank of Lieutenant-Colonel of the Forty-first Battalion (of which the Brockville Rifles was always No. 1 Company), the duties of which position he filled with great ability and credit for twenty-seven consecutive years, retiring on July 1st, 1898.

The Brockville Rifle Company was selected by the Government as one of the units to form the regiment organized in 1864, under command of Lieut.-Col. W. Osborne Smith, to guard the St. Clair and Detroit River frontiers (extending from Sarnia on the north to Amherstburg on the south) for the purpose of preventing raids from Canadian territory on the United States by organized gangs of desperate men from the Confederate States, who had come north for that purpose.

The Canadian regiment had its headquarters at Windsor, with detachments posted at that point, and at Sarnia, Chatham, Sandwich and Amherstburg. To the latter point the Brockville and Belleville Rifle Companies were sent in command of the following officers:—

Brockville Rifle Company—Major James Crawford, Lieut. W. H. Cole, and Ensign Edmund W. Windeat.

Belleville Rifle Company—Capt. Charles G. Le Vesconte. Lieut. James Brown, and Ensign Mackenzie Bowell.

The two companies at Amherstburg improved their time by engaging in constant drill, and by the maintenance of strict discipline and close attention to the duties required of them, they became very efficient. After five months of frontier service the regiment was relieved on the 4th of May, 1865, and returned to their homes.

In the fall of 1865 the Fenians began to get very active, and the feeling prevailed among the people of Brockville that some provision should be made for the protection of that town. The Brockville Rifles at that time was in a very efficient condition, having four officers and 85 rank and file, as follows:—Major James Crawford in command, Lieut. W. H. Cole, Ensign E. W. Windeat and 65 non-commissioned officers and men, with an additional gun detachment composed of one officer and 20 men, equipped with a 6-pound brass field gun, under command of Lieut. Robert Bowie, who had been at Amherstburg with the company the year previous. (Lieut. Bowie was born a soldier, his father having held an important command in the Tower of London, and had private quarters there with his wife when Robert, his only son, was born.)

Major Crawford called his officers together, and after a discussion of what might happen to Brockville in its unprotected condition, it was decided to make the following offer to the Militia Department:—As the Company was now 85 strong, they would enlist 15 more men, making a total of 100. The men would be called out at 6.30 p.m. every day, given a two hours' drill; an officer's guard to be mounted, to consist of one sergeant, one corporal and 24 men; sentries to be posted at seven of the most exposed places, including one at each of the two banks; the non-commissioned officers and men to be paid 25 cents each per day, the officers giving their services free, and if the Department would furnish the necessary bedding the Company would have 60 of the remaining men sleep in the Armory every night, to be ready for any emergency. This would enable the men to attend to their usual daily avocations and not interfere with the business requirements of their employers. This patriotic offer was at once accepted by the Government, and orders were issued to have the duties carried out as above stated, which was done in every detail from the 15th of December, 1865, to the eventful day in March, 1866, when the first general call was made on the Volunteer Force for service on the frontier.

CHAPTER III.

THE FIRST ALARM—CANADIAN VOLUNTEERS PROMPTLY RESPOND
TO THE CALL OF DUTY—THE CAMPO BELLO FIZZLE—
FENIANS GATHER ON THE BORDER—OPERATIONS ON THE
NIAGARA FRONTIER.

Early in the month of March, 1866, considerable activity
was observable among the Fenians in both the United States and
Ireland, and it became known to the authorities that a "rising"
was contemplated, to occur on St. Patrick's Day. That a simultaneous raid on Canada had been planned was evident, and as
the Government maintained a force of secret service agents in
the principal American cities to keep watch on the movements
of the Fenians, reliable information was furnished which was
regarded of sufficient importance by the Canadian authorities
to warrant prompt action in putting the country in a state of
defence. Accordingly on the 7th of March a General Order was
issued by Col. P. L. Macdougall, Adjutant-General of the Canadian Militia, calling out 10,000 volunteers for active service.
The summons was flashed across the wires to all points in the
Provinces of Upper and Lower Canada, and fourteen thousand
men promptly responded to the call. By 4 o'clock on the following day these forces were all assembled at their respective
headquarters, awaiting further orders. So eager were the young
men of Canada to perform their duty in those trying times that
a force of 50,000 could have been raised as easily as the number
called for. Most of the companies and battalions were reported
"over strength" when the returns were received at headquarters, and the Government decided to retain the whole 14,000 on
service pending developments of the enemy's movements. Lieut.-
General Sir John Michel (then commanding Her Majesty's
forces in North America) was placed in supreme command. with
Major-Gen. James Lindsay in command of the troops in Canada
East, and Major-Gen. G. Napier, C.B., in charge of the forces
in Canada West.

On the 8th of March, the following companies were ordered to report for duty to Major Crawford at Brockville for the purpose of forming a Provisional Battalion:—

Perth Rifle Company—Capt. Edmund Spillman.
Gananoque Rifle Company—Capt. Robert McCrum.
Carleton Place Rifle Company—Capt. James Poole.
Perth Infantry Company—Capt. Thomas Scott.
Almonte Infantry Company—Capt. James D. Gemmill.
Brockville Infantry Company—Capt. Jacob D. Buell.

The above units promptly reported, and the organization of the Battalion was effected by a mergement of them with the Brockville Rifles, which was placed on full service and divided, the right half forming a company of 50 men under Capt. W. H. Cole, and the left half (50 men) placed in command of Lieut. Windeat. Lieut Robert Bowie was appointed Adjutant of the new Battalion thus created.

Thirty Spencer rifles were issued to the Brockville Rifles, and given to Capt. Cole's company. That officer compiled a drill manual which instructed the men armed with the repeating rifles to act on the same words of command issued to those who had the muzzle-loading Enfields, which was so excellent in practice that he was afterwards highly complimented by Major-General Lindsay when the Battalion was inspected by him in the following May. This Battalion remained on duty at Brockville until about the 16th of May, when they were released from further service and permitted to return to their homes.

For several weeks the country was kept in a state of feverish excitement, as all sorts of rumors of intended raids at different points were prevalent. Constant drilling and vigilance was maintained, and all the avenues of approach to the frontier towns and exposed points were closely guarded. The weather was very severe that winter, especially during the period the troops were on duty, and many of the survivors of those eventful days will doubtless remember the frost-bites they received while pacing their dreary beats on guard duty, and the many other discomforts which fell to their lot.

The 17th of March passed without the anticipated attacks being made, however, and the fears of the people were gradually allayed. The Fenians had evidently reconsidered their plans so far as Canada was concerned, as the Frost King held sway with rigid severity, and decided to delay their invasion until early summer. On the 28th of March the force on active service was reduced from 14,000 to 10,000 (the original prescribed number), and on the 31st of March all were relieved from permanent duty with the exception of the advanced frontier posts, but were required to parade and drill on two days of each week at local headquarters.

Meanwhile the Fenians kept up their drill and warlike preparations. Immense quantities of arms and ammunition were purchased and shipped to various points in the United States contiguous to the Canadian frontier, where they could quickly be obtained by the invaders when wanted.

During the early part of April a number of Fenians gathered in the towns of Eastport and Calais, in the State of Maine, with the avowed purpose of capturing the Island of Campo Bello, a British possession at the mouth of the St. Croix River, on the boundary line between the Province of New Brunswick and the United States. This expedition was under the direction of "General" Dorian Killian, who was one of the leading lights of the O'Mahony faction of the Fenian Brotherhood. This move was made contrary to the fixed policy of the Stephens-O'Mahony wing of the Fenian organization, but something had to be done to satisfy the impatient people who were providing the funds to inaugurate the war and were clamoring for immediate action. So after considerable deliberation and hesitation, General O'Mahony gave his consent to the proposed invasion, and preparations were hurriedly made. A vessel was chartered at New York, and being loaded with arms and ammunition, sailed for Eastport, Maine. The rank and file of the Fenian force gathered quietly at Eastport, Calais and adjacent towns, and awaited the arrival of their armament. In the meantime the Canadian military authorities were getting ready to meet the filibusters, and strong forces of volunteers were posted along the New Brunswick frontier to watch events and be prepared for action as soon as the Fenians attempted to make a landing. Three British war vessels steamed quietly into the St. Croix River, ready for instant service, and a couple of American gunboats were also on guard to prevent a crossing. General Meade, with a battalion

of United States troops, arrived at Eastport, with orders from
the American Government to see that a breach of the Neutrality
Act was not committed. On the same day the vessel with arms
for the Fenians sailed into Eastport harbor and was promptly
seized by the United States officials. This was "the last straw"
to break the hopes of the Fenians, and they left for their homes
without accomplishing anything, utterly dejected, hungry and
weary, and bitterly cursing their leaders, and the American
authorities particularly, for preventing them from crossing the
line. This fiasco was a mortifying blow to General O'Mahony
and his supporters. and the cohorts of Roberts and Sweeny
gained more confidence and support as the star of the Stephens
faction grew dimmer.

The remainder of April and the month of May passed away
quietly, and the people of· Canada had almost dismissed the
Fenian "bugaboo" from their minds, and were enjoying a period
of peace and prosperity, when again the Demon of War loomed
up on the border more terrible than ever. This time it was the
Roberts-Sweeny section of the Fenian Brotherhood who were
bent on making trouble for Canada, and if possible carry out
their elaborate plan of campaign for conquering our Provinces.
All during the winter and spring the Fenian leaders had been
secretly and sedulously at work making preparations for simultaneous raids on Canada at different places, and towards the
end of May the Irish Republican Army began massing on the
border for that purpose. At strategic points all along our extensive frontier the Fenian forces were quietly gathering, evidently
with the purpose of trying to work out the wide scheme of Gen.
Sweeny to capture Canada and hand us over body and bones to
the United States.

At St. Albans, Vermont, and adjacent villages, a large
force gathered for the purpose of making a raid from that
quarter. in the possible hope that with the reinforcements they
expected, they might be able to hold that section of country and
operate against the City of Montreal with some degree of success, in conjunction with two other columns which were expected
to carry the St. Lawrence line.

At Malone, New York, another strong force assembled under
the command of the Fenian Gen. M. J. Heffernan. who announced

his intention of making an attack on Cornwall. Gen. Murphy and Gen. O'Reilly, both veteran officers of the Union Army in the Civil War, were attached to this column, and were very assiduous in their efforts to make it an efficient fighting force.

At Ogdensburg, New York, Gen. Sweeny personally supervised the mobilization of a large contingent of his warriors. This column was organized for the purpose of attacking Prescott, Brockville, and other points along the St. Lawrence, and after taking possession of the Canadian shore and the Grand Trunk Railway, be available for his plan of sweeping the whole country east as far as Montreal, and join with the other columns (which were to start from Malone and St. Albans) in capturing that city.

Cape Vincent, Oswego, Rochester and other points along the Upper St. Lawrence and Lake Ontario were places of rendezvous for the Fenian troops who were steadily arriving from the interior of New York State, while the Western and Southern contingents gathered at Detroit, Toledo, Cleveland, Erie and Buffalo.

As the Niagara frontier possesses many attractions for an invading force (as in the days of 1812 and 1814), it was decided to again make that historic territory one of the arenas for hostile operations. Gen. Sweeny fondly nursed the hope that while our forces were busily engaged there, that he would be able to make crossings at two or three other points along the border. As the scene of the first active operations was presented on the Niagara Peninsula, I will relate those events first, and then return to a description of what was occurring on the St. Lawrence and Vermont borders.

For some days previous to the 31st of May large numbers of mysterious strangers were noticed to be gathering in some of the towns and cities adjacent to the Niagara frontier. In Buffalo particularly this mobilization of men with a purpose was observable, but so reticent were they, and so careful of their movements causing comment, that suspicions were partially disarmed. Yet these strangers were all Fenian soldiers, who were silently and quickly gathering from various States of the Union with a determined intention to make a quick dash on Canada, which they hoped to capture, and set up their standards upon our soil. All preparations for the *coup* had been made, and yet the people of Canada seemed to dream not of their peril.

Towards midnight on the 31st of May those strangers in Buffalo were noticed to be assembling in groups, squads and companies, and moving as if by a pre-arranged programme in the direction of Black Rock, two or three miles north of the city, on the Niagara River. Suspicious-looking waggons and furniture vans were also moving in the same direction. These were loaded with arms and ammunition for the use of "the Army of Conquest," but no attempt was made by the United States authorities to stop the expedition, although it was a clear breach of the Neutrality Act then in force between the two countries. At the hour of midnight, when the peaceful citizens on the Canadian side of the Niagara River were slumbering in their beds, the Fenian hordes were steadily gathering on the other side of the shimmering stream and making preparations to effect a crossing. Two powerful tugs and several canal boats had been chartered to convey the Fenians across to Canada, and these were quickly and quietly loaded with men and munitions of war. As the grey dawn of day was breaking on the morning of the 1st of June, the Fenian transports started across the river. The troops consisted of one brigade of the Irish Republican Army, under command of Gen. John O'Neil, a veteran soldier who had seen much active service and hard fighting in the American Civil War. This brigade was composed of the 13th Regiment (Col. O'Neil), from Tennessee; 17th Regiment (Col. Owen Starr), from Kentucky; 18th Regiment (Lieut.-Col. John Grace), from Ohio; the 7th Regiment (Col. John Hoye), from Buffalo, N.Y., and a detachment of troops from Indiana. The whole number was estimated to be about 1,500 men, who were principally veteran soldiers of the Northern and Southern armies.

This was the "forlorn hope" who were expected to make the first landing and hold the country until sufficient reinforcements could be rushed across the border to enable them to make a success of the campaign. Buffalo was full of Fenians and their sympathizers at that time, and thousands were coming into the city every day to take part in the invasion.

It was an opportune time for such a movement, as the popular feeling of the American people was not altogether amicable or friendly to the British nation, and it was the hope of the promoters of the raid that something might occur which would give them the countenance and support of the United States. It is a well-known fact that under the political system of America the Irish vote is a dominant factor in elections, and all classes of citizens who aspire to public office are more or less controlled by that element. Consequently the vigilance of many of Uncle Sam's officials was relaxed, and they winked the other eye as the invaders marched towards Canada, instead of endeavoring to stop them from committing a breach of the law of nations in regard to neutrality.

It was asserted in the public press of the United States and proclaimed by the Fenians themselves at that time, that Andrew Johnson (who was then President of the United States) and Secretary of State Seward openly encouraged the invasion for the purpose of turning it to political account in the settlement of the Alabama Claims with Great Britain. In view of the fact that he held back the issuance of his proclamation forbidding a breach of the Neutrality Act for *five full days after* the Raid had been made, there was manifestly some understanding between President Johnson and the Fenian leaders, as the American authorities were perfectly cognizant of what was intended long before Gen. O'Neil crossed the boundary, and might have been prevented from doing so, had the United States officials at Buffalo exercised such due vigilance as Gen. Meade did in the Campo Bello affair.

CHAPTER IV.

THE LANDING IN CANADA—PRELIMINARY OPERATIONS OF THE
FENIAN FORCES NEAR FORT ERIE—ADVANCE INTO THE
INTERIOR.

About half-past three o'clock on the morning of June 1st
the peaceful shores of Canada were reached by the invaders.
The embarkation was made at Pratt's Iron Furnace Dock on
the American side, and the landing took place at what was then
known as the Lower Ferry Dock, about a mile below the village
of Fort Erie. Just as the boats struck the shore, the color-
bearers of Col. Owen Starr's 17th Kentucky Regiment sprang
on to Canadian soil and unfurled their Irish flags amid terrific
cheering by the Fenian troops. This was the first intimation
that the people of the quiet vicinity received that an invasion
had actually occurred, and it was a terrible awakening from
peaceful slumber to most of them. There were no Canadian
troops whatever within 25 miles of Fort Erie, and the invaders
had it all their own way. The war material was quickly un-
loaded from the canal boats, and Gen. O'Neil at once began
making dispositions of his force to hold his ground. The total
number of troops that came over by the first boats was stated
to be 1,340, with 2,500 stand of arms. This force was rapidly
augmented during the day by reinforcements, so that by evening
the strength of the Fenian army in Canada amounted to about
2,000 men.

After posting guards and throwing out pickets in various
directions, Gen. O'Neil marched up to the village of Fort Erie
with the main portion of his brigade, which he occupied without
resistance. He then made requisition on the village authorities for meals for his men. He stated that he would do no personal injury to private citizens, but wanted food and horses,
and these he proposed to take forcibly if they were not furnished
willingly. Dr. Kempson, the Reeve of the village, in order to
protect the citizens and prevent pillage, at once called a meeting of the Municipal Council, who decided to provide the food

demanded. In some cases Fenian bonds were offered in payment for articles, but were not acceptable to the Canadian people, and were courteously and firmly refused.

Immediately after breakfast had been served and rations distributed, Gen. O'Neil made details of troops for various purposes. Guards were posted all along the river front, from the ruins of old Fort Erie to a point below Haggart's Dock, who were instructed to shoot any person who attempted to interfere with them. Detachments were sent to cut the telegraph wires and destroy part of the Buffalo and Lake Huron railway track (now the Grand Trunk), which was quickly done. A detail under command of Capt. Geary, of the 17th Kentucky Regiment, was despatched to burn Sauerwine's Bridge, on the railway track between Fort Erie and Ridgeway, and tear up the rails. This was only partially accomplished, as after the Fenians left some of the people residing in the vicinity rallied and extinguished the flames in the burning bridge before much serious damage was done. The railway track, however, was torn up for a considerable distance by the raiders.

An early morning train on the B. & L. H. Railway narrowly escaped capture by a detail of troops sent for that purpose. The train had just succeeded in transferring its passengers to the ferry boat "International" and was starting back westward empty, when the Fenians put in their appearance. The plucky engineer, seeing the danger, pulled the throttle of his engine wide open and saved the train from capture by a narrow margin.

After committing sundry other depredations in the way of cutting telegraph wires and destroying public property, Gen. O'Neil marched the main body of his troops down the River Road to Frenchman's Creek, where they encamped in an orchard on Newbigging's Farm, about half a mile north of the Lower Ferry. Here the Fenians began work on the construction of a line of breastworks and entrenchments, which kept them busily employed all afternoon.

A detachment of the 7th Buffalo Regiment, under command of Capt. Donohue, made a reconnaisance in the direction of Chippawa during the afternoon, and after discovering a party of mounted farmers, who they mistook for Canadian cavalry, fired a volley at them without effect and then retreated valiantly back to the Fenian camp, bombastically boasting that they had routed a strong force of British troops.

Other details had been busy seizing horses and food supplies, and mounted scouts galloped for miles in all directions, scouring the country seeking information as to the whereabouts of the Canadian forces, and at the same time distributing copies of the following proclamation:—

"To the People of British America:

"We come among you as the foes of British rule in Ireland. We have taken up the sword to strike down the oppressors' rod, to deliver Ireland from the tyrant, the despoiler, the robber. We have registered our oaths upon the altar of our country in the full view of heaven and sent up our vows to the throne of Him who inspired them. Then, looking about us for an enemy, we find him here, here in your midst, where he is most vulnerable and convenient to our strength. . . . We have no issue with the people of these Provinces, and wish to have none but the most friendly relations. Our weapons are for the oppressors of Ireland. Our bows shall be directed only against the power of England; her privileges alone shall we invade, not yours. We do not propose to divest you of a solitary right you now enjoy. . . . We are here neither as murderers, nor robbers, for plunder and spoliation. We are here as the Irish army of liberation, the friends of liberty against despotism, of democracy against aristocracy, of the people against their oppressors. In a word, our war is with the armed power of England, not with the people, not with these Provinces. Against England, upon land and sea, till Ireland is free. . . . To Irishmen throughout these Provinces we appeal in the name of seven centuries of British iniquity and Irish misery and suffering, in the names of our murdered sires, our desolate homes, our desecrated altars, our million of famine graves, our insulted name and race—to stretch forth the hand of brotherhood in the holy cause of fatherland, and smite the tyrant where we can. We conjure you, our countrymen, who from misfortune inflicted by the very tyranny you are serving, or from any other cause, have been forced to enter the ranks of the enemy, not to be willing instruments of your country's death or degradation. No uniform, and surely not the blood-dyed coat of England, can emancipate you from the natural law that binds your allegiance to Ireland, to liberty, to right, to justice. To the friends of Ireland, of freedom, of humanity, of the people, we offer the olive branch of peace and the honest grasp of friendship. Take it Irishmen, Frenchmen, American, take it all and trust it. . . . We wish to meet with friends; we are prepared to meet with enemies. We shall endeavor to merit the confidence of the former, and the latter can expect from us but the leniency of a determined though generous foe and the restraints and relations imposed by civilized warfare.

"(Signed) T. W. SWEENY,

"Major-General Commanding the Armies of Ireland."

During the afternoon and evening there was considerable excitement and uneasiness in the Fenian camp, caused by rumors of the near approach of the Canadian troops, and officers and men steadily prepared for any emergency. Gen. O'Neil had been expecting heavy reinforcements all day, but they failed to appear, although it was estimated that there were over 10,000 Fenians then assembled in Buffalo and vicinity, with a plentiful supply of arms and ammunition. A few came over in rowboats as evening approached, but the large forces that were expected remained on the other side, cautiously awaiting developments.

It was the evident intention of the Fenian army to penetrate the country and capture and destroy the Welland Canal, and subsequent events confirmed that as part of their plan of campaign.

As the shades of night fell, strong guards were posted around the Fenian camp, and the roads leading thereto were effectively picketed. From reports brought in by his scouts and spies, Gen. O'Neil learned that two Canadian columns were being mobilized—one at Chippawa and the other at Port Colborne—and he resolved to make a quick dash on one of these before a junction could be effected between the two, counting upon a surprise and the prestige of his men as veteran soldiers to win a victory. A council of war was therefore held by O'Neil and his officers, and it was resolved to make an advance immediately.

About 10 o'clock that night the men were aroused and commanded to "fall in" for the movement forward. A large quantity of arms and ammunition which had been brought over for the use of the expected reinforcements was now found to be an impediment, and O'Neil decided to destroy them to prevent their falling into the hands of the Canadians. Consequently hundreds of rifles and other munitions of war were burned or thrown into Frenchman's Creek before leaving their camp.

The Fenian column then started down the River Road towards Black Creek. On arrival at a point near that stream they bivouacked by the roadside and awaited reports of scouts. It was here that Gen. O'Neil learned that a force of Canadian volunteers would leave Port Colborne for Ridgeway early on the morning of June 2nd, and he decided to go forward and attack them. It was just about daybreak that he put his brigade in motion and moved west by an old bush road until he struck the Ridge Road, which bears south-west from the river to Ridgeway. As they marched along the latter highway in the early

hours of a bright, beautiful morning, the Fenians were in fine
fettle and "spoiling for a fight." They had some mounted
scouts in advance, cautiously feeling the way. When within a
few miles of Ridgeway Station this advance guard heard the
whistle of a locomotive, and soon after bugle calls, which signified the arrival of the Canadian troops. The scouts galloped
back to O'Neil with the information, and he at once halted his
brigade, closed up his column, and began making preparations
for battle.

Gen. O'Neil's experience in the military campaigns of the
Civil War had taught him many useful lessons, which he had
evidently profited by, as his choice of a battleground on Limestone Ridge was admirable, and the skillful disposition he made
of his forces was commensurate with the ability of a high-class
tactician.

Limestone Ridge, along which the so-called "Ridge Road"
runs, has an elevation of about 35 feet over the surrounding
country, and at the point where O'Neil took up his main position is about half a mile wide, with patches of bush and clumps
of trees alternating with open fields. On both sides the country
is comparatively cleared, so that an extensive view is obtainable
from the summit of the ridge, which was of decided advantage
to O'Neil, as he could watch the approach of advancing troops
from almost any direction. Here he posted his brigade and
hastily began the construction of breastworks and barricades of
fence rails and earth. A force of sharpshooters and skirmishers
were thrown out well to the front and along the flanks of this
position, and after all dispositions for battle had been carefully
made, Gen. O'Neil coolly awaited the arrival of the Canadian
troops, who were advancing from Ridgeway totally ignorant of
the fact that there was a lion in their path.

CHAPTER V.

THE SECOND ALARM—GRAND UPRISING OF THE CANADIAN PEOPLE
—DEPARTURE OF TROOPS FOR THE FRONT—GEN. NAPIER'S
PLAN OF CAMPAIGN.

Late on the night of the 31st of May, 1866, the second call
to arms was telegraphed from Ottawa, and within an hour the
sound of bugles and alarm bells was heard echoing and ringing
in nearly every city, town and village in the country. The alacrity with which our volunteers responded to the summons on
that eventful night is without a parallel in the history of any
nation. The whole country was aroused, and all were eager to
go to the front. Many young men pleadingly begged for a
chance to join the already "over strength" companies who could
not be accommodated, and were reluctantly obliged to satisfy
their military ardor by enrolling themselves in the Home Guards
and shouldering rifles for patrol duty.

In the town of St. Catharines the excitement was intense,
on account of its near proximity to the border and the alarming
reports that were being circulated of the near approach of the
enemy. The town companies of the 19th Lincoln Battalion,
under command of Lieut.-Col. J. G. Currie, and the St. Catharines Battery of Garrison Artillery, under Capt. George Stoker
and Lieut. James Wilson, were speedily mustered, and all
through the night kept faithful vigils on guard duty, anxiously
awaiting orders to move to the frontier. A Home Guard was
hastily organized and equipped, and every citizen vied with his
neighbor to shoulder his share of the responsibility in defending
their homes and kindred from the attacks of the invaders.

At Toronto the Queen's Own Rifles, the Tenth Royals, the
Toronto Garrison Battery, and the Toronto Naval Brigade, were
quickly assembled at the drill shed and preparations made to
leave for the front at a moment's notice. The citizens of the
loyal old city of Toronto, who had on many previous occasions
rallied around the flag of their country when danger threatened,
were so strongly imbued with that patriotic feeling which pre-

vailed everywhere that they immediately enrolled a Home Guard
to defend the city in the absence of the volunteer regiments,
and faithfully and well was that duty performed.

The same intense patriotism was manifested by the people
of Canada generally, and a general muster of all military commands prevailed wherever organized.

LIST OF TROOPS CALLED OUT FOR ACTIVE SERVICE.

As a matter of record and interest to the survivors of the
Fenian Raid of 1866, copies of the General Orders issued by
the Militia Department, designating the troops that were called
out for active service on the 1st and 2nd of June, 1866, together
with a list of the new companies organized, are herewith given:

HEADQUARTERS, OTTAWA, 1st June, '66.
GENERAL ORDERS, No. 1.

The Governor-General and Commander-in-Chief directs that the following named corps be called out for active service, and that the said corps
be immediately assembled and billeted at their respective headquarters,
there to await such orders for their movement as may be directed by the
Commander-in-Chief:

UPPER CANADA.

Windsor Garrison Battery.
Goderich Garrison Battery.
St. Catharines Garrison Battery.
Toronto Garrison Battery.
Port Stanley Naval Company.
Dunnville Naval Company.
Hamilton Naval Company.
Toronto Naval Company.
Mount Pleasant Infantry Company.
Paris Rifle Company.
Brantford Rifles, 2 Companies.
Kincardine Infantry, 2 Companies.
Paisley Infantry Company.
Southampton Rifle Company.
Vienna Infantry Company.
St. Thomas Rifle Company.
Windsor Infantry Company.
Sandwich Infantry Company.
Leamington Infantry Company.
Amherstburg Infantry Company.
Gosfield Rifle Company.
Durham Infantry Company.
Mount Forest Rifle Company.
Leith Rifle Company.
Dunnville Rifle Company.
York Rifle Company.

20th Battalion, St. Catharines, 5 Com-
panies.
7th Battalion, London, 6 Companies.
Komoka Rifle Company.
Villa Nova Rifle Company.
Simcoe Rifle Company.
Port Rowan Rifle Company.
Walsingham Rifle Company.
Ingersoll Infantry Company.
Drumbo Infantry Company.
22nd Battalion Oxford Rifles, Wood-
stock, 4 Companies.
Brampton Infantry and Rifle Com-
panies.
Albion Infantry Company.
Derry West Infantry Company.
Alton Infantry Company.
Grahamsville Infantry Company.
Stratford Infantry Company.
Bradford Infantry Company.
Barrie Infantry and Rifle Companies.
Collingwood Rifle Companies.
Cookstown Rifle Company.
Orangeville Infantry Company.
Fergus Rifle Company.
Elora Rifle Company.

Caledonia Rifle Company.
Stewartown Infantry Company.
Georgetown Infantry Company.
Norval Infantry Company.
Oakville Rifle Company.
Seaforth Infantry Company.
Chatham Infantry, 2 Companies.
Blenheim Infantry Company.
19th Battalion, St. Catharines, 6 Companies.

13th Battalion, Hamilton, 6 Companies.
Aurora Infantry Company.
Lloydtown Infantry Company.
King Infantry Company.
Scarborough Rifle Company.
2nd Battalion, Queen's Own Rifles, Toronto, 11 Companies.
10th Battalion (Royals), Toronto, 8 Companies.

LOWER CANADA.

Franklin Infantry Company.
Durham Infantry Company.
Hinchinbrooke Rifle Company.
Athelstan Infantry Company.
Rockburn Infantry Company.
Huntingdon Infantry, 2 Companies.
Hemmingford Infantry Company.
Roxham Infantry Company.
Lacolle Infantry Company (21st Battalion).

St. John's Infantry Company (21st Battalion).
Havelock Rifle Company.
Granby Infantry, 2 Companies.
Waterloo Infantry, 2 Companies.
Freleighsburg Infantry Company.
Phillipsburg Infantry Company.
Montreal Infantry, 6 Companies.

OTTAWA, 2nd June. 1866.

GENERAL ORDERS, No. 2.

The Governor-General and Commander-in-Chief has been pleased to call out for active service the following corps in addition to those called out by General Order No. 1, of yesterday's date:

UPPER CANADA.

1st Frontenac Troop Cavalry, Kingston.
1st Squadron Volunteer Light Cavalry, County of York.
Grimsby Troop Cavalry.
London Troop Cavalry.
St. Thomas Troop Cavalry.
Governor-General's Body Guard, Toronto.

King-Kingston Field Battery.
Hamilton Field Battery.
Welland Canal Field Battery.
London Field Battery.
14th Battalion Rifles. Kingston.
Brockville Rifle and Infantry Companies.

LOWER CANADA.

Varennes Infantry Company.
Napiersville Infantry Company.
St. Remi Infantry Company.
St. Luc's Infantry Company, 21st Battalion.
Sherbrooke Rifles, 2 Companies.

Danville Rifle Company.
Bury Infantry Company.
Richmond Infantry Company.
Melbourne Infantry Company.
2nd Lennoxville Rifle Company.

On 2nd June the following new companies were placed on the list of the Volunteer Militia of Canada:

UPPER CANADA.

Oil Springs Infantry Company.
Bayfield Infantry Company.
Galt Infantry Company.
Oro Infantry Company.
Aylmer Infantry Company.
Strathroy Infantry Company.

Orillia Infantry Company.
Woodstock Infantry Company.
Wolfe Island Infantry Company.
Tamworth Infantry Company.
Kemptville Infantry Company.
Sydney Infantry Company.

Hillsboro Infantry Company.
Dundas Infantry Company.
Bobcaygeon Infantry Company.
Bearbrook Infantry Company.
St. Mary's Infantry Company.
Clinton Infantry Company.
Huntley Infantry Company.
Widder Infantry Company.
Peterboro Infantry Company.
Edwardsburg Infantry Company.
Parkhill Infantry Company.

Stirling Infantry Company.
Ottawa Garrison Artillery (3rd Battery).
Waterloo Infantry Company.
Warwick Infantry Company.
Amherst Island Infantry Company.
Napanee Garrison Artillery.
Port Hope Garrison Artillery.
10th Royals, Toronto (2 additional Companies).

LOWER CANADA.

Stanstead Infantry Company.
Coaticooke Infantry Company.
Ste. Hyacinthe Infantry Company.
Sorel Infantry Company.
Tingwick Infantry Company.
Winslow Infantry Company.
Clarenceville Infantry Company.
Elgin Infantry Company.
Longueuil Infantry Company.
Boucherville Infantry Company.

Vercheres Infantry Company.
Abercorn Infantry Company.
Huntingdon Infantry (3rd Company).
St. Pie Infantry Company.
Vaudreuil Infantry Company.
St. Martine Infantry Company.
St. Athanase Infantry Company.
Beauharnois Infantry Company.
Knowlton Infantry Company.
Sutton Infantry Company.

On the evening of the 2nd of June the whole of the Volunteer Force not already called out or enumerated in the above-mentioned lists, was placed on active service, and on Sunday, the 3rd of June, the Province had more than 20,000 men under arms, besides the numerous companies of Home Guards. The entire force turned out not only willingly, but eagerly, although at a season of the year when their business interests suffered greatly by their absence. It was enough for every militia man to know that the country needed his services, and personal interests were cheerfully sacrificed. Instances of devotion to Queen and country were general. Business matters were but a secondary consideration. Merchants and their clerks left their shops, students their colleges, professional men their offices, while factories were shut down and farmers left their ploughs in the furrows to take up their rifles to assist in the national defence. Those who were obliged by age or infirmities to stay at home were not idle, but nobly did their part in raising funds to assist the families of those bread-winners who had gone to serve on the frontier posts. All over the country large sums were raised for this purpose, and the patriotic Relief Committees were exceptionally busy attending to the proper distribution of food and supplies, both among the volunteers and the needy families who were depending upon them.

In the order calling out the troops for active service the Governor-General placed the whole force under the command of Lieut.-Gen. Sir John Michel, and added:

In former times the Commander-in-Chief has had occasion to call for the active services of the volunteer force to maintain international obligations, and as a precaution against threatened action. These threats have now ripened into actual fact. The soil of Canada has been invaded, not in the practice of legitimate warfare, but by a lawless and piratical band in defiance of all moral right, and in utter disregard of all the obligations which civilization enforces on mankind. Upon the people of Canada this state of things imposes the duty of defending their altars, their homes and their property from desecration, pillage and spoilation. The Commander-in-Chief relies on the courage and loyalty of the volunteer force and looks with confidence for the blessings of Providence on their performance of the sacred duty which circumstances have cast upon them.

MAJOR-GEN. NAPIER'S PLAN OF CAMPAIGN.

As the Niagara district was chosen by the Fenians to be the theatre of their first operations, Gen. Napier quickly made preparations to occupy the salient points of this important territory. The Welland Canal, connecting Lake Erie with Lake Ontario, runs from Port Colborne on the former lake to Port Dalhousie on the latter (a distance of 26 miles), and lies at an average distance of about 13 miles inland from the Niagara River. The Welland Railway also connected these two points, running nearly parallel with the canal. To protect these two arteries of commerce from destruction was a desideratum to the General commanding, and his plan of campaign was framed on these lines. Port Colborne lies about 19 miles west of Fort Erie, and Gen. Napier decided to mobilize a force at that point and another at St. Catharines, 10 miles west of the Niagara River. These were two very strategic points at which to concentrate troops for the defence of the Niagara frontier, as they possessed excellent advantages as bases of supply for the sustenance of columns operating in any quarter of the district. On account of the favorable rail communication with each of those places, troops could be moved rapidly by trains from the interior, and would always be within easy striking distance of an invading force on any portion of the Niagara frontier. Therefore orders were issued to commanding officers to assemble their corps immediately at their respective local headquarters, and await further instructions.

The first body of troops which left for the front was the Queen's Own Rifles. of Toronto, with a total strength of 480 of all ranks. The regiment was assembled at the Drill Shed on Front Street at 4 o'clock on the morning of June 1st, and received orders to proceed to Port Colborne without delay. At 6.30 a.m. they embarked on board the steamer "City of Toronto" for Port Dalhousie, where they entrained on the Welland Railway for Port Colborne. Lieut.-Col. J. S. Dennis, Brigade Major of the Fifth Military District, was in command. This officer had received orders from Gen. Napier to occupy Port Colborne, and if necessary entrench a position there and await reinforcements and further orders before an attack was made on the enemy. The Queen's Own arrived at Port Colborne about noon, and there being no indications of the enemy in the near vicinity, the men were billetted among the citizens for dinner, as by somebody's oversight no rations or food supply of any kind had been forwarded for the sustenance of the troops.

Lieut.-Col. Dennis sent out couriers and mounted scouts to glean information of the whereabouts of the enemy, who he finally located at their camp near Fort Erie. During the afternoon the Thirteenth Battalion, of Hamilton, under command of Lieut.-Col. A. Booker, arrived at Port Colborne from Dunnville, accompanied by the York and Caledonia Rifle Companies. These reinforcements made a total force of about 850 troops at Port Colborne, and as Lieut.-Col. Booker was the ranking officer present, he took command of the column.

Meanwhile other troops were on the move towards the frontier. As before mentioned, Gen. Napier had decided to also mobilize a force at St. Catharines, and orders were given to Col. Geo. Peacocke, commanding Her Majesty's 16th Regiment, to proceed thither with the forces at his command, and assume charge of the operations for the defence of the fron-

---

KEY TO MAP ON NEXT PAGE.

(a) Where Fenians landed. (b) Fenian Camp 1st June. (c) Fenian bivouac night of 1st June. (d) Point at which Fenian pursuit was abandoned. (e) Fenian Camp near the old Fort, night of 2nd June, from which point they evacuated Canada. (f) Col. Peacocke's forces, night of June 1st. (g) Col. Peacocke's Camp at noon, June 2nd. (h) Col. Peacocke's bivouac at Bowen's Farm, night of 2nd June.

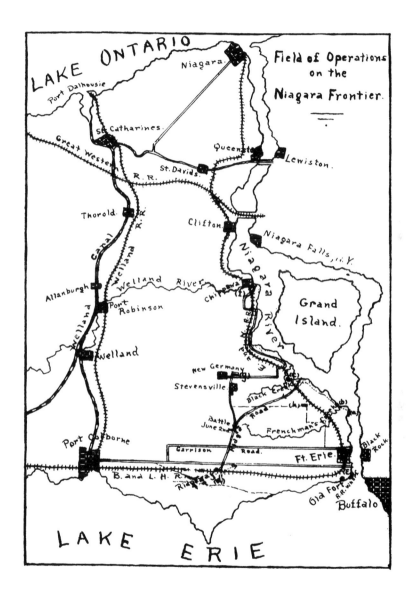

tier. At 12.40 o'clock (noon) a force consisting of three companies of Her Majesty's 47th Regiment, under command of
Major Lauder, and the Grey Battery of Royal Artillery, commanded by Lieut.-Col. Hoste, C.B., left Toronto via the Great
Western Railway for St. Catharines. At Hamilton this contingent was joined by Col. Peacocke with 200 men of the 16th
Regiment, and the whole force proceeded to their destination.
On arrival at St. Catharines Col. Peacocke received telegrams
advising him that a strong body of Fenians were marching
towards Chippawa, so he resolved to move forward his
force at once to that point and endeavor to save the bridges
across the Welland River (or Chippawa Creek) from destruction. He issued immediate orders for the Tenth Royals,
of Toronto, two more companies of H. M. 47th Regiment, the
Nineteenth Lincoln Battalion, and Capt. Stoker's Battery of
Garrison Artillery, from St. Catharines, to reinforce him at
Chippawa. These troops moved promptly forward, and before
daylight all were bivouacked on the streets of the quiet village
of Chippawa. No provision had been made for sheltering our
volunteers, as neither tents or blankets had been issued, so the
weary, jaded troops were content to lie out on the green sward
under the star-lit canopy of heaven, with the gentle June dew
falling on their sleeping forms, until at sunrise the bugles
sounding the reveille awoke them to a realization of the hard
fare of a soldier's life on active service. By some blunder of
somebody no food had been provided for the volunteer battalions, nor haversacks to carry it in if they did have it, so
fortunate indeed was he who received breakfast that morning.
As the majority of the men had left their homes early the day
before, and had eaten very little since, they keenly felt the
pangs of hunger. But the patriotic people of Chippawa did
their best to cater to their needs, and were unsparing in their
efforts to provide the meals so urgently required, while the
regular troops shared their rations of hard tack, cheese, meat
and tea cheerfully with their Canadian comrades.

Although the Fenians had openly flaunted their intention
of invading Canada, and the secret service agents had made
minute reports of the determination of the marauders to make a
raid, still the Canadian military authorities seemed apathetic.

and took very little heed of the warnings until the eve of the event. Plenty of time was accorded the Government to have the whole force properly equipped and in readiness, but when the bugles sounded the alarm and the volunteers promptly assembled to meet the foe, there was a woeful lack of the necessaries which are indispensable to a successful campaign, namely, an available supply of military stores, commissary and medical supplies. Many of the companies and battalions which moved promptly to the front were totally unprovided even with canteens or water bottles, and had to depend on creeks or roadside ditches for a drink of water wherewith to allay their thirst, which they scooped up in their hands or caps as best they could. But "Johnny Canuck" never murmured, and marched cheerfully onward in the shoes in which he usually stood, without provisions and weighted down with heavy padded uniforms (which were designed for winter wear), carrying a heavy rifle and accoutrements, with forty rounds of ball cartridges in his pouch and twenty more in his pockets for ballast. Still he had a stout heart within his breast, and a resolute determination to do his duty in assisting to drive the invaders from the shores of his native land served to impel him onward as he marched through the choking dust of clay roads on a blazing hot June day, gaily joining in the refrain of the old marching song:—

> "Tramp, tramp, tramp, our boys are marching,
>   Cheer up, let the Fenians come!
> For beneath the Union Jack we'll drive the rabble back
>   And we'll fight for our beloved Canadian home."

Those were stirring days, and many an old volunteer who participated in the forced marches and hardships of the campaign on the Niagara frontier particularly, still retains vivid recollections of that strenuous period.

On the evening of the 1st of June, Col. Peacocke received definite reports that the Fenians were still occupying their camp at Frenchman's Creek, and at once conceived the plan of uniting the forces at Port Colborne with his own column at Stevensville (a small country hamlet about seven miles south-west of Chippawa) and make a combined attack on Gen. O'Neil's position as soon as the junction of the two columns was effected. He accordingly dispatched Capt. Chas. S. Akers (an officer of the Royal Engineers) across the country about midnight with orders to Lieut.-Col. Booker to leave Port Colborne for Ridgeway by rail at five o'clock next morning, and after detraining his troops at that station to march by the nearest road to Stevensville, where he expected to meet him with his column about 10 o'clock. Capt. Akers was given minute instructions by Col. Peacocke as to the time he proposed to leave Chippawa (6 o'clock) and also the route of his march, so that Lieut.-Col. Booker could be thoroughly informed of his plans.

Capt. Akers arrived at Port Colborne about 2 o'clock a.m., on June 2nd, and after delivering his dispatches and verbal orders, had a conference with Lieut.-Col. Booker and Lieut.-Col. Dennis as to the situation of affairs at the front, which resulted in a proposal by Lieut.-Col. Dennis that Col. Peacocke's plans should be altered (contingent on that officer's consent) and that Lieut.-Col. Booker's column should advance on Fort Erie direct and join Col. Peacocke near Frenchman's Creek, instead of at Stevensville. This proposal was telegraphed to Col. Peacocke, who promptly negatived any change in his plans, and insisted on his original orders being obeyed.

Previous to the issuance of his order to Lieut.-Col. Booker, Col. Peacocke had telegraphed to Lieut.-Col. Dennis that he had ordered the International Ferry steamer to proceed from Fort Erie to Port Colborne, and instructed him to put a gun detachment on board and patrol the Niagara River from Fort Erie to Chippawa. As this steamer had not arrived at 10.30 p.m., Lieut.-Col. Dennis availed himself of the patriotic offer of Capt. Lachlan McCallum, owner of the powerful tug "W. T. Robb," to place that boat at his disposal. Capt. McCallum was the commanding officer of the Dunnville Naval Brigade, and the boat was lying at her dock at that place when he received a telegram from Lieut.-Col. Dennis shortly after midnight to proceed to Port Colborne without delay. He quickly mustered his crew and the members of his Naval Brigade and left Dunnville at 2 o'clock a.m., arriving at Port Colborne at about 4 a.m. Meanwhile the Welland Canal Field Battery, under command of Capt. Richard S. King, of Port Robinson, had reported at Port Colborne, and received orders to embark on the "W. T.

Robb,'' for the proposed reconnaisance to the Niagara River. For some unaccountable reason the field guns of this splendid Battery, which was one of the most efficient in the Province at that time, had been removed to Hamilton a few months previously, and their only armament on this occasion was short Enfield rifles with sword bayonets. They mustered three officers and 59 men when they joined the Dunnville Naval Brigade on board the tug. The latter corps consisted of three officers and 43 men, armed with Enfield rifles and equipment, but were without uniforms. Thus the total strength of the combatant forces which left Port Colborne on the ''W. T. Robb'' was 108 of all ranks. Without waiting for a reply from Col. Peacocke relative to the change in plans suggested by the conference, Lieut.-Col. Dennis, accompanied by Capt. Akers, went on board the tug, and assuming command of the expedition, ordered the vessel to proceed at once to Fort Erie.

Shortly after the ''W. T. Robb'' left the harbor, a telegram was received by Lieut.-Col. Booker from Col. Peacocke, ordering him to adhere to his original instructions, and to leave Port Colborne for Ridgeway not later than 5.30 a.m., to disembark there and march to Stevensville, so as to effect the junction with his column at the specified hour. Lieut.-Col. Booker's troops were already on board the train, having remained in the cars nearly all night with very little sleep, and after being served a hasty and very meagre breakfast, the train started from Port Colborne about 5 o'clock. The total strength of the forces (which consisted of the Queen's Own Rifles, the Thirteenth Battalion, and the York and Caledonia Rifle Companies) was about 840 men. Preceded by a pilot engine the train moved carefully eastward until it reached Ridgeway station, where the force was detrained and formed up in column of march. It was then found impossible to obtain horses and waggons at Ridgeway for the transport of the stores, so that a large quantity of supplies and other material which was urgently required had to be sent back to Port Colborne by the returning train. This was a lamentable state of affairs, which did not reflect much credit on the ability of some officer whose duty it was to look after such matters.

Although Col. Peacocke had notified Lieut.-Col. Booker that he would leave Chippawa with his column at 6 o'clock on his march for Stevensville to form the proposed junction of forces, he was nearly two hours late of his scheduled time in doing so, which had an important bearing on the fortunes of the day, and the events which might have been averted. The reinforcements (consisting of two companies of H. M. 47th Regiment, the 19th Lincoln Battalion, the 10th Royals of Toronto, and Stoker's Battery of Artillery, from St. Catharines) had arrived during the night and early hours of the morning. Some time was lost in getting the column ready for the advance, and it was not until 7 o'clock that the "assembly" was sounded for the companies to "fall in." The troops hurriedly bundled on their accoutrements and equipments, and in a quarter of an hour were ready for the march. Another half hour was lost in inspection, "telling off" the battalions, serving out ammunition and other preliminaries, so it was nearly 8 o'clock when the bugle sounded "the advance" and the column was put in motion.

H. M. 16th Regiment supplied the advance guard, with the usual look-out and flanking files. The main body of the advance was commanded by Capt. Horne and Lieut. Taylor, and the support by Lieut .Reid. The remainder of the column was formed in the following order: The right wing of H. M. 16th Regiment, under command of Major Grant; the Grey Battery of Royal Artillery (with six Armstrong guns), under Col. Hoste; H. M. 47th Regiment, under Lieut.-Col. Villiers and Major Lauder; the Nineteenth (Lincoln) Battalion (seven companies, with a strength of 350), and the Tenth Royals of Toronto (417 strong. The volunteer battalions were officered as follows:

NINETEENTH BATTALION—Lieut.-Col. James G. Currie in command; Majors, John Powell and T. L. Helliwell; Adjutant, Silas Spillett. No. 1 Co.—Capt. Ed. Thompson, Lieut. Johnson Clench. No. 2 Co.—Capt. Fred W. Macdonald, Lieut. F. Benson. No. 3 Co.—Capt. Wm. Kew, Lieut. J. K. Osborne, Ensign Kew. No. 4 Co.—Capt. Mathias Konkle, Lieut. G. Walker, Ensign Wolverton. No. 8 Co.—Capt. Henry Carlisle, Lieut. Edwin I. Parnell, Ensign Josiah G. Holmes. Surgeon, Edwin Goodman, M.D.; Quartermaster, Wm. McGhie. (The Clifton and Port Dalhousie Companies of this Battalion were left to guard the Suspension Bridge, and the Thorold Company was sent to Port Colborne to guard the Welland Canal).

THE TENTH ROYALS—Lieut.-Col., A. Brunel; Majors, James Worthington and John Boxall (in command during march); Adjutant, C. H. Connon. No. 1 Co.—Capt. Geo. McMurrich, Lieut. John Paterson, Ensign F. Barlow Cumberland. No. 2 Co.—Capt. Geo. R. Hamilton, Lieut. Fred Richardson.

Ensign Alex. Macdonald. No. 3 Co.—Lieut. H. J. Browne in command, Ensign Walter H. Barrett. No. 4 Co.—Capt. Wm. A. Stollery, Lieut. Arthur Coleman, Ensign W. D. Rogers. No. 5 Co.—Capt. Geo. W. Musson, Lieut. Chas. S. Musson, Ensign J. Widmer Rolph. No. 6 Co.—Capt. J. W. Laurence, Lieut. C. J. H. Winstanley, Ensign Hayward. No. 7 Co.—Capt. J. W. Hetherington, Lieut. G. Brunel. No. 8 Co.—Lieut. T. Brunel in command, Ensign L. Sherwood. Surgeon, Dr. J. H. Richardson; Assist. Surgeon, Dr. James Newcombe; Paymaster, Capt. John H. Ritchey; Quartermaster, Capt. Rufus Skinner.

The St. Catharines Garrison Battery of Artillery, under command of Capt. George Stoker and Lieut. James Wilson, was left at Chippawa to hold that place and guard the bridges.

A very grave error or oversight was made by the General Commanding in not providing a force of cavalry to thoroughly scour the country in advance of both of these columns before they started feeling their way through a district that was practically unknown to the commanding officers, and which was reported to be occupied by marauding parties of the enemy. Had this been done on the first of June, and cavalry scouts been employed on all the leading roads and highways gathering information of the whereabouts and doings of Gen. O'Neil and his forces, the events which subsequently transpired might have ended more happily. At the eleventh hour the Militia authorities saw the necessity of employing cavalry in the operations, and called out a portion of that extremely useful branch of the service. One of these cavalry troops (the Governor-General's Body Guard, of Toronto, under command of Major Geo. T. Denison), performed splendid service in this direction. an account of which will be given in a subsequent chapter.

Col. Peacocke marched from Chippawa by the River Road for Black Creek on his way to Stevensville, a rather round-about route, which added some miles to his journey and caused considerable loss of time. The day was an oppressively close one, with not a breath of air stirring, and as the sun rose higher in the heavens it cast forth a brassy heat that was almost unbearable, and had a telling effect on the men, who were soon drenched with perspiration and covered with dust. By 11 o'clock the heat became more intense and the dust more denser, and the jaded soldiers began to show signs of weariness, when Col. Peacoke resolved to halt his column at New Germany, a point about three miles from Stevensville, having covered 12¼ measured miles on this strenuous march.

CHAPTER VI.

THE BATTLE OF RIDGEWAY—A BAPTISM OF FIRE AND BLOOD FOR THE CANADIAN TROOPS—SPLENDID COOLNESS AND HEROIC COURAGE OF THE VOLUNTEERS AT THE BEGINNING OF THE FIGHT ENDS IN DISASTER.

The second of June, 1866, was an eventful day for the Canadian troops who were operating on the Niagara frontier. They had hurriedly left their homes, the majority of them wholly unprovided with the means of subsistence, and illy equipped for campaigning, to combat a band of veteran troops who were bent on capturing Canada. A large proportion of our volunteers were mere youths who had left their colleges, office work, mercantile and other occupations, to go forth at their country's call, and had never encountered the perils of war or seen a hostile shot fired in their lives. But the high spirit of courage and patriotism which animated the hearts of all, rendered them self-reliant and determined to do their utmost in performing their sacred duty to their Queen and country.

In the preceding chapter a general idea of Col. Peacock's plan of campaign was given, and as Lieut.-Col. Booker's force was the first to move in carrying out that plan, it will be necessary to describe the operations of this command in detail, so that the reader may acquire a comprehensive knowledge of the exciting events which succeeded each other rapidly during the time this gallant force was in action.

A few minutes after 7 o'clock Lieut.-Col. Booker put his column in motion from Ridgeway station. The troops had previously been instructed to "load with ball cartridge," and all were keen to meet the enemy. Just before leaving, Lieut.-Col. Booker had been informed by several farmers of the neighborhood that the Fenians were only a short distance in his front, but he could scarcely believe so many conflicting stories, as the last official information he had received was that O'Neil was still at his camp at Frenchman's Creek. Although he considered the information unreliable, still he resolved to be prudent, and keep a sharp lookout for "breakers ahead." The usual military precautions which govern an advance into a hostile country were taken by him, and the advance guard and commanding officers warned to be on the alert.

The Queen's Own Rifles, under command of Major Charles T. Gillmor, led the van, followed by the York Rifle Company (Capt. Davis), the Thirteenth Battalion, under command of Major Skinner, and the Caledonia Rifle Company, under Capt. Jackson, in the order named. No. 5 Company of the Queen's Own (who were armed with Spencer repeating rifles) formed the advance guard, and the Caledonia Rifles the rear guard.

After proceeding about two miles along the Ridge Road the advance guard signalled back the intelligence that there were indications of the enemy in front. The column was then halted on the road, and flanking parties were detailed to scour the woods to the right and left. Proceeding a little further it became apparent that the Fenians were in position about half a mile north of the Garrison Road.

As the Canadian troops carefully moved forward, the advance guard (No. 5 Co., Q.O.R.), extended from its centre, with No. 1 Company on its left and No. 2 Company on its right as skirmishers. No. 3 Company acted as centre supports, No. 4 Company left supports, No. 7 Company as a flanking party to the left, supported by No. 8 Company, and No. 6 Company flanking to the right. Nos. 9 and 10 Companies were in reserve. After an advance of about half a mile in this formation No. 6 Company was sent as a support to No. 2 Company on the right.

The Canadians bravely advanced until they were met by a heavy fire from the Fenians' sharpshooters, who were extended behind rail fences and clumps of bushes, their main force being posted behind breastworks in a wood some distance in their rear. The Queen's Own promptly returned the fire and continued to advance steadily. The firing then became general, being most galling on the right and centre of the Canadian line.

The first Canadian to fall by a Fenian bullet was Ensign Malcolm McEachren, a brave officer of No. 5 Co., Q.O.R., who was mortally wounded in the stomach and died on the field about twenty minutes later.

For over an hour the gallant Queen's Own continued to drive the enemy before them, and one after another of their positions was carried, until they had the Fenians forced back to their main breastworks in the woods. By this time the Queen's Own had nearly exhausted their ammunition, and No. 5 Company had fired every round of their Spencer rifle cartridges. So that it became necessary for Major Gillmor to ask for relief.

The Thirteenth Battalion was the reserve force of the column, and it now became their turn to go into action. Lieut.-Col. Booker at once ordered the right wing of the reserve to deploy on the rear company to the right and extend. Major Skinner commanded the Thirteenth, and acted very courageously. He executed the movement with great skill and ability. No. 1 Company of the Thirteenth Battalion was on the right of the line and the York Rifles on the left. The troops advanced with coolness and bravery and were heartily cheered by the Queen's Own as they took their place in the battle line. The left wing of the Thirteenth moved up as the supports of their comrades of the same Battalion, and the Queen's Own then became the reserve. The fighting line of the Thirteenth continued the "drive" of the enemy into their entrenchments, and their hearty cheers as they pushed on to the attack were answered by the yells of the Fenians, who were preparing to make a charge.

Observing a movement on the part of O'Neil which threatened his right flank, Lieut.-Col. Booker requested Major Gillmor to keep a sharp lookout for the cross-roads on which the reserve rested, and to send two companies from the reserve to occupy and hold the woods on the hill to the right of his line. Major Gillmor sent the Highland Company of the Queen's Own to perform that duty.

Just at this time (about 9.30 a.m.) two telegrams were handed to Lieut.-Col. Booker by a gentleman who had then arrived from Port Colborne. Both messages were from Col. Peacocke, one stating that he could not leave Chippawa until 7 o'clock, and the other advising him to "be cautious in feeling his way for fear obstacles should prevent a junction." This was disappointing news to Lieut.-Col. Booker. He had already

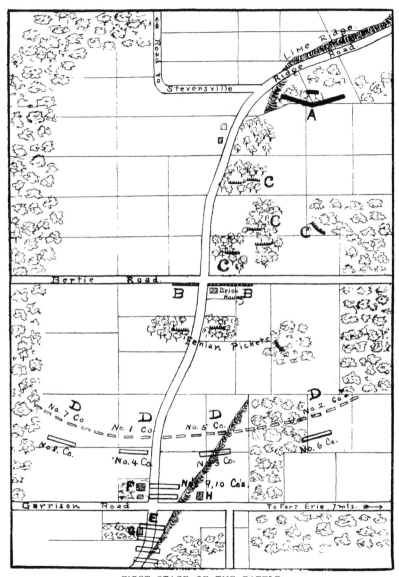

FIRST STAGE OF THE BATTLE

A—Main position of the Fenians.   B—Advanced position of Fenians at the Cross Roads from
whence they where driven by the Queen's Own.   C—Fenian Pickets and Skirmishers.
D—Queen's Own line of skirmishers and supports.   E—Col. Booker's column of reserve.
F—Hoffman's Tavern.   G—Baker's house, used as an Hospital.   H—School House.

struck an "obstacle," and had to overcome it alone, as there was now no chance of any succor from Col. Peacocke.

To make matters worse, a few moments later Major Gill-mor reported that the Highland Company had been compelled to leave the woods on the right of his position, as they had found that point occupied by Fenians. Almost simultaneously the cry of "Cavalry! Look out for cavalry!" came down the road, and some of our men were observed doubling down the hill. As the alarm was repeated when a few Fenian horsemen were observed advancing from around the corner of a piece of bush, Lieut.-Col. Booker ordered the reserve (which was composed of the Queen's Own) to "Prepare for Cavalry," and Companies Nos. 1, 2, 3, 5 and 8 promptly "formed square" on the road. As soon as it was discovered that the alarm was a false one, the order was given to "Reform Column," and for the two leading companies (Nos. 1 and 2) to "extend." On reforming, the reserve, being too close to the skirmish line, was ordered to retire. The left wing of the Thirteenth, who were in rear, seeing the four companies of the Queen's Own reserve retiring, and thinking a general retreat had been ordered, broke and retired in a panic, on seeing which the Queen's Own reserve also hurriedly retired. The bugles now having sounded the "Retire," Nos. 1 and 2 Companies of the Queen's Own fell back and seeing their comrades in disorder they too became demoralized. The Fenians, who were about ready to quit the fight and flee from the field when this unfortunate circumstance occurred, now saw their opportunity, and were quick to avail themselves of it. Their rifle fire became hotter and more incessant than ever, and as the Canadian troops were all huddled up in a narrow road, their murderous volleys were very destructive. It was a vain effort on the part of the officers to check the retreat and rally the men for the first few hundred yards, but after a while they cooled down and retired in an orderly manner, occasionally turning around to take a parting shot at the Fenians, who were pursuing them. Occasionally a squad or company would halt and deliver a well-directed volley, but no general formation could be accomplished. as the troops were practically demoralized.

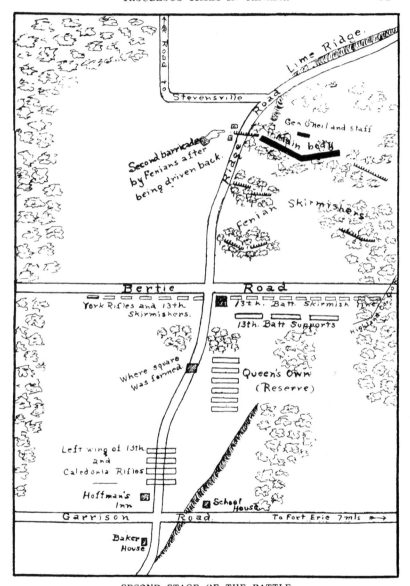

SECOND STAGE OF THE BATTLE

Position of the Canadian Troops when the fatal order to "Form Square" was given. No. 1 and 2 Companies, Q.O.R. were extended as Skirmishers, and covered the retreat, supported by a portion of the 13th. The Highland Co. (No. 10) was on the extreme right of the Canadian Line.

The Fenians followed in pursuit as far as Ridgeway Station, when they turned east and retreated to Fort Erie, no doubt thinking that a fresh column of Canadian troops would endeavor to effect their capture. Lieut.-Col. Booker, seeing that it was impossible to get the troops in good fighting condition again that day, decided to order a retreat to Port Colborne, where they arrived during the afternoon, utterly worn out from loss of sleep and their strenuous exertions during the day.

THE HONOR ROLL.

The following is a list of the Canadians killed and wounded in the action at Ridgeway:

QUEEN'S OWN RIFLES.

Killed.

Ensign Malcolm McEachren, No. 5 Company.
Lance-Corporal Mark Defries, No. 3 Company.
Private William Smith, No. 2 Company.
Private Christopher Alderson, No. 7 Company.
Private Malcolm McKenzie, No. 9 Company.
Private Wm. F. Tempest, No. 9 Company.
Private J. H. Mewburn, No. 9 Company.
Sergt. Hugh Matheson (died on June 9th), No. 2 Company.
Corporal F. Lackey (died on June 11th), No. 2 Company.

Wounded.

Ensign Wm. Fahey (in knee), No. 1 Company.
Private Oulster (calf of leg), No. 1 Company.
Private Wm. Thompson (neck), No. 2 Company.
Capt. J. B. Boustead (contusion), No. 3 Company.
Lieut. J. H. Beaven (thigh), No. 3 Company.
Private Charles Winter (thigh), No. 3 Company.
Private Chas. Lugsdin (lung and arm), No. 4 Company.
Private Chas. Bell (knee), No. 5 Company.
Private Copp (wrist), No. 5 Company.
Lieut. W. C. Campbell (shoulder), No. 6 Company.
Corporal Paul Robbins (knee, leg amputated), No. 6 Company.
Private Rutherford (foot), No. 6 Company.
Sergt. W. Foster (side), No. 7 Company.
Private E. T. Paul (knee), No. 9 Company.
Private R. E. Kingsford (leg), No. 9 Company.
Private E. G. Paterson (arm). No. 9 Company.

Private W. H. Vandersmissen (groin), No. 9 Company.
Color-Sergt. F. McHardy (arm), No. 10 Company.
Private White (arm, amputated), No. 10 Company.
Private Alex. Muir (arm dislocated), No. 10 Company.
Sergt. Forbes (arm), No. 10 Company.

THIRTEENTH BATTALION.

Died.—Private Morrison, No. 3 Company.

Wounded.—Lieut. Routh, severely in left side; Private Mc-
Kenzie, wound in foot; Private George Mackenzie, left arm; Private Edwin Hillier, wound in neck; Private Stuart, flesh wound
in neck; Private Powell, wound in thigh; Sergt. J. M. Young,
H. W. Simons, B. W. Sutherland, Alex. Henderson, John Cross-
man, James Cahill, W. Irving, W. T. Urquhart, and W. B.
Nicholls.

YORK RIFLES.

Wounded.—Sergt. Jack, in thigh; B. J. Cranston, Oneida.

The unfortunate termination of the battle of Ridgeway was
a great disappointment to the rank and file in Lieut.-Col. Booker's force, and he was severely condemned for having given the
fatal order which resulted in huddling up his men in a "square"
in an exposed position, and finally resulted in the retrograde
movement. But under similar circumstances any other officer
might have done likewise, and to his credit it may be recorded
that he did his best afterwards to retrieve the consequences of
his error, and by personal courage on the field endeavored to
stop the retreat. He had no staff to assist him, and was the only
mounted officer on the Canadian side, so that he was at a dis-
advantage. Moreover, he had never previously manoeuvred a
brigade, even on parade, and to handle one in battle was a trying
ordeal to an inexperienced officer who had never before been
under fire.

It was a most disastrous occurrence, for in another ten
minutes of fighting Gen. O'Neill's forces would have been defeated and in full retreat. In fact, O'Neil himself afterwards
admitted this, and stated that if the Canadians had fought five
minutes longer his forces would have given way, as they were
fast becoming demoralized and were making preparations for
flight. He complimented our men highly on their courage and
steadiness, and said that he had mistaken them for regular British troops, and could not believe that they were merely Canadian
volunteers, without any previous experience in warfare.

An observer who was present at the battle states that ''there were no faint hearts in the whole Canadian line while under fire, but with the steadfastness of old soldiers trained in battle, the gallant youths stood up to perform honorably and creditably the stern task which they saw was before them. The officers. by word and act, gave their men whatever slight encouragement was needed, and each vied with the other in enthusiasm and firmness of purpose.''

On the retreat from Ridgeway the dead and severely wounded were of necessity left on the field, but during the afternoon and evening were collected by the people residing in the vicinity and conveyed to near-by houses, where the wounded received every attention that it was possible to bestow until the arrival of medical aid. As soon as it became known in Toronto that a battle had been fought, the following surgeons left for the front by the 1 p.m. train: Doctors Tempest, Rowell, Stevenson. Howson, Agnew, Pollock, De Grassi and Dack. They arrived at Port Colborne at 9 a.m., and Dr. Tempest immediately conferred with Dr. Thorburn, Surgeon of the Queen's Own, who had retired to Port Colborne with his regiment. It was just at this moment that Dr. Tempest received the sad intelligence that his own son had been killed in the engagement, which was a crushing blow to the patriotic father. He, however, remained at his post of duty, carefully supervising details in the movement of several surgeons to the battlefield, fourteen miles distant, and directed affairs at Port Colborne to receive the wounded on their arrival at that point. No vehicles were available at Port Colborne, but Doctors Stevenson and Howson, noticing a farmer's waggon passing by. impressed it into the service and started together for the battle ground, where they arrived about 2 o'clock Sunday morning. They found our wounded in the houses in the neighborhood, and with the assistance of Dr. Clark, of St. Catharines, Doctors Brewster and Duncan, of Port Colborne, and Dr. Allen, quickly dressed the wounds of all of the wounded. The dead were sent on to Port Colborne in waggons, and a train was ordered to proceed to Ridgeway to bring back the wounded. This train left Ridgeway in charge of Doctors Stevenson and Howson at 1 o'clock on Sunday, and soon after arrived at Port Colborne, where it was met by Doctors Tempest. Beaumont and other medical men. Several of the most severely wounded, whose cases demanded rest and more careful surgical treatment, were left in charge of the surgeons at Port Colborne, while others were removed to the improvised hospital in the Town Hall at St. Catharines, and the remainder conveyed to Port Dalhousie, where they were carefully carried on board the "City of Toronto." After the wounded had been comfortably placed on mattresses and stretchers, the bodies of six of the dead soldiers (Ensign McEachren, Corporal Defries, and Privates Smith, Alderson, McKenzie and Tempest), encased in the plain wooden coffins which had been provided for them at Port Colborne, were reverently carried on board, and the steamer started on its sorrowful trip to Toronto.

A Toronto paper, in reciting the circumstance of the sad home-coming of the dead and wounded heroes, said:

At 9 o'clock in the evening the bells of the city began to toll mournfully as the lights of the "City of Toronto," freighted with dead and wounded from the battle field, were seen entering the harbor, and every street and avenue began to pour their throngs of sympathizing citizens to Yonge street wharf, where strong pickets of volunteers were drawn up to keep the dense crowd already assembled from pressing over the dock. Ominous files of hearses, with cabs and carriages, passed over the wharf, and the pickets again closed upon the multitude, vast numbers betaking themselves to the neighboring wharves and storehouses and literally swarmed over every post of observation. We do not think that gloomy Sunday night will soon be forgotten by any of the myriads who, as the soft southeastern wind dashed the waves against the esplanade, awaited in melancholy expectation the approaching steamer. The wharf was densely crowded with an anxious crowd to witness the arrival of the poor fellows. A strong guard had to be stationed across the street at the entrance of the wharf, and no one was allowed to pass except the committee and those privileged with a pass. At half past nine the steamer arrived, and the committee immediately went on board and assisted in the removal of the wounded, many of whom were lying on mattresses with their legs and arms in bandages, some of them apparently in great pain. A company of the 47th was in waiting with ambulances to convey the wounded out of the boat to cabs. Six dead bodies were brought down in coffins, their names being McEachren, Defries, Alderson, Tempest, McKenzie and Smith. The wounded who arrived were Capt. Boustead, Ensign Fahey, Kingsford, Lakey, Robins, VanderSmissen, Patterson, Webster, Muir and Elliott. Lugsden and Mathieson were left at Port Colborne, they being too much injured to be removed. The wounded were conveyed in cabs to their residences, and the dead to the houses of their friends.

INCIDENTS OF THE BATTLE.

A daring deed of bravery was performed by Private John H. Noverre, of No. 5 Co., Q.O.R., while the battle was at its hottest stage. When Ensign McEachren received his fatal wound, his belts and sword were removed from his body and left in a fence corner. As the Fenians were working up in that direction, Mr. Noverre determined to run the risk of recovering his dead comrade's equipments, rather than have them fall into the hands of an exultant enemy. Therefore he ran across the line of fire amid a storm of bullets, secured the sword and belts, and regained the Canadian lines unscathed just as the retreat began. The exertion of the race and the excessive heat proved too much for him, however, and he suffered sun-stroke, which necessitated his being carried from the field and borne to Port Colborne by his comrades, from whence he was sent to the hospital at St. Catharines for treatment, and soon recovered.

Ensign Wm. Fahey, of No. 1 Company, was about the last man struck, while assisting to cover the retreat. He was using the rifle of a fallen comrade on the firing line when he was struck in the knee. He was assisted to a neighboring house and was kindly treated by the Fenians when they took possession.

Private R. W. Hines, of No. 8 Co., Queen's Own, was taken prisoner by a squad of Fenians and his rifle taken from him and handed to one of their officers. The officer took the rifle, and after eyeing it critically, grabbed it by the barrel and with a profane remark that it would never shoot another Fenian, smashed the stock against a boulder. The Canadian gun, being loaded and at full cock, went off with the concussion, and the bullet passed through the Fenian's body, killing him instantly.

It is related that a private of the Queen's Own was in conflict with two Fenians, who pressed him at the point of the bayonet. He retreated across a fence and fell, when one of the Fenians dashed at him with his bayonet and pinned him to the ground, the bayonet passing through his arm. He pulled a revolver with the other hand and shot the Fenians one after another and escaped.

Private Graham, of the Queen's Own, in getting over a fence, caught his foot between the top rails and swung over, his head downwards, and was unable to extricate himself. A shower of Fenian bullets whistled around him without injury, when a comrade came to his rescue and relieved him, but was himself seriously wounded.

Private R. E. Kingsford, of No. 9 Co., Queen's Own (now Police Magistrate at Toronto), was wounded and taken prisoner. The Fenians carried him to a farm house, procured him refreshments, and took great care of him while he was in their hands.

Major Cattley, of the 13th Battalion, had a spur knocked off his heel by a bullet while climbing a fence, and a private of the same battalion had the ball on the top of his shako shot away.

Private Shuttleworth, of the 13th, had a narrow and extraordinary escape. While he was in the act of firing, the muzzle of his rifle was shot into by a Fenian musket ball and torn open.

It is recounted that Lieut. Routh, of the 13th Battalion, turned his company towards the enemy three times during the retreat and delivered volleys at the advancing foe. He called out to the men to stand their ground, but just at that moment he was struck by a spent ball on the hip. He rallied, and said it was lucky it was no worse, and exclaimed, "I will not run, I will die first," but he was again struck by a ball through the left side, when he dropped and was carried off the field by two of his men.

Capt. Sherwood, of No. 8 Co., Q.O.R., had the band taken off his collar and a piece taken out of the sleeve of his tunic by a bullet, without being even wounded.

Sergt. Foster, of No. 7 Co., Q.O.R., was struck by a bullet over the heart, tearing his tunic and grazing the skin, but leaving him otherwise uninjured.

Mr. P. E. Noverre, of No. 5 Co., Q.O.R., relates that during the progress of the fight a patriotic lady and her little daughter, who resided in the neighborhood of the battlefield, were busy carrying water for the thirsty soldiers to drink. They were right in the line of fire, but seemed to disdain the danger. Suddenly a Fenian bullet perforated the tin pail the little girl was carrying, and she remarked, "Mother, the pail is leaking; it won't hold water." Mr. Noverre was being served with a drink by the lady at the time, when another bullet whizzed past his ear and severely wounded a soldier of the 13th Battalion who was standing behind him.

C. H. Murdock, a bugler attached to No. 10 Co., Q. O. R., was conspicuous for his gallantry in carrying water to the men of the Highland Company during the hottest part of the action. and had several narrow escapes from the Fenian bullets which rattled around him.

Mr. Phil. E. Noverre was an eye-witness to the interment of eleven Fenians in a field near Fort Erie. These bodies were found by our troops on arrival at Fort Erie on Sunday, and it is supposed the men were killed during the two actions at Ridgeway and Fort Erie. Five or six more were buried on the Ridgeway battlefield.

A correspondent of the Toronto *Leader*, who was present during the engagement at Ridgeway, gave the following vivid account of his personal experiences:

At the time the disastrous retreat of our troops commenced I was requested by his comrade to assist a wounded soldier of the Queen's Own to Hoffman's tavern, then about half a mile distant. The whole force rushed past us. We found on reaching the tavern that, with the exception of some more wounded whom we found there, we were the only parties left. We had barely time to deposit our burden when the advance guard of the Fenians rushed up and surrounded the tavern, flushed with apparent victory, and wild with excitement. They presented such an appearance as I certainly shall not soon forget. They were the most cut-throat-looking set of ruffians that could well be imagined. Supposing me to be the landlord, they immediately demanded liquor. In vain I urged that I was as much a stranger as themselves. Their leader presented a revolver at me, and ordered me behind the bar; every decanter was empty. They insisted that I had hid everything away. I examined every jar, without success. Fortunately I discovered a small keg, which on examination I found to contain about a gallon of old rye whiskey. This I distributed among them and think I must have treated about fifty. This mollified them in some degree, and after slaking their thirst at the well that party proceeded on its way without molesting me further. I then, assisted by the young volunteer whose comrade we had brought in, proceeded to render what assistance we could to the wounded men, one of whom was Private Lugsden of the Queen's Own, badly wounded in the chest, when we were interrupted by the arrival of another detachment under the command of a Capt. Lacken, who marched my assistant off a prisoner. I remonstrated with him upon the cruelty of leaving me alone with all the wounded, when he detailed one of his own men to assist me and went his way. About one hundred yards from the tavern, on the west side of the road, I found a poor fellow of the Queen's Own lying on his face near the fence. I knelt down beside him and found that he was sensible. He told me his name was Mark Defries, and that he was shot through the back. He knew that he was dying. He requested me to take a ring from his finger and send it with a message to a young lady in Toronto. He also requested me to take his watch and send it to his father, whose address he gave me. This I attempted to do, but he could not endure to be touched. He told me it would do to take it after he was dead. I conversed with him for some time, when I left him to try to obtain some assistance to have him removed into

HOFFMAN'S TAVERN, KNOWN AS "THE SMUGGLER'S HOME."

the house. I was then placed under arrest by a Fenian, by order of his commanding officers, and conveyed to a farm house, where I found two of our wounded men, young VanderSmissen, of the University Rifles, badly wounded in the thigh, and Corporal Lakey, shot through the mouth. With the assistance of the Fenian sentry I had them both put to bed and rendered them all the assistance in my power; for, be it noticed, that we could not find man, woman nor child in a circuit of miles, all fled in terror. When I could not do any more in that house, I requested the sentry to march me to the commanding officer, who was then at the tavern. He rode a sorrel horse, which was then at the door, and about half a mile from where we then were. I found him to be a very mild-looking young man, civil and courteous, evidently well educated. I stated my business at once, which was that I might obtain from him a written authority to go through their lines and visit the wounded on both sides without molestation. This he readily consented to, and gave me a document to that effect, signed Major McDonnell, commanding Division F. B. I had now perfect freedom to go wherever I wanted to. I immediately went in search of young Defries, but found that he had been removed. I returned to the tavern and found him lying in a back room dead. I then asked the landlord, who had by this time returned, to witness me taking the watch at his request, but after feeling him all over, the watch was gone. It had been taken from him, no doubt, by some Fenian marauder. I sent the ring, enclosed in a letter, to the young lady; I also wrote to his father's address, stating all the circumstances.

I found there were more of our wounded men in another frame house about a mile further, on the Fort Erie road. I proceeded there and found the place guarded with Fenian sentries, but my protection was all potent. They, supposing me to be a surgeon, gave me every facility. I found, among others whose names I failed to ascertain, young Kingsford, of the

University Rifles, lying on a lounge, badly wounded in the leg, but remarkably cheerful. I also found a young man named Hamilton, of the 13th Battalion, with a very bad wound in the right side. He had been attended to by a Fenian surgeon; he was lying on his face and suffering much. At his request I examined his wound and placed a bandage around it to stop the bleeding. There was also another young man of the Queen's Own lying on the floor in strong convulsions, evidently in a dying state, singular to say, without a wound upon his body. In another room in the same house I found another young man badly wounded. At this time a Fenian was brought in on a stretcher in a dying state. I ordered his comrades to cut his shirt open, when I found an ugly wound just under his left arm, which I have no doubt penetrated a vital part. I got water and washed the wound; he was sensible and able to tell me that his name was James Gerrahty, from Cincinnati, and that one of his own comrades had shot him by mistake, and that he freely forgave him. He died in about thirteen minutes, one of his comrades holding a crucifix before him as long as he could see it. We buried him in an orchard adjoining, the same evening.

Another Fenian was now brought in with a very bad wound in the neck. He was a very rough-looking fellow. I washed his wound also. He was afterwards removed to the hospital at St. Catharines. On leaving the house my attention was called to the dead body of one of the Queen's Own lying across the road, a very powerful man. He was shot through the head and presented a horrid spectacle. A little further on I found a group of three armed Fenians, who were watching over a wounded comrade. I was called upon to assist him. His comrades stripped him, and I found a gunshot wound in the hip, having passed right through, leaving two very ugly wounds. I washed him also and left him.

I now returned to the tavern. By this time the main body had returned, after having pillaged the village of Ridgeway, ransacking the principal stores, taverns, etc., and were now resting on a rising ground almost immediately opposite the tavern. The green flag, on which was emblazoned a large golden harp, was floating to the breeze in their centre. An officer, whom I soon found was their Adjutant, rode across to me and told me that two of our wounded men were lying on the road about fifty rods from us, nearer Ridgeway, a circumstance I was not before aware of. Desiring that I should procure some assistance to have them removed from the sun's scorching influence, which at that time was very powerful, I told him I had not a man left but the wounded. I suggested to him to detail four of his stoutest fellows and place them under my authority for a few minutes, which he readily agreed to. I marched them off, but before reaching the poor fellows their bugle sounded the assembly, when they all started off and left me without assistance. I may mention here that this officer gave me an authority in writing to remove the wounded to where they might obtain proper medical assistance. Accompanied by a young man of the Queen's Own, who was slightly wounded in the wrist, I proceeded to the poor fellows who were lying on the road. We were unable to remove them, but gave them water to drink and put the overcoats that we picked up on the road in such a way as to shelter them from the sun. We then proceeded to Ridgeway to try to obtain assistance to remove those that were able, or nurses to attend upon the poor fellows, or men to move the dead and wounded that were still exposed on the road, as well as to try to procure teams to take them to Port Colborne, but with the exception of three men who agreed to go and move the men off the road, and one colored woman, whom I pressed into service, I could get no further assistance. The horses had been all driven away for fear of them being taken. In going into a farmer's house in the immediate neighborhood of Ridgeway I knocked and could not obtain admission. I then went to the kitchen door, and opening another door, I found lying on the bed a poor young volunteer of the Queen's Own. I learned from himself that he was a son of the Rev. Mr. McKenzie, and was badly wounded, I think, in the arm. He was lying there alone, the house being deserted by all its inhabitants. I promised to send him assistance, which I did.

Returning from my fruitless errand, I met Dr. Elliot, of Port Colborne, who in the interim had been visiting the wounded men. He agreed to find ways and means to convey me to Port Colborne to report to the medical staff, with a view to sending immediate relief. On returning to Ridgeway I fortunately found a farmer's horse and buggy, and immediately drove to Port Colborne, when I reported to Dr. Thorburn, of the Queen's Own, who authorized me to press into the service all the teams necessary to bring up the dead and wounded, which was accomplished with little delay. A medical staff, consisting of Dr. Clark, of St. Catharines; Dr. Fraser, of Fonthill; Dr. Downie, Dr. Allen, of Brantford, and others, proceeded at once to the battle-ground, attending carefully to the wounded, but it was deemed advisable for the medical men to remain with them and accompany them by railway next day to Port Colborne. We, however, brought with us two wounded Fenian prisoners, who were taken to the hospital at St. Catharines. We also brought the bodies of the honored dead. We arrived at Port Colborne with our melancholy burden, about six o'clock a.m. on the 3rd. I may mention that two of the wounded men, whom I left alive in the afternoon, were dead when we returned in evening. Thus terminated the day of horrors. God grant that it may never be my lot to relate similar experiences.

As an evidence of the coolness and courage which was exemplified by many of our citizen soldiers, it is related by one of his men that Ensign Wm. Fahey, of No. 1 Company of the Queen's Own, when that company was advancing in skirmishing order in the face of a hot fire, kept continually encouraging his comrades in both words and action. When the bullets were flying around them he shouted, "Boys, keep a stiff upper lip!" and when a little later he was shot through the left knee and was being carried off the field, he again encouraged them by shouting, "No. 1, do your duty!" Such bravery under such circumstances will tend to show the sort of material of which our volunteers was composed.

An officer who fell on the firing line during the final stage of the battle was taken prisoner by the Fenians. When asked by the officer in command of the enemy what troops confronted them, and being told they were Canadian volunteers, he would hardly believe it. Their Adjutant said that during his experience in the Civil War he had never seen troops extending in

such order and steadiness as our men did that morning. He was
under the impression that they were British regulars.

PUBLIC FUNERALS FOR THE DEAD.

On Tuesday afternoon, June 5th, the bodies of Ensign Mc-
Eachren, Corporal Defries and Privates Smith, Alderson and
Tempest were interred in St. James' Cemetery, Toronto, with
full military honors. It was a public funeral, and one of the
most solemn and imposing *corteges* that ever passed through the
streets of Toronto.   The bodies of the five dead heroes were
placed upon a catafalque which had been specially prepared to
convey the remains to their last resting places, and at 3.50 p.m.
the procession started from the Drill Shed to the Cemetery. preceded by the Band of the 47th Regiment, playing the Dead
March. The Lloydtown Rifle Company acted as the firing party,
and the *cortege* included all the military units in the city. besides fraternal societies, the Mayor and Corporation, Major-Gen.
Napier and staff, and citizens on foot and in carriages.   All
along the line of march the shops were closed and buildings
draped in mourning. An immense concourse of people lined the
streets, and a general feeling of mournfulness and sadness pervaded the community as the procession moved slowly on to the
solemn strains of the band and the tolling of all the bells in the
city. After the service at the Cemetery had been concluded, the
usual volleys were fired over the remains by the Lloydtown
Rifles, and all that was mortal of those five heroes who had sacrificed their lives on the field of battle for their country were laid
away to eternal rest.

The body of Malcolm McKenzie was sent to his old home at
Woodstock for burial, and that of Private J. H. Mewburn to
Stamford.   Both of these dead soldiers were buried the
same day, with full military honors. and were laid to rest with
the deepest reverence by their comrades and the people of the
communities in which they had lived and been honored.

On the 9th of June Sergt. Hugh Matheson, of No. 2 Company. Queen's Own Rifles, died in the hospital at St. Catharines, from wounds received at Ridgeway, and on the 11th Corporal F. Lackey, of the same company, died in Toronto, from
the effects of a cruel wound in the upper jaw, received in the
same battle. The remains of these two soldiers were also given
a public funeral, as large and imposing as had been accorded to

their dead comrades a week previously. At St. James' Cemetery the same service took place as at the previous funerals, Rev. Mr. Grasett reading the burial service of the Church of England, after which the Upper Canada College Company of the Queen's Own fired the customary volleys over the remains, which were then placed in the vault of the Cemetery Chapel.

Thus were laid to rest the bodies of nine Canadian heroes whose names and deeds are engraved deeply on the tablets of their country's history, and whose memory is warmly preserved in the hearts of their surviving comrades, who annually decorate their graves with flowers, flags and garlands on each recurring anniversary of the battle in which they gave up their lives.

A handsome monument was erected in the Queen's Park, Toronto, to perpetuate their memory, while at the entrance of the Ontario Parliament Buildings the Provincial Government has also erected a brass memorial plate in commemoration of their patriotic deeds in shedding their life's blood for the honor of their country and its flag. *"Dulce et decorum est pro patria mori."*

LIST OF OFFICERS WHO PARTICIPATED IN THE BATTLE.

The following is a list of the officers in command of the battalions and companies which formed Lieut.-Col. Booker's column, all of whom were present at the battle of Lime Ridge and took part in the action:—

QUEEN'S OWN RIFLES.

Major Chas. T. Gillmor in command.

No. 1 Company—Capt. John Brown, Lieut. Joseph Davids, Ensign Wm. Fahey (wounded).

No. 2 Company—Capt. Fred. E. Dixon, Lieut. Farquhar Morrison, Ensign James Bennett.

No. 3 Company—Capt. J. B. Boustead, Lieut. James H. Beavan, Ensign Wm. Wharin.

No. 4 Company—Capt. John Douglas, Lieut. Wm. Arthurs, Ensign John H. Davis.

No. 5 Company—Capt. John Edwards, Lieut. Alex. G. Lee, Ensign Malcolm McEachren (killed).

No. 6 Company—Capt. G. M. Adam, Lieut. Wm. C. Campbell, Ensign T. A. McLean.

No. 7 Company—Capt. A. Macpherson, Lieut. John G. R. Stinson, Ensign Smith.

No. 8 Co.—Capt. L. P. Sherwood, Lieut. John O'Reilly.

No. 9 (Trinity Coll.) Co.—Acting Captain Geo. Y. Whitney.

No. 10 (Highland) Company—Capt. John Gardner, Lieut. Robert H. Ramsay, Ensign Donald Gibson.

Staff Paymaster, Capt. W. H. Harris; Quartermaster, Capt. James Jackson; Adjutant, Capt. Wm. D. Otter; Surgeon, James Thorburn, M.D.; Assistant Surgeon, Samuel P. May, M.D.

THIRTEENTH BATTALION.

Major James A. Skinner in command; Major Stephen T. Cattley.

No. 1 Company—Capt. Robert Grant, Lieut. John M. Gibson, Ensign McKenzie.

No. 2 Company—Capt. John H. Watson, Lieut. Chas. R. M. Sewell.

No. 3 Company—Lieut. John W. Ferguson; Ensign Charles Armstrong.

No. 4 Company—Lieut. Percy G. Routh (severely wounded), Ensign J. B. Young.

No. 5 Company—Capt. Alex H. Askin, Lieut. F. E. Ritchie.

No. 6 Company—Ensign W. Roy.

Adjutant, Capt. John Henery.

YORK RIFLES.

Capt. Robert H. Davis, Lieut. Davis, Ensign Jeffrey Hill.

CALEDONIA RIFLES.

Capt. William Jackson, Lieut. Robert Thorburn, Ensign Chrystal, Ensign Ronald McKinnon (attached).

Many of those above mentioned have passed away to eternal rest, yet their memories linger lovingly in the hearts and minds of their surviving comrades, who are personally cognizant of their patriotic deeds in defence of their country. By those old soldiers they will never be forgotten while life remains.

Of those old comrades who still survive, there are some who have achieved honor and distinction in the service of their country, among whom may be mentioned the Hon. John M. Gibson (Lieutenant-Governor of Ontario), and Brigadier-General Wm. D. Otter, C.V.O., C.B., Chief of the General Staff of the Active Militia of Canada, both of whom were under fire at Lime Ridge. In other walks of life many of those old veterans have achieved fame and success, and have proved an honor and a credit to the country they have spent their lives in endeavoring to upbuild.

CHAPTER VII.

THE EXPEDITION ON THE STEAMER "W. T. ROBB"—FIERCE FIGHT
AT FORT ERIE—STIFF RESISTANCE OF A GALLANT BAND OF
CANADIANS AGAINST A FENIAN FORCE TEN TIMES THEIR
NUMBER.

After the steamer "W. T. Robb" cleared from the mouth
of the harbor at Port Colborne, her prow was turned eastward,
and under full steam the staunch little craft proceeded to the
Niagara River. The morning was a most beautiful one, and the
surface of Lake Erie was as calm and glassy as a mill-pond. All
on board were in the best of spirits, and their stout hearts beat
high in the hope that they would be able to render their country
some signal service in faithfully performing the duty for which
they had been detailed.

After a quick run the "W. T. Robb" entered the inlet of
the Niagara and started down stream. The expedition had not
proceeded far when the boat was stopped by an armed patrol tug
from the United States man-of-war "Michigan." The officer in
command, on becoming acquainted with the nature of the Canadian steamer's mission, courteously gave Lieut.-Col. Dennis what
information he possessed regarding the operations of the Fenians, and stated that Gen. O'Neil had "broke camp" at the Newbigging Farm during the night and moved off down the River
Road.

The "W. T. Robb" continued on down the river to Black
Creek, where Lieut.-Col. Dennis learned that the Fenian forces
were then at a point about two miles south of New Germany.
A messenger was despatched to Col. Peacocke, giving all the information obtainable, and as Lieut.-Col. Dennis was of the opinion that the modified plans arranged by the conference of officers
at Port Colborne had been assented to by Col. Peacocke, and that
the two columns were working in unison along these lines, he
ordered the "Robb" to return to Fort Erie to meet Lieut.-Col.
Booker's force as arranged. But on arrival there he was disappointed to find that the connection had not been made, and as

he was in ignorance of Col. Peacocke's definite orders to Lieut.-Col. Booker, after he had left Port Colborne that morning, he was somewhat nonplussed at the failure of Lieut.-Col. Booker to join him at Fort Erie.

But as the plan had seemed to have mysteriously miscarried, Lieut.-Col. Dennis resolved to do something on his own account. He therefore decided to employ his force in patrolling the river, and endeavor to intercept the retreat of any Fenians who might attempt to escape back to the American shore. Capt. Akers having assented to this programme, a force was landed at Fort Erie. who picked up a number of Fenian stragglers. These men were placed on board of the ''Robb'' under guard, and while the steamer slowly drifted down the stream the Welland Canal Field Battery and a portion of the Naval Brigade patrolled the shore and scoured the woods and by-roads for some miles, in the course of which ''round up'' they gathered in another batch of prisoners. On arrival of the patrol parties at a point on the river about two miles above Black Creek, all were taken aboard the steamer by means of rowboats, and after securing the prisoners in the hold, the ''Robb'' was again headed for Fort Erie. On arrival there she was moored to the dock, when a detachment of the Welland Canal Battery again landed and brought in still another squad of Fenian prisoners. who were confined in the hold with the rest of their comrades.

After the boat had lain at the wharf for some time, Lieut.-Col. Dennis conceived the idea of landing all of the prisoners and leaving them under guard of the Welland Canal Battery at Fort Erie. while he and Capt. Akers would go around to Port Colborne with the ''Robb'' on a reconnoitering expedition and obtain further instructions and orders. This cool proposition did not appeal favorably to Capt. King, and he naturally remonstrated strongly against such action. especially in regard to leaving so many prisoners in his charge. as they outnumbered the strength of his command. and in his isolated position there was a strong possibility that they might be rescued by their friends from the other side of the river before assistance could reach him. Lieut.-Col. Dennis, however, was obdurate. and was making arrangements to billet the Welland Canal Battery in the village when the intelligence came that a battle had been fought at Ridgeway, and that the Fenians were on their way back to Fort Erie, moving rapidly.

Lieut.-Col. Dennis did not place much reliance on this rumor, and seemed determined to carry out his plan of leaving the Battery on shore. But Capt. King was solicitous for the safety of his men and the prisoners, and after some parley Lieut.-Col. Dennis allowed the Battery to go aboard the steamer. But they were scarcely at their quarters when he changed his mind and ordered them all on shore again, together with a portion of the Naval Brigade. Altogether the force landed consisted of 76 combatants, consisting of three officers and 54 men of the Welland Canal Field Battery, and two officers and 18 men of the Dunnville Naval Brigade.

Meanwhile (about 2 p.m.) Capt. Akers had secured a horse and buggy and drove up to the Buffalo & Lake Huron Railway telegraph office, seeking information. While there the Fenian forces suddenly appeared, and he was cut off from returning to the steamer by the rapid advance into the village of the Fenian skirmishers. By sheer good fortune he escaped capture, and by taking a secluded route along the lake shore reached Port Colborne safely about 7 o'clock in the evening.

Then Lieut.-Col. Dennis perceived his error, and with a realization that the warnings he had received of the near approach of the Fenians were correct, he appears to have become excited and confused. He had about 60 prisoners on board the "Robb," and after securing them well in the hold, ordered the Captain to cast off his lines and get out into the stream, which was speedily done.

About 2.15 o'clock he formed up his little command and advanced up the main street about 150 yards to meet the advancing Fenian forces, who were coming down the street in large numbers. When they approached within a distance of 200 yards they commenced a fusilade of rifle fire on the Canadians, who immediately retaliated by delivering a volley, which was executed with such precision that the Fenian advance was checked. Another volley from the Canadians also had a telling effect, and several of the enemy dropped in their tracks. By this time the

Fenians were approaching from several directions, and a severe flank fire was opened on the Canadians, who were exposed on the road in close formation. Opposed to them on the street was a detachment of 150 Fenians, led by Col. Bailey, while the main body of Gen. O'Neil's forces were coming down over the hill from the west in large numbers.

The firing was now terrific, and bullets were flying thick and fast, with men falling on both sides. About half- past 2 o'clock the Fenians fired a general volley, and Gen. O'Neil ordered a charge with fixed bayonets. With a wild Irish cheer the Fenians dashed down the village street, but were promptly stopped by another volley from the Canadians, and more men dropped. Among those who fell was Col. Bailey, the Fenian leader, who received a bullet through his breast. Fearing another charge and the ultimate capture of his force, Lieut.-Col. Dennis then ordered his men to retreat, and do the best they could to get safely away, each man for himself. He set the example and vanished. But his soldiers were made of different timber. The Welland and Dunnville men stood up to their work and contested every foot of ground, as they slowly and doggedly retired from one position to another, dodging from cover to cover, and firing into the enemy's ranks as fast as they could load.

Capt. King rallied a portion of his battery behind a pile of cordwood on the dock, and made a determined stand against the enemy until he fell with a bullet through his ankle, which shattered the bone. Still he fought on, and even while lying on the dock, grievously wounded, he emptied his revolver at the Fenians and kept cheering his men on to fight to the last. This they did courageously and nobly until they were flanked out of their position and taken prisoners.

Another portion of the Battery, under Lieut. A. K. Scholfield, and some of the Naval Brigade, under Capt. McCallum and Lieut. Angus Macdonald, retreated northward along the street stubbornly fighting every yard of the way until they reached the large frame residence of Mr. George Lewis, adjoining a small building which was used as the village post office. Here about thirty of their number took possession of the building, while the remainder (under command of Capt. McCallum) continued on down the River Road under a galling fire.

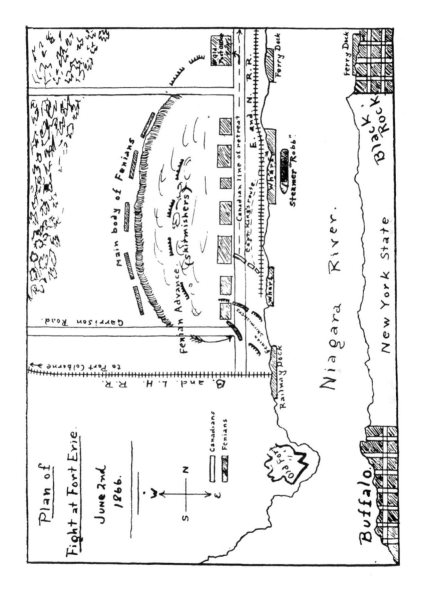

Plan of
Fight at Fort Erie.
June 2nd
1866.

The men who occupied the Lewis mansion resolutely continued the battle, firing through the doors and windows with such steadiness that the Fenians were glad to get under cover behind a pile of cordwood, from which place of security they fairly riddled the house with bullets. How the Canadians in this old frame building escaped the deadly missiles is a miracle, for, strange to say, none were injured, although exposed to a perfect hail-storm of bullets which crashed through the thin boards, lath and plaster, in all directions. After this gallant band had fired their last round of ammunition, they saw that further resistance was useless, and discreetly surrendered.

While the battle was in progress the American shore was lined with spectators, who cheered the Fenians lustily whenever it appeared to them from a safe distance that the Canadians were suffering losses or being defeated.

In the meantime Capt. McCallum and his detachment had fought themselves clear of the range of the Fenian rifles and retired down the River Road about three miles, where they were discovered by Lieut. Walter T. Robb, sailing master of the steamer, and taken on board. Capt. McCallum then decided to proceed to Port Colborne and send the captured Fenian prisoners who were in the hold of the vessel to a place of safety. He accordingly ordered the boat to head for that port, and while going past Fort Erie village was obliged to run the gauntlet of a heavy Fenian rifle fire for more than a mile. Although many bullets struck the boat, and some passed through the wheel-house uncomfortably near the heads of Capt. McCallum and Lieut. Robb, no person was injured by any of them.

Capt. McCallum arrived at Port Colborne at 6.30 o'clock that evening with 59 prisoners, who he handed over to Lieut.-Col. W. McGiverin, of the 20th Battalion, with a full list of their names and commitment papers. These men were sent to Brantford the same evening in charge of the Special Service Company of the St. Catharines Home Guard, and lodged in the jail at that place for safe keeping.

While the Canadians were still fighting desperately in the streets of Fort Erie, encompassed by a force of fully 800 Fenians (as nearly the whole of O'Neil's brigade was there by that time),

THE LEWIS HOUSE AND POST OFFICE AT FORT ERIE.

Lieut.-Col. Dennis succeeded in reaching the residence of a Mr. Thomas, in the village, where he lay concealed until evening, when he disguised himself, and getting through the Fenian lines without being detected, struck across the country in search of Col. Peacocke's column, which he found in bivouac at Bowen's Farm (about three miles north-west of Fort Erie) at 3 o'clock the next morning, and reported his mishap.

The Canadians who were captured at Fort Erie were well treated by Gen. O'Neil, who complimented them highly on the bravery and courage they had displayed during the battle, and bestowed upon them kind attentions.

The Fenian losses were heavy in comparison with the Canadian casualties at Fort Erie. Four of their number were killed, five more mortally wounded, and a large number sustained wounds from rifle balls and bayonet thrusts at the hands of the Canadians.

Although the engagement only lasted for less than an hour, it was hot and spirited throughout, and the valiant phalanx of 70 men who held their own under such trying circumstances, in the face of fully 800 veteran soldiers, fully deserve the greatest honor and credit that can be given by the Canadian people, and are well worthy of having their heroic deeds handed down to posterity on the pages of our country's history.

The following is a list of the casualties on the Canadian side during the engagement at Fort Erie:

Welland Canal Field Battery.—Killed—None. Wounded— Capt. Richard S. King, in ankle (leg amputated); Gunner John Bradley, above knee (leg amputated); Gunner Fergus Scholfield, below knee (leg amputated); Gunner John Herbison, wounded severely in leg; Gunner R. Thomas, wounded in thigh severely.

Dunnville Naval Brigade.—Nelson Bush, bayonet wound in chest.

Welland Canal Field Battery.—Lieut. A. K. Scholfield. Lieut. Chas. Nimmo. Sergt.-Major Wm. Boyle. Farrier-Sergeant Isaac Drew, Gunners Robert Offspring, Gideon Griswold. Wm. Brown, John Waters, Patrick Roach, Samuel Cook, Thomas Boyle, Stephen Beattie. Vilroy McKee, Joseph Reavly, Jonathan W. Hagar, Isaac Pew, William Black, Robert Armstrong, Jacob Gardner, Edward Armstrong. J. H. Boyle, James Coleman, Chas. Campbell, Isaac Dickerson. S. Radcliffe, Morris Weaver.

Dunnville Naval Brigade.—Second Lieut. Angus Macdonald. Samuel McCormack, James Robertson, Abram Thewlis, Geo. B. McGee, Thomas Arderly, Wm. Burgess, Harry Neff. Wm. Nugent, and Joseph Gamble.

The following Canadians were also prisoners in the hands of the Fenians, having been captured at Ridgeway and brought back to Fort Erie by Gen. O'Neil, who subsequently abandoned them when he made his flight back across the river:

Thirteenth Battalion—Jas. S. Greenhill and Joseph Simpson.

Queen's Own Rifles—R. W. Hines (No. 8 Company), Wm. Ellis (No. 9 Company). D. Junor (No. 9 Company), and Colin Forsythe (No. 10, Highland Company).

The casualties of the Fenians were heavy in both engagements. but the exact number is unobtainable, as no record was kept, and many of their wounded were removed to the United States and lost track of. At Ridgeway it is known that at least ten Fenians were killed, and quite a number severely wounded, some of whom afterwards died in Buffalo from their injuries. During the Fort Erie fight nine Fenians lost their lives and fourteen were wounded, most of them seriously.

The bravery and courage of the men who composed the Welland Canal Field Battery and the Dunnville Naval Brigade in standing up before an enemy nearly ten times their number, and fighting valiantly until the last round of their ammunition was expended and they were obliged to succumb to overpowering forces, will serve to show the resolute spirit and determination of these gallant troops. They were truly "a Spartan band," who were ready to sacrifice their lives on the spot, and their valor won the admiration of even the Fenians themselves, who complimented them highly on the stiff resistance they made, in the face of unequal odds, in the engagement.

The following personal narration of the fight, which was given by a member of the Dunnville Naval Brigade who participated in the engagement, is so vivid and graphic that I am pleased to reproduce it, as it gives a faithful and accurate account of the operations of the small Canadian force at Fort Erie on that eventful occasion:

On Friday, June 1st, at 10 p.m., Captain McCallum received a telegram to ship his men on the tug Robb, and proceed immediately to Port Colborne. About 2 a.m. on Saturday (2nd) we started, and arrived there a little after 4 a.m. We then took on the Welland Field Battery, numbering 59 men and 3 officers, commanded by Capt. King, of Port Robinson, which, together with the 43 men and 3 officers composing the Naval Brigade, made a total of 108 men. Col. Dennis, of the volunteer force, then came on board and took command of the expedition, when we at once started for Fort Erie, to co-operate with the gallant Queen's Own and the 13th Battalion, who were to leave Port Colborne early that morning for the same place. As we approached the village of Fort Erie all the men were sent below, leaving no one on deck but an officer dressed in civilian clothes. Nothing could be seen but the Fenian pickets and some stragglers. We went down the river nine miles, and received information that the main body of the Fenian army had fallen back to a wood some six or seven miles distant; but could gain no positive information as to their whereabouts. The movement was made about 3 o'clock a.m.; but in order to guard against surprise, they left their pickets behind. These our officers determined to capture, as well as all the stragglers. The boat then steamed back to Fort Erie, when a party of four men went ashore and succeeded in taking seven prisoners the first haul. The Welland Field Battery was also landed, with instructions to scour the woods along the river bank for stragglers. The boat was then headed down the stream, and was proceeding very slowly, keeping a sharp lookout along the bank. We had not gone far before discovering a small body of eight or ten Fenians ahead of us, armed with rifles and bayonets fixed, who were about to get into a small boat and recross to the American shore. The speed of our boat was immediately increased, and on arriving opposite them an officer and eleven men got into a yawl and pulled for the shore. The enemy looked at us for a moment or two and then took to their heels and ran, thinking, no doubt, that we had a large gun on board to support our men. This, however, was not the case; but had the authorities placed one on board at Port Colborne, the casualties to be hereafter mentioned would never have occurred. Two of the squad were captured, however, and we proceeded down the river, sending out small parties of from eight to ten men until there were no more men to be spared. The parties were instructed to pick up all the stragglers and pickets they could, and hold them until the boat returned. On our return we picked up our men and their prisoners, together with the Battery and their prisoners, and proceeded to Fort Erie and tied up to the wharf of the Niagara River Railroad. We had not been there long before intelligence reached us that the Fenians were coming down the Garrison Road in force, and would be in the village in ten minutes. Col. Dennis seemed confused, and like the rest of us, thought they were being driven by the Queen's Own (at that time we were ignorant of the repulse of those forces). The moment they were seen approaching the Field Battery (which had been landed) were ordered aboard, and in another minute was again ordered ashore. Capt. McCallum was then asked how many of the Naval Brigade could be spared for a support. He replied that he thought it very imprudent to attempt an attack upon so large a force with his small body, and advised Lieut.-Col. Dennis to retire to the boat, and push out into the stream and endeavor to ascertain their strength and movements. The Colonel, however, decided to meet them. Capt. McCallum then said he would give him 25 men, himself and 2nd Lieutenant (leaving only seven men besides the crew on board to guard the prisoners (59 in number). The Colonel formed his line in the open street opposite the hill in the rear of the village, but partially hid from him by some buildings on his right flank. In a moment the enemy appeared, coming over the hill in every direction; the buildings before mentioned hid them from view until they were upon him. From our position on the boat we could see all that was going on, and Lieut. W. T. Robb, of the Naval Brigade, seeing the small band was in great danger of being cut off, called to the Colonel that he was being outflanked and pointed to the hill, but he was not heard, and in a moment more the whole body were surrounded. It was, you may be sure, sickening to see one's friends and neighbors in such a perilous position, but even in this trying moment they did not at once surrender. Captains McCallum and King called on the Colonel to order the men to fire. He said no, but ordered them to the "right about," instead of "left half face," towards the boat; he, I suppose, mistaking the lower wharf for the one the boat was moored to, and started on a run, the men following. The enemy fired a volley in their rear, making one poor fellow kiss the dust, the balls striking the ground at their feet. The Captains called on their men to turn and fire, which they did with some effect. The next volley from the Fenians brought poor Capt. King down, and two others. Capt. McCallum called out to scatter, which was done; the enemy at this time were within 40 or 50 yards of them. We on the boat, with the aid of the crew who had rifles, tried to draw the fire of the Fenians, who were coming down Front street, on the boat, which we succeeded in doing. Their Adjutant, who was on horseback, here fell, and after picking him up they directed their fire at us and made a furious attempt to capture the boat. In this they were foiled by our cutting the line and backing down the stream, receiving at the same time a volley by way of a parting salute. By this time our men and the Battery had got into a house attached to the Post Office, from which they continued to resist the attack by every means in their power. Not a great deal of injury was inflicted upon the attacking party owing to a wood pile in the vicinity, behind which the enemy took shelter until our men had emptied their pouches and all the ammunition with them was gone. The Fenians then came up and demanded their surrender, which was at first refused. On the answer being given, fire was applied to the house in two places, the enemy standing around with bayonets fixed to prevent any one from escaping. Our men, seeing no way of escaping, then surrendered, determined to run the chance of being shot to being roasted. After disarming our men, some of the lowest of the Fenians threatened to shoot the prisoners for making a resistance while in the house. Col. O'Neil and the other officers prevented any violence being done, and at the same time threatened to shoot the first one who ill-treated the prisoners. In the meantime 15 men of the Battery, with Capt. McCallum and two of the Naval Brigade, were retreating down the river, a body of Fenians in full pursuit, exclaiming "Shoot the b——y officer." One who had got within ten feet of the Captain shot at him twice with a revolver, missing him each time, when one of the Brigade, named Calback, bayoneted him in the neck, turned and shot another through the heart, and then said to the Captain that the balls were coming too thick for comfort, advising him at the same time to take care of himself. Seeing our boat coming to the rescue of the Captain and the others, the enemy gave up the chase. It was high time for some more to come on board. As I have before mentioned, there were but seven left to take care of the 59 prisoners and work the ship. No doubt they would have attempted to rise had it not been for a few rifles at full cock pointed at them. Seeing our own perilous position with an enemy numbering 900 at Fort Erie, and thousands of sympathizing spectators on the opposite shore, our Captain determined to run the gauntlet and proceed to Port Colborne with his prisoners, fearing that the enemy might get a tug or two in Buffalo and attempt their rescue, thus causing more loss of life than was necessary. We then steamed up the river, close to the American shore, in silence, having been forbidden to fire while in American waters. As soon as we arrived opposite Lower Black Rock, the Fenians opened a furious fire upon us, and continued firing while we were going a distance of three-quarters of a mile. Their whole aim seemed to be the pilot-house, through which six shots passed, one of them grazing the head of our gallant Lieutenant Robb, who remarked to the wheelsman to jump up and take his place in case he fell. Those six shots struck the boat, doing no further injury than disfiguring the woodwork and painting. We arrived safely at Port Colborne and marched our prisoners to the railway station amid the deafening cheers of the volunteers and the citizens. Our officer delivered them to Lieut.-Col. Wm. McGiverin, who escorted them to Brantford, guarded by thirty men of the St. Catharines Special Service Company of Home Guards. A more rascally set of vagabonds were never congregated together. There were a great many Dunnville people at the Port on our arrival, and when they heard of the capture of our men volunteered to go and attempt their rescue; but owing to the scarcity of arms we could not accept them, besides we could not move without orders. These we received after waiting some time, which was to cruise along the lake as far as Windmill Point and no further. (It was a great pity we had not a gun on board and gone to Fort Erie, for if we had we could have captured or sunk the whole of the Fenian army, either of which would have given us great pleasure). On our return again to Port Colborne we received orders to proceed to Fort Erie, the Commander offering us as many men as we wanted. Our Captain said twelve good ones were all he wanted; these were immediately furnished him and we started. On our way down we built breastworks of cordwood along the bulwarks of the boat. These were impregnable to rifle bullets. When within six miles of Fort Erie two volunteers were called for to go ashore without arms and proceed cautiously down the lake and gather what information they could. All offered, but young Murdy and Edie were the chosen ones, two as brave boys as ever sun shone on. They went ashore, and then the boat resumed her journey. On turning into the river we saw the place was occupied by our troops, and the enemy in a scow made fast to the U. S. steamer Michigan, on the American shore. You may imagine the satisfaction this state of things gave us, nearly as much as if we had captured them ourselves. Our boys were much disappointed on finding the bird flown. We had heard of the repulse of the "Queen's Own" at Port Colborne, and every one went down with the determination to do all in their power to avenge their loss. Our joy was unbounded when we reached the wharf at finding our Second Lieutenant, Angus McDonald, and the greater part of our men, together with the most of the men belonging to the Battery. There were not many of our men taken, as they had no uniform, except the officers, and after slipping off their belts, they looked like civilians, in which capacity they effected their escape, and at once proceeded to Port Colborne and Dunnville to report themselves. Strange to say, the only one of our company touched was by a bayonet in the breast; not so bad as to prevent him from doing duty. The Welland Canal Field Battery was not so fortunate, having five wounded, namely: Captain King, leg, below the knee, amputated; Fergus Scholfield, foot amputated; John Bradley, leg amputated; John Herbison, wounded in the leg, and another with a flesh wound through the thigh. The Fenian casualties were Major Bigelow, with five balls through his breast, an Adjutant and six men killed, all shot through the breast, besides fourteen wounded, making in all twenty-two casualties— *the gallant Queen's Own were avenged.* The Fenian officers and men told the prisoners at the camp that their strength was 640 engaged in the fight, and 260 on the top of the hill as a reserve, and if all the Canadians fought as well as they did, they feared it would be a hard struggle, but they were determined to conquer.*

CHAPTER VIII.

THE GOVERNOR-GENERAL'S BODY GUARD—DENISON'S RAPID RIDE
—COL. PEACOCKE'S MOVEMENTS—ARRIVAL OF COL. LOWRY
WITH REINFORCEMENTS.

It was not until late in the afternoon of June 1st that the
Militia Department considered the necessity of calling on the
services of cavalry troops for duty on the frontier. Had this
been done twenty-four hours earlier the calamity which occurred at Ridgeway and the disaster at Fort Erie might have
been averted, and the whole campaign had a different termination. The omission was a serious mistake, which was subsequently realized. It is perilous and suicidal to move columns
of infantry in war times without having the advance and
flanks well protected by mounted troops, and scouts employed
to glean information of the location and strength of the enemy.
Therefore this branch is indispensable, as they are rightly
termed "the eyes and ears of an army," ever watchful and on
the alert for impending danger, or for an opportunity to strike
a crushing blow.

In the Niagara District campaign this omission was pain-
fully in evidence. At Chippawa, Col. Peacocke had to rely on
meagre and conflicting reports of the whereabouts of the
enemy which were brought in to him from various sources,
more or less unreliable, while Col. Booker was in a similar
position before advancing on the Fenian force at Ridgeway.
Had an efficient troop of cavalry scouts been employed to thoroughly scour the country in advance of these two columns, a
different tale might be related of their operations.

It was after 3 o'clock on June 1st when Major Geo. T.
Denison received orders to assemble the Governor-General's
Body Guard, and proceed to the front next morning. The
Major moved quickly, and during the evening and night had
his non-commissioned officers riding hard through the country
warning out his troopers. The place of rendezvous was the

Toronto Exhibition Grounds, and by day-break the troop was all mustered in saddle, and ready for service. At 8 o'clock a.m. on June 2nd they left by the steamer "City of Toronto" for Port Dalhousie, where they arrived about 11.30. Major Denison immediately entrained his men and horses on the Welland Railway and proceeded to Port Robinson, being under orders to report to Col. Peacocke. At Port Robinson the troop detrained, and after hastily feeding the horses and men, started for Chippawa on a gallop. On arrival there the troop halted for an hour or two, to have the horses' shoes reset, which being attended to, the command again took the road for New Germany, where he reported to Col. Peacocke about 5.30. This gallant corps had moved with such celerity that within ten hours after leaving Toronto they were at the extreme front, a good deal of the distance having been covered by hard and rapid riding.

Col. Peacocke was just on the point of moving off to resume his march from New Germany when the Body Guard arrived, and that officer ordered Major Denison to lead the advance of the column. Without dismounting, although the men and horses were both jaded and tired, they promptly spurred on to the front, and threw out scouts to the right and left. Major Denison was restrained from pushing ahead too rapidly, as he was obliged to regulate his march by the pace of the infantry, and his men chafed with the tardiness, as they were all eager to get into a brush with the enemy.

After a march of about nine miles they arrived at Bowen's Farm, about three miles northwest of Fort Erie. It was just getting dusk, and the troopers were approaching a piece of dense bush which flanked both sides of the road. When within about 200 yards of the bush the advance files of the cavalry discovered some men in the road, and signalled back the information. A halt was then ordered and Major Denison personally galloped forward, and on inquiry learned from his videttes that a force of the enemy were in front, and that several men had been observed going into the woods on the right. A search was made of the bush, but as the shades of night had fallen fast it was impossible to grope through the woods, and fearing an ambuscade Col. Peacocke resolved to halt his column for the night. In the meantime he had sent two companies of the 16th Regiment to scour the woods, but owing to the darkness they were unable to do so. Having been told by some person that a bridge on the road had been broken down, which rendered it impassable for his troops, Col. Peacocke decided to bivouac where he was, so recalled the two companies of the 16th, and made dispositions of his force to guard against a night attack. The 47th Regiment was formed in line to the right of the road, with one company of the same corps about 200 yards in advance, extended as skirmishers. The 10th Royals, of Toronto, were formed up as a support for the 47th, with two companies of that battalion wheeling to the right and extending as skirmishers, so as to fully cover the right flank of the column. The 16th Regiment was placed in a similar position on the left of the road, supported by the Nineteenth Lincoln Battalion, in the same formation. These troops laid in a ploughed field all night, sleeping on their arms, while the guards and sentinels were exceedingly watchful and vigilant. The cavalry and artillery remained in column on the road, with the baggage wagons in their rear.

About dark the St. Catharines Battery of Garrison Artillery, under command of Lieut. James Wilson, arrived at the bivouac, and was placed as the rear guard. This command, which had been left at Chippawa when Col. Peacocke's column had marched out in the morning, had been relieved at 4 p.m., and ordered to proceed at once to the front. They made a wonderfully quick march, covering the entire distance of about 17 miles in less than five hours, without a halt, and arrived at their destination with every member of the Battery in line—a feat which earned for them the title of "Stoker's Foot Cavalry." This battery had left their field guns at St. Catharines, and were armed with short Enfield rifles, acting as infantry. So they were formed up across the road, facing to the rear, and after posting the usual guards and sentinels, the remainder were glad to lie down in the dusty road and go to sleep supperless.

As it was generally supposed that the enemy were in force in the near vicinity, no fires were allowed to be lighted, and as the night was pretty cool and no blankets were available, the situation was not altogether comfortable. Yet the boys made the most of it, with the hope that by daylight they would have an opportunity of meeting the Fenians and proving the quality of their mettle.

As the night wore on Col. Peacocke received information that 2,000 or 3,000 reinforcements had crossed over from the American side and joined the Fenians. Lieut.-Col. Dennis had also come in to the Canadian lines and told of his defeat at Fort Erie the day before, while the reports received of the Ridgeway fight, with numerous other rumors of impending dangers, all combined to lead Col. Peacocke to believe that he would soon be up against a serious proposition.

About 4.30 o'clock in the morning (June 3rd) the soldiers arose from their rude couches on mother earth and began the task of getting the stiffness out of their joints as they moved about in quest of rations. Fortunately during the night some wagons loaded with bread, beef and groceries had arrived, but the necessities of hunger were so keen that the men could hardly wait for a proper distribution of the supplies. There was no means of cooking meat except by toasting it on the end of a ramrod poked over a fire of fence rails, but that was only a trifling matter to a hungry soldier. Loaves of bread were torn asunder in chunks, as bread-knives were not in evidence, while butter was spread by means of a chip. But the absence of table etiquette was not considered, so long as the purpose was served. There were no utensils for making tea or coffee, so the men had to dispense with these comforts and content themselves with a drink out of a roadside ditch.

Shortly after 5 o'clock Lieut.-Col. the Hon. John Hillyard Cameron (an old-time politician of prominence) arrived at Col. Peacocke's headquarters on horseback, and reported that the main body of the Fenian army had evacuated Canada, but that there were yet some of their forces straggling in the neighborhood.

Immediately the "assembly" was sounded, and Col. Peacocke formed up his column for an advance toward Fort Erie. Major Geo. T. Denison was ordered to scour the country with the Governor-General's Body Guard, and to enter the village and send back reports. Shortly afterward Major Denison reported that he was informed there was still a body of Fenians about the Old Fort, while farmers residing in the neighborhood said there were a number of stragglers lingering in the woods.

Accordingly Col. Peacocke made his arrangements to sweep the whole southeast angle of the Peninsula clear up to the Old Fort. On leaving the bivouac the column moved out by the Gilmore road, leading towards the Niagara River. The Grey Battery of Royal Artillery was ordered to the head of the column, in anticipation of having some shelling to perform. As the infantry halted by the roadside to allow this gallant battery to pass to the front on a gallop, the sight was inspiriting and elicited hearty cheers. The magnificent horses, throwing into play their splendid muscles, whisked the heavy guns along like so many feathers, while the drivers and gunners maintained their seats like centaurs, notwithstanding the bumps and jolts they encountered while bounding over the ruts and roadside ditches of a rough country highway. On arrival at a cross road leading south from the Gilmore road towards Lake Erie, a portion of the column, consisting of the 47th Regiment and the 19th Battalion moved off to the right, while the 16th Regiment, the 10th Royals and the St. Catharines Garrison Artillery continued on eastward. By this means all egress from the village of Fort Erie was effectually cut off. After traversing these roads for a short distance, lines of skirmishers were thrown out, and an advance through the fields in a sweeping semi-circle was begun. The troops had not proceeded far when two men were seen getting over a fence on the edge of a piece of bush. Both were carrying guns, and being in civilians' dress, were mistaken for Fenians. A volley was fired by the 47th, when both were observed to fall over the fence. On arrival of the skirmishers at the spot it was found that the two men were loyal Canadian citizens (Messrs. Bart. McDonald and A. Dobbie, of Thorold) who had armed themselves as Home Guards and gone to the front to assist in driving the enemy from our shores. Unfortunately they were too zealous and imprudent in getting beyond our lines, and drew upon themselves the fire of their friends. Mr. McDonald was so badly wounded that he died shortly afterwards, but Mr. Dobbie miraculously escaped injury.

As the skirmish lines moved onward the woods were thoroughly searched, and quite a number of Fenian stragglers were discovered in hiding and taken prisoners. During the time the drag-net of skirmishers was spread about fifty Fenians were gathered in.

At the home of "Major" Canty (a B. & L. H. railway section foreman who held a commission in the Fenian army) several prisoners were taken, among them being Rev. John McMahon (a Catholic priest) and two wounded Fenians named Whalen and Kiely. In the barn adjoining Canty's house was stretched the body of Lieut. Edward K. Lonergan, of the ·7th Irish Republican Regiment, of Buffalo. He had been killed at Ridgeway and the body brought back to Canty's barn and abandoned there. Several more Fenians were discovered under the barn, and more in a haystack near by, all of whom were taken in charge.

In the loft of Major Canty's house were found a number of overcoats belonging to the Queen's Own, and also some rifles which the retreating Fenians had carried back from the battle-field of Ridgeway. The "Major" was not at home when the Canadians called, so his guests were quietly placed under guard, and in due time conducted to a place of safety to stand their trial with the rest of the prisoners.

On arrival in the village of Fort Erie, the Canadian troops were much mortified and chagrined to find that O'Neil and his followers had escaped, and the only satisfaction they had was to gaze across the waters of the Niagara and see a scow-load of Fenians lying astern of the United States man-of-war "Michigan" as prisoners of the American Government.

On leaving Bowen's Farm, Major G. T. Denison started direct for the River Road with the Governor-General's Body Guard on a reconnaisance. Details were made by him to scour the country roads, which was thoroughly done, and being informed that there were a number of Fenians still at Fort Erie he proceeded on a gallop to the village, where he arrived at about 6 a.m. Major Denison's troop was the first Canadian force to reach Fort Erie after the battle, and they were received with great joy and delight by the citizens and also the Canadians who were prisoners in the hands of Gen. O'Neil the day previous.

A number of Fenians were gathered in by the troopers, and placed under guard. This command did excellent service subsequently in patrolling the river bank and providing cavalry pickets for the force which occupied Fort Erie during the next few weeks.

On the afternoon of June 2nd, Lieut.-Col. R. W. Lowry, of Her Majesty's 47th Regiment, received orders to proceed to the front with reinforcements, and left Toronto at 2 p.m. via the Great Western Railway with Capt. Crowe's Battery of Royal Artillery, equipped with four field guns. He was accompanied by Col. Wolseley (afterward Field Marshal Lord Wolseley). who was then serving in Canada as Assistant Quartermaster-General on the staff of the Lieut.-General commanding Her Majesty's Forces in British America; and by Lieut. Turner, R.E.; Lieut. Dent, 47th Regiment, and Lieut.-Col. Cumberland. A.D.C., of Toronto. At Oakville he was joined by Capt. Chisholm's Rifle Company, 52 rank and file. On arrival at Hamilton Col. Lowry learned that the detachments of the 16th Regiment and 60th Royal Rifles which were under orders to join him there. had already left for the Niagara frontier to reinforce Col. Peacocke, who had twice telegraphed for reinforcements. Col. Lowry therefore decided to proceed to Clifton, and from thence move to the support of Col. Peacocke. During the evening he was joined at Clifton by a provisional battalion composed of the Barrie, Cookstown. Scarboro, Columbus, Whitby and Oakville rifle companies. about 350 strong, under command of Lieut.-Col. Stephens.

At 3.40 a.m. on June 3rd, Col. Lowry, with Capt. Crowe's Battery and Lieut.-Col. Stephens' battalion, left Clifton by the Erie and Niagara Railway for Black Creek. Shortly after his arrival there (at daybreak) he was joined by 200 rank and file of the 60th Rifles under Capt. Travers, and 140 of the 16th Regiment under command of Capt. Hogge, which troops had bivouacked at New Germany overnight. On the report of Lieut.-Col. John Hillyard Cameron that the Erie and Niagara Railway was passable to a point near Fort Erie, Col. Lowry moved his column by rail as far as Frenchman's Creek (Gen. O'Neil's old camp ground). Here he detrained his troops, and throwing out an advanced guard and flanking lines of skirmishers, moved promptly forward towards Fort Erie. Col. Wolseley had preceded the column on horseback, and meeting Major Denison's troopers, who already had possession of the village, found that Gen. O'Neil and his army had left the country and were beyond the pale of punishment by our forces.

Col. Lowry's column reached Fort Erie about 8 o'clock, and shortly after Col. Peacocke's force swept in from the west, bringing with them the spoils of victory in the shape of about sixty prisoners, being part of the picket line which Gen. O'Neil had abandoned during the night.

The whole force was then placed in position on the high ground in rear of the village and went into camp. Guards, patrols and pickets were posted in every direction, and all precautions taken that the occasion demanded.

During the afternoon Capt. Akers arrived from Port Colborne with the Queen's Own Rifles, 7th Battalion of London, four companies of the 22nd Oxford Rifles (with the Drumbo Infantry Company attached), the Caledonia Rifle Company, the Thorold Infantry Company, and the St. Catharines Home Guards, about 1,000 men altogether.

When the three columns were all assembled on the heights at Fort Erie they presented a formidable and imposing spectacle to the many thousands of Americans and Fenians who crowded the river banks and points of vantage for sight-seeing on the American side. It seemed as if the whole population of

Buffalo and surrounding country were gathered on the river shore that pleasant Sunday afternoon to gaze upon the British camp and watch the movements of the soldiers. The rows of white tents, the scarlet uniforms of the infantry, and the blue of the cavalry and artillery, intermingled with the dark green of the rifle companies, certainly gave a variety of color, while the steadiness and regularity with which the different units performed their evolutions must have convinced the on-lookers (especially the Fenians) that it was just as well for them that they were safely out of harm's way.

In the course of the day a steam launch arrived at the Fort Erie dock with a message from Captain Bryson, commander of the U. S. steamer "Michigan," to Colonel Lowry. inviting him to go aboard that vessel and have an interview with himself and Mr. H. W. Hemans (the British Consul at Buffalo) regarding matters in connection with the Fenians. To this proposal Col. Lowry immediately assented, and accompanied by Col. Wolseley, Capt. Crowe. R.A., and Lieut. Turner. R.E.. proceeded on board the American steamer. They were courteously received by Capt. Bryson, who introduced Mr. M. Dane. the United States District Attorney; General Barry, the commander of the United States troops on the frontier, and Mr. H. W. Hemans, the British Consul. An interesting conference was held, in the course of which the American officials expressed their reprehension of the infraction of international law by the Fenians, and assured Col. Lowry that nothing in their power had been or would be neglected to arrest such infraction, and that they had prevented many Fenian reinforcements from getting across to Canada during the two previous nights. In the meantime Col. Lowry was assured that the 600 or 700 prisoners who had been captured by the "Michigan" would be rigidly guarded until instructions were received from Washington as to their disposal.

After the conference Col. Lowry and his staff returned to camp, where orders were waiting to dispatch Capt. Crowe's Battery, with four field guns. and 200 men of the 47th Regiment under command of Major Lauder. to Kingston without delay. as that point was threatened. This force left Fort Erie by rail at 7 o'clock that evening, taking with them 22 Fenian prisoners who had been committed to the Toronto jail.

Shortly afterward another telegram arrived ordering that the detachment of the 60th Rifles, one company of the 16th Regiment and the 7th Battalion of London volunteers be forwarded to London as soon as possible. Owing to lack of railway transport these troops were unable to leave Fort Erie until 10.30 the following morning, when 800 men were dispatched to London by the Erie & Niagara and Great Western Railways, via Clifton and Hamilton.

At 1.30 a.m. of June 5th, the Queen's Own and the York and Caledonia Rifles were quietly aroused and ordered to strike tents, parade, and entrain on cars which were in waiting to convey them to Stratford. The work of packing up was quickly accomplished, and at 6 o'clock the train left Fort Erie for its destination, the troops being accompanied by Col. Garnet S. Wolseley, A.Q.M.G., of Her Majesty's Forces. They arrived at Stratford at 5 p.m., and were immediately billetted among the citizens. At this time it was feared that the Fenians contemplated an attack on the frontier of the western portion of the Province, and it was deemed advisable to have a sufficient force mustered at a convenient point, to be available in case of emergency. The force collected at Stratford consisted of Capt. Gore's Battery of Royal Artillery, two companies of H. M. 16th Regiment, the Queen's Own and the York and Caledonia Rifles, the whole being under command of Col. Wolseley.

The withdrawal of these troops from Fort Erie reduced Col. Lowry's force to about 2,000 men, but they were sufficient to over-awe the 8,000 Fenians who were still hanging around Buffalo and vicinity with the intention of making another raid as soon as they could escape the vigilance of the United States authorities, who were now determined to prevent any further incursions if possible.

The Thirteenth Battalion, of Hamilton, under Major Skinner, garrisoned Port Colborne, and guarded the approach to the Welland Canal.

At Clifton and Suspension Bridge a provisional battalion consisting of the Collingwood, Aurora, Bradford, Derry West

CANTEEN OF THE NINETEENTH BATTALION AT
FORT ERIE. JUNE, '66.

and Grahamsville companies were assembled under command
of Lieut.-Col. Robert B. Denison, while two more companies were
stationed at Chippawa, so that the whole Niagara frontier was
carefully guarded.

At St. Catharines several other companies were billetted,
who were ready to move in any direction that their services
might be required.

Toronto was also well garrisoned with troops which ar-
rived on Sunday, among which were the following:—The
Cobourg Cavalry, Col. Boulton, 40 men and 40 horses; Cobourg
Battery, Capt. Dumble, 46 men; Ashburnham Infantry, Capt.
Rogers, 32 men; Peterboro Infantry, Capt. Kennedy, 50 men;
Campbellford Infantry, Capt. Lin, 40 men; Lakefield Infantry,
Capt. Leigh, 31 men; Cobourg Infantry, Capt. Elliott, 45 men;
Peterboro Rifles, Capt. Poole, 44 men; Cobourg Rifles, Capt.
Smith, 47 men; Bowmanville Rifles, Lieut.-Col. Cubitt, 40 men;
Port Hope Rifles, Capt. Williams, 42 men, and several other
companies which arrived later.

CHAPTER IX.

HURRIED EVACUATION OF CANADA BY GEN. O'NEIL—CAPTURE OF
THE ESCAPING FENIANS BY THE UNITED STATES GUNBOAT
MICHIGAN.

After the smoke of battle had wafted away from the streets
of Fort Erie, and the dead and wounded removed, Gen. O'Neil
gathered his troops together and marched up to the ruins of the
"Old Fort," situated on a point at the inlet of the Niagara
River from Lake Erie. Here they went into camp, and began to
make preparations for defence, as they fully expected to be
attacked early next morning by Col. Peacocke's column and other
forces who were advancing from the interior. It was a very
anxious time for Gen. O'Neil and his officers, and they spent
some hours in earnest deliberation as to what would be the best
course for them to pursue. They were now between "the devil
and the deep sea," with the wide river and lake in front of
them, and an avenging army of British and Canadian troops,
well equipped with cavalry, artillery and trained infantry,
gradually tightening the coils around their position from the
rear, in which direction there was no avenue of escape. It was
indeed a serious predicament, and the only hope of the Fenians
rested in the possibility of being able to escape across the river
and abandon their project to capture Canada, at this point at
least. To guard against surprises, Gen. O'Neil had left his
picket lines extended over a large area of country, and scouts
and patrols were still on duty on the country roads and along
the river bank. Reinforcements were expected over from Buffalo that night, and O'Neil personally felt disposed to fortify
his brigade in the ruins of the Old Fort and fight to a finish.
But by this time the American authorities had aroused, and
instructed Gen. W. F. Barry (the United States officer in command at Buffalo), to stop any more Fenian troops from crossing
into Canada, and in the performance of this duty he exhibited
great energy. There were thousands of Fenians ready and
eager to cross the border to reinforce O'Neil, but the presence
of the United States gunboat "Michigan" and several regiments

and batteries of American regular troops. prevented the movement. Therefore the Fenians who were marooned in Canada,
with visions of a hangman's noose dangling before them, became
desperate and despondent. They knew very well that a concentration of the Canadian forces was going on, and that at the
first break of day an attack was likely to be made, from which
there would be no alternative but to ''die in the last ditch'' or
surrender. They had encountered the raw Canadian volunteers
and experienced two bitter tastes of hard fighting during the
day, and were quite satisfied. So they decided to get out of
Canada as quickly as possible. The officers and men were dispirited and crestfallen, and bitterly blamed Gen. Sweeny and
other high Fenian officials for not having sent over the promised
reinforcements in ample time to ensure the success of the expedition. When the twilight deepened and the darkness of night
fell, a feeling of gloom pervaded the Fenian camp. The men
had eaten their evening meal, which had about exhausted their
Quartermaster's stores, and there was nothing in sight for breakfast on the morrow. As they gathered around their camp-fires
or lay upon the grass in groups, discussing the day's events and
their possible chance of succor, the suspense became terrible.
The conviction finally became forced upon them that without
reinforcements or rescue they would be utterly lost, and many
of them were not prepared to take any chances, so before 10
o'clock quite a number deserted their standards and wandered
down along the water front in search of some means of getting
back across the river. Boats were seized wherever found, and,
loaded to the gunwales, the fugitives plied their oars vigorously
in their haste to cross the stream. Others trusted themselves
to single planks upon which to gain support while they endeavored to swim across the current. The covering of one of the
docks afforded the means for this purpose. It was a very risky
method of navigation, and it is generally supposed that several
of the Fenian ''Leanders'' who attempted the passage of the
Niagara ''Hellespont'' in this way lost their lives in doing so, as
they were reported ''missing'' afterwards.

Late that night signal lights were displayed from the American shore, which by the Fenian code signified to Gen. O'Neil
that a movement was on foot in Buffalo to attempt to run the

blockade with reinforcements. But the remnant of the Fenian army which was bivouacked in the ruins of old Fort Erie was too much demoralized to take any further interest in the campaign, and signalled back the information that the reinforcements were too late—that they intended to evacuate the country, and needed speedy relief.

About midnight two steam tugs, with a couple of canal boats in tow, quietly slipped out of Buffalo Creek, and escaping the vigilance of the American authorities, headed for the Canadian shore. These boats contained about 500 reinforcements for the Fenians, but when about half way over the river the transports were met by a messenger in a rowboat with an order from Gen. O'Neil, directing them to return to Buffalo, disembark all the troops, and immediately proceed back to Fort Erie to carry off the remainder of his men. The order was obeyed, and at 1 o'clock on the morning of June 3rd all in the camp were shipped on board of the canal boats and started back across the river. When about half way over, and in American waters, the retreating army was hailed by the armed tug "Harrison," under command of Acting Master Morris of the gunboat "Michigan," who demanded an immediate surrender to the United States authorities. The order not being promptly obeyed, it was repeated with a threat to sink the canal boats if not immediately complied with. Gen. O'Neil, realizing that resistance was useless, then surrendered the remnant of his command. The "Michigan" was signalled, and having steam up and anchor tripped, came alongside, and taking the tug and canal boats in tow, proceeded down the river to a point opposite Black Rock, where she dropped anchor in mid-stream and placed a guard over the prisoners. Gen. O'Neil and his principal officers were taken on board the "Michigan," while the rank and file were left huddled up on the canal boats for the night.

When the main body of the Fenians evacuated Canada their movement was executed so hurriedly that the officers did not take time to notify their pickets and patrols, who were still faithfully performing their duties, so that about 150 of these "patriots" were deserted by their comrades and exposed to the halter. Great indignation was manifested by these men at being left as they were on outpost duty without any notification of the proposed withdrawal of the Fenians from Canada. Had it not been for the approach of Major Denison's cavalry, which encountered their picket line at Bowen's Farm and caused their retreat to Fort Erie, none of them would probably have learned of the evacuation in time to escape. As it was, a large number of these men were captured by the Canadians the next day and consigned to prison, while the remainder managed to get across the border in various ways.

Commander Bryson, of the "Michigan," at once telegraphed to the United States authorities at Washington, reporting the capture of the main portion of Gen. O'Neil's forces, and asked for instructions regarding their disposition. Pending official correspondence between the two Governments relative to the prisoners, they were kept under close guard for a day or two. But as the British Government made no immediate demand for their extradition, the rank and file were liberated on their own recognizances to the amount of $500 each, binding them to appear if a complaint was lodged against them.

Gen. O'Neil and the other officers who were captured by the "Michigan" were released on bail, to appear when called on for trial on charges of violations of the neutrality laws, but the proceedings were quietly dropped, and thus the matter ended.

This disposal of the prisoners captured by the "Michigan" did not meet with popular approval in Canada, where our people were mourning the loss of some of our bravest and best young volunteers, and feelings of resentment held sway for some time. It was thought that an example should have been made of the leaders at least, but the diplomats who had charge of the matter evidently felt that a policy of moderation and leniency might be exercised with beneficial results at that particular time, and the raiders were not further molested.

The City of Buffalo, on the 4th of June, was full of Fenians. They had been arriving from all parts to take part in the raid, and only for the vigilance of the United States troops, were prepared to make another attempt to cross the line. But General Meade was firm in his resolve to prevent further disturbances, and issued the following order:

Headquarters Mil. Div. Atlantic.

Buffalo, June 3, 1866.

Brevet Maj.-Gen. Barry:

General,—Orders will be sent you from Headquarters, Department of the East, assigning you to the command of the District of Ontario, extending from Erie, Pa., to Oswego, New York, both places included, Headquarters at Buffalo. In advance of the orders and accompanying instructions, I direct you to use the force at your command to preserve the neutrality by preventing the crossing of armed bodies, by cutting off reinforcements or supplies, by seizing all arms, munitions, etc., which you have reason to believe are destined to be used unlawfully—in fine, taking all measures precautionary and otherwise to prevent violation of law. For this purpose you will move the forces under your command to such points as are threatened, and you will employ vessels, tugs, or others, such as can be procured, for watching the river and lake shores, and taking all such measures as in your judgment the emergency requires.

Very respectfully,

GEO. G. MEADE,

Major-General Commanding.

In accordance with the above instructions, Gen. Barry very thoroughly guarded the United States frontier with troops, while the United States man-of-war "Michigan," the "Fessenden," and other armed steamers, patrolled the lakes and the Niagara River with the full determination to rigidly carry out Gen. Meade's orders. This was a crushing blow to the hopes of the rank and file of the Irish Republican Army, and there were many who were inclined to defy the Federal authorities and fight their way over the border. But wiser counsels prevailed, and the fiery subordinates were obliged to submit to the law and await another opportunity.

During the following ten days the people of Buffalo had a horde of very undesirable guests within their gates. The majority of the Fenian troops were without means of subsistence, and became a charge upon the authorities and their sympathizers. The question of their disposal was at last decided by the United States Government offering transportation to their homes to all who would agree to sign the following:

FORM OF PAROLE.

We, the undersigned, belonging to the Fenian Brotherhood, being now assembled in Buffalo, with intentions which have been decided by the United States authorities as in violation of the neutrality laws of the United States; but being now desirous to return to our homes, do severally agree and promise to abandon our expedition against Canada, desist from any violation of the neutrality laws of the United States, and return immediately to our respective homes.

This offer was largely taken advantage of, and muster rolls were made out as rapidly as possible. The number of signatures obtained to the written paroles was 5,166 during the afternoon of June 15th, and that night these men departed for their homes, much to the relief of the citizens of Buffalo, who had become weary of their guests.

Previous to the departure of the disappointed warriors from Buffalo, the Fenian General Burns issued the following farewell address:

Buffalo, June 14, 1866.

To the Officers and Soldiers of the Irish Republican Army in Buffalo:

Brothers,—Orders having been received from President Roberts, requesting you to return to your homes, it becomes my duty to promulgate said order in this department. Having been but a few days among you, and witnessing with pride your manly bearing and soldierly conduct in refraining from all acts of lawlessness on the citizens of this city, it grieves me to part with you so soon. I had hoped to lead you against the common enemy of human freedom, viz., England, and would have done so had not the extreme vigilance of the United States Government frustrated our plans. It was the United States, and not England, that impeded our onward march to freedom. Return to your homes for the present, with the conviction that this impediment will soon be removed by the representatives of the nation. Be firm in your determination to renew the contest when duty calls you forth; the cause is too sacred to falter for a moment. Let your present disappointment only prompt you to renewed energy in the future. Be patient, bide your time, organize your strength, and as liberty is your watchword, it will finally be your sword. In leaving this city, where you have bountifully shared the hospitality of the citizens, I beg of you to maintain the same decorum that has characterized your actions whilst here.

(Signed) M. W. BURNS.
Brigadier-General Commanding Irish Army at Buffalo.

CHAPTER X.

THE CHICAGO VOLUNTEERS—A NOBLE BAND OF PATRIOTS RETURN HOME TO DEFEND THEIR NATIVE LAND—A STRIKING EXAMPLE OF CANADIAN PATRIOTISM.

No matter where you find a true Canadian, he holds in the depths of his heart a love and reverence for his native land and its flag which cannot be uprooted. He may "roam 'neath alien skies" or tread a foreign shore, but his heart ever beats true to his homeland, and when his services are required in defence of her shores he does not as a rule require to be summoned hence. He acts on the impulse of the occasion, and quickly buckles on his armor to take the field for the honor of his country.

This national trait was never more spontaneously illustrated than during the perilous periods of the Fenian Raids. Many of the stalwart sons of Canada were temporarily residing in the United States at these times, and had exceptional opportunities of noticing the constant preparations that were being made by the Fenian plotters to invade the land of their birth. Ofttimes, perhaps, they were reminded by their American and Fenian shopmates or fellow-employees, of the fact that they were aliens, who were only permitted to reside in the United States on sufferance, and insults and epithets would be hurled at them because they were "bloody Canucks." But the Canadian boys always kept a stiff upper lip, and when insolence became too intolerable they were not afraid to assert their manhood by the use of a little physical force. and teach their tormentors that a Canadian has rights which *all* men are bound to respect.

Quite a colony of Canadians resided in the City of Chicago, Illinois, in 1866, many of them holding lucrative positions in employment where brains, energy and confidence were the chief essentials required. As a natural result these loyal boys chafed in spirit. and their breasts heaved in indignation. when they observed the open encouragement and financial assistance which was being given to the Fenians by the citizens of that metropolis to enable them to carry out their nefarious plans to conquer Canada.

For the purpose of meeting together for mutual counsel, and more firmly welding the bonds of loyalty and unity among themselves, these young men organized the "Chicago Canadian Society," with Mr. John Ford (an old Toronto boy) as President. The formation of this Association in one of the hottest hot-beds of Fenianism in America, required men of courage and reliance to uphold its principles, and in this they were specially fortunate. From the President down to the most youthful member they were all "hearts of oak"—men who unflinchingly stood by their principles, and had their love of country so deep at heart that they resolved to sacrifice their positions and return to their native land to offer their services to the Government as soon as occasion demanded. They accordingly organized a military company, with the sturdy patriot, John Ford, as their Captain, and began drilling.

They had not long to wait before the news was received in Chicago that the Fenians had landed in Canada, and that the time for action had arrived. So the "Chicago Volunteers" at once decided to individually resign their situations and leave for "the Land of the Maple" to fight for their flag. While the Company was making preparations for their journey, Capt. Ford was sent ahead to make the necessary arrangements at Windsor for their reception, and to formally offer their services to the Government. Capt. Ford had a dangerous trip *en route*, as many of the most violent Chicago Fenians knew him personally and were inclined to "put him out of business." But the Captain was a stalwart, determined young man, full of fire and courage, and being ready for any emergency, he succeeded in getting through to Windsor without any serious trouble, although dogged all the way by Fenians, who only waited an opportunity to assault him. On arrival at Windsor he consulted with Mr. Gilbert McMicken, the Police Magistrate, who advised him to proceed on to Toronto with his Company. He then telegraphed his comrades to come along, and they quickly answered the summons. That night the whole Company of 57 men left Chicago for Canada, and great was their delight when they lined up at Windsor the next morning under the folds of the

Union Jack, and gave three hearty cheers for their Queen and country. Two companies of volunteers, accompanied by the Mayor and a large concourse of citizens, were at the railway ferry dock to meet the boys, and gave them a great reception.

They then proceeded by the Great Western Railway to Toronto, receiving hearty ovations at London, Hamilton and every station at which they stopped, until they arrived at their destination at 10 o'clock on the night of June 5th. They were met at the depot by a guard of honor composed of two companies of volunteers, His Worship Mayor Metcalfe, and a large number of citizens, and escorted to the Drill Shed, where short addresses were delivered to them by the Mayor, Hon. George Brown, Mr. T. M. Daly, and others, thanking them warmly for their patriotism and manly conduct in making personal sacrifices to return to their native soil and defend their country in a time of peril.

Capt. Ford and Lieut. G. R. Kingsmill replied in suitable terms on behalf of their Chicago comrades, saying that they could vouch that every man would do his duty fearlessly, should their services be required. They both stated that if necessary an entire regiment could have been raised in Chicago for the defence of Canada, so ardent were the Canadians in that city to assist in driving out the invaders.

After hearty cheers had been given for the Queen, the Chicago Volunteers, and the men on duty at the front, the Chicago men were marched to the Metropolitan Hotel and the Robinson House, where refreshments and lodgings had been provided for them for the night.

On the following morning this band of patriots formally tendered their services to the Government as a company to be enrolled as volunteers for the defence of the Province. The Mayor and Col. Durie (Assistant Adjutant-General) called on Gen. Napier, and presented the offer, which was immediately accepted by the General on behalf of the Government. At the same time he spoke in the most complimentary terms of the patriotic spirit evinced by these gallant young men, and desired Col. Durie and the Mayor to convey his views to them.

The corps was named "*No. 1 Company of Volunteers for Canada,*" and the following officers were chosen: Captain, John

Ford; Lieutenant. George R. Kingsmill; Ensign. Hector Ross; 1st Sergeant. Samuel Ridout; 2nd Sergeant. T. D. Skinner; 3rd Sergeant, W. F. Collins; 4th Sergeant. J. H. Cornish; 1st Corporal, John Allen; 2nd Corporal, G. J. Fitzsimmons; 3rd Corporal, John Ginn; Lance Corporal, George McKay. The privates were: C. T. Wright. B. Baskerville, R. Gilbert. T. English. R. Mason, J. Moore. F. Gatrell. T. G. Rice. R. S. Shenston, W. E. Richards, W. Crain, W. Skinner. C. J. Mitchell. S. Langford. J. Cavers, S. McKay, G. B. Roberts. J. Hillman. F. Baker, J. C. Keighley, J. J. Innes. C. Rubidge, L. Werden, W. Orr. J. Fraser, J. Wickens, J. G. Kinnear, W. H. Rice. George Morehead, John Travers. W. Beck. Luke E. Kingsmill. S. Gordon. E. Smith, G. Mothersill. W. S. Cottingham. S. Langford. A. Babley. J. W. Dunn. S. McCallum, W. Ford. O. S. Hillman. J. Healey, C. C. Baines. James J. James, and F. W. Nation.

The Chicago Volunteers remained on guard duty at Toronto until all danger was passed. when they were relieved from service and permitted to return to their homes. Previous to their departure a grand reception was given in their honor at the Music Hall. where an immense concourse of people assembled to assist in paying them a royal tribute of praise for their loyal service.

His Worship Mayor Metcalfe presided. and after delivering a splendid patriotic oration. presented Capt. Ford and his comrades with an address from the Mayor and Corporation of the City of Toronto, expressive of the high opinion of their patriotism that prevailed among the citizens and their countrymen generally.

The address was accompanied by the presentation of a handsome Union Jack. on which was inscribed, "Presented to the Chicago Volunteers by the City Council. Toronto."

Capt. Ford and his officers replied in fitting terms to the sentiments expressed by the Mayor. and assured him that should occasion ever again arise to necessitate their services. they would promptly respond to the summons.

Capt. John Ford (who at the date of issue of this book is still alive and as full of fire and patriotism as in days of yore) is a well-known and highly respected citizen of Toronto. whose

friends are many.   By request of the author he has given the
following personal recollections of the organization of ''The
Chicago Volunteers'' and their trip home to Canada, which I
feel will prove of great interest to the reader :—

"As all old citizens of Toronto will well remember, they had for
neighbors years ago some who were keen sympathizers with the Fenians,
and whose relatives were seen in Fenian processions in Chicago and other
American cities. As circumstances took many young men from Canada
to the States, we found on foregathering on one occasion in the old Post
Office in Chicago, in 1864, that we numbered 75, all former citizens of Toronto.   We then organized the "Chicago Canadian Society," meeting
weekly for drill and social purposes in the hall of the American Protestant
Association. Our drill instructors were Military School cadets, holding first
and second-class certificates. We found that the Fenian organization was
raising money and manufacturing pikes, and in the year 1864 they held
an Irish National Fair for the purpose of increasing their fund. Quite
a number of Canadians visited the Fair, and saw soil or turf from Ireland
sold in envelopes for 25 cents each, and also ''Irish bonds,'' to be re-
deemed on the consummation of the object of the Fenian organization, or
the capture of Canada; and to show the ease in which they expected to
accomplish this end, a stuffed lion was shown with its tail between its
legs, and head down, covered with a calf-skin. On lifting the calf-skin
the calf's head appeared, their idea evidently being to cast ridicule on
the bravery of the British lion or the nation.

"On the evening of May 24th, 1865, we held a banquet in the Washington Coffee House, which was largely attended, and the toast of 'The
Queen and Royal Family,' and other patriotic sentiments, were enthusiastically honored.

"On attending one of the Fenian recruiting meetings in Metropolitan
Hall, we saw upwards of 1,000 veteran cavalry men enrolled for service,
who, it was announced, were to be mounted on horses between Hamilton and
Toronto. This enrollment was only part of the 37,000 guaranteed by the
delegates from Illinois at the National Convention of the Fenian Brotherhood in 1865, when the total guarantee was 250,000 men. Needless to
say, we were thoroughly alarmed, and prepared to leave for home on short
notice.

"On the day of the Raid (June 2nd, 1866) at about 3 p.m., it was
reported in Chicago that 30,000 men had crossed into Canada, had destroyed
the Welland Canal, and were advancing on Stoney Creek, expecting to be
in Hamilton that night. We had wired Toronto for information, and went
from one telegraph office to another in vain for answers. We found out
afterwards that our telegrams were lying unopened on Mayor Metcalfe's
table on the following Tuesday, as that gentleman was away at the front.

"We held a meeting at Chicago on Saturday, June 2nd, 1866, and
organized a second company to follow the first to Canada, provided their
services would be accepted and they could get to the front. The St. George's
Society guaranteed to organize more companies, which would total 1,000
men.

"Comrade Forbes and myself were appointed delegates to proceed to
Detroit and open communications with the military authorities at Windsor,
and offer our services. We arrived at Detroit at early dawn on Monday,

June 4th, and were very much relieved, on looking across the river through the haze, to recognize the scarlet coats of the soldiers on duty on the Canadian shore. We crossed to Windsor, and met Col. McMicken, who immediately wired Hon. John A. Macdonald, Minister of Militia, tendering our services. The answer arrived in Windsor between 3 and 4 o'clock, when Col. McMicken advised me to wire the company in Chicago, and to avoid international complications he instructed us to do this in a private manner. We then sent the following message to the company: 'Ship what you have, and buy up the rest.' In Chicago the company awaited instructions in the A. P. A. Hall, and on receiving our telegram they marched to the depot through enthusiastic crowds of sympathizers, singing, ''Rule, Britannia'' and other patriotic songs. On arrival at the depot, Dr. Bigelow, a sympathizer, took off his Panama hat, placed a $5 greenback in it, and passed it around, raising $20 more than was required to pay the Michigan Central Railroad for two first-class coaches, which had been arranged for by Lieut. Kingsmill with the General Manager of the Michigan Central, who very courteously allowed us the same rates charged the United States Government when moving troops. Lieut. Kingsmill agreed to place a guard at each end of the coaches, and allow no one to enter except members of the company.

''The company arrived at Detroit early on Tuesday morning, June 5th. Col. McMicken gave Comrade Forbes and myself a pass to go to Detroit and meet the company, advising us to allow no demonstration until we had passed the centre of the river and were in Canadian waters. The company followed the advice, and when the steamer crossed the line the men went wild with enthusiasm, and were royally received in Windsor by the military authorities. This was repeated at London and Hamilton. The company arrived in Toronto on the night of Tuesday, June 5th. It took the entire police force to get the men off the train, owing to the delight of their friends and the cheering crowds who came to welcome us home. The company was then escorted to the Drill Shed by the military companies, where patriotic speeches were made by Mayor Metcalfe, Hon. Geo. Brown, and others.''

Chicago was not alone in the matter of exemplifying Canadian patriotism during this trying period, as loyal sons of Canada came trooping home from nearly every quarter of the United States, and gallantly took their places in the ranks wherever a vacant place could be found. Thousands of others wrote home, volunteering their services if necessity required. These men deserve special mention on the pages of Canadian history, and it is a pleasure to the author of this book to put on record the splendid spirit of patriotism they displayed when their beloved Canada was in danger. Very many of them have passed away from earth, but their memories and worth will long be remembered by those who knew them best. To their descendants, and to all young Canadians, the loyal spirit which animated them should strongly appeal, and their deeds be emulated whenever danger threatens their native land.

CHAPTER XI.

JOHNNY CANUCK AFLOAT—SPLENDID SERVICE ON BOARD THE
GUNBOATS—THE BEGINNING OF THE CANADIAN NAVY—
ARRIVAL OF BRITISH TARS.

Concurrent with the mustering of troops to act on land, the need of naval forces to patrol our lakes and rivers was fully realized, so preparations were quickly made in that direction. The Toronto Naval Brigade, commanded by Capt. W. F. McMaster, was a very efficient and well-disciplined corps of brave and hardy men, who were among the first to respond to the call of duty. The Government chartered the powerful steam tug "Rescue," which being properly armed, was placed in commission as the first boat in the Canadian Navy. She was manned by the Toronto Naval Brigade, and sailed out of Toronto Harbor on June 4th under sealed orders. She arrived at Port Dalhousie the same evening and proceeded through the Welland Canal and Lake Erie to Windsor, where trouble was expected. Her officers and crew were a resolute and able lot of men, who were patriotic to the core, and were keen to get into action with the enemy. It had been rumored that a Fenian fleet was being fitted out on the Upper Lakes to assist in Gen. Sweeny's programme, therefore all on board the "Rescue" were vigilant and expectant that they would have an opportunity to meet a Fenian gunboat on Lake Erie and prove their mettle.

The roster of the Toronto Naval Brigade on this expedition was as follows: Captain. W. F. McMaster; Lieutenant, Alex. McGregor; Sub-Lieutenant. E. B. Vankoughnet; Surgeon, N. McMaster; Gunner. John Field; Boatswain. R. Montgomery; Chief Engineer, J. Nicholson; Midshipmen, R. Wilson and A. Miller; Paymaster. Joseph Fletcher; Quartermaster, George Wyatt; Assistant Engineers, James Findlay and John Young; Gunner's Mate, James Morrison; Boatswain's Mates, James Ford and Richard Ardagh; Carpenter. Joseph Smith; Carpenter's Mate, John Clendinning; Armorer. Fred. Oakley; Seamen. Thos. G. Cable, George Mackay. Wm. A. Wilson, John Bolam. Harry

Sewart Crewe, George Fox, Wm. W. Fox, George Poulter, Samuel Crangle, Ed. Metcalfe, Fred Walker, Samuel Mountain, Charles Corin, Wm. Miles, Ed. Scadding, Joseph Fetters, Thos. Hutchinson, James Humphrey, Wm. Dillon, Wm. Maclear, Chas. Callighan, R. Y. Ellis, Joseph Bywater, John Graham, James Ferguson, Fred Yates, Harry Y. Young, George Mutton, Edward Turner, Wm. Pedlow, Samuel Pettigrew, W. J. McClure, Ben. Cope, Thos. Spence, James Craig, Clarence Cooch, W. Cooch, T. Mulholland, Sam. Parker, E. J. Hobson, J. G. Hutchinson. Thos. Lunday, Geo. Williams, George Oakley; Powder Boys. F. H. Moulson and Gus Ellis.

Mr. E. B. Vankoughnet (a Toronto boy, who was then serving as a midshipman on board Her Majesty's warship ''Aurora,'' lying at Quebec, and who was home on a visit at the time) wired his commanding officer for leave to join the ''Rescue,'' and being granted permission, reported for duty to Capt. McMaster and was attached to the Toronto Naval Brigade as Sub-Lieutenant on board the ''Rescue'' before she sailed.

As an example of the alacrity which marked the men of the Toronto Naval Brigade, it may be mentioned that when they received orders to go on board the ''Rescue'' on Sunday morning, June 3rd, and fit her up for service, they responded so promptly that before evening they had put 67 tons of coal on board, besides transforming the boat from a peaceful tug to a veritable gunboat by making such alterations as were necessary for that purpose. All were workers, and ''handy men'' either ashore or afloat, and that night everything was so snug and secure that they took up their quarters on board, fully provisioned for a cruise. Early next morning the ''Rescue'' steamed up to the Queen's Wharf and took on board her armament and ammunition. A large 32-pound gun was mounted on the main deck, in a position available for service in any direction required, while the projectiles were placed in pyramidal piles near-by, so as to be convenient for quick action.

On the afternoon of the 5th of June, while proceeding up Lake Erie, a suspicious-looking steamer was seen approaching from the west. Heavy clouds of black smoke belched forth from her funnels, and she appeared to be heading for the ''Rescue'' under full speed. As rumors of a Fenian flotilla on the Upper

Lakes had prevailed, it was conjectured that this strange craft might be one of the enemy's gunboats, and consequently its appearance caused some excitement on board the "Rescue." The men were called to quarters, the 32-pounder loaded and charged with chain-shot, and every preparation made to give battle in case the approaching steamer should happen to be a foe. As it came nearer it was seen that she was a side-wheeler, and was evidently crowding on all steam. Jack Fields (an experienced gunner) took charge of the 32-pounder, which he carefully trained on the stranger, and remarked: "We will take that walking-beam out of her." All were now expectant, and ready for action, awaiting orders to fire. But as the steamer approached closer it was learned that she was the United States revenue cutter "Fessenden," which was on patrol duty on Lake Erie, on the look-out for Fenians also, and her commander had intended to overhaul the "Rescue," as he likewise thought her suspicious-looking. After a friendly "hail" and mutual explanations, both steamers proceeded on their way.

At about 12 o'clock that night, when about off Port Stanley, a heavy storm of wind and rain arose, and the crew of the "Rescue" experienced a very rough time. The boat pitched and rolled in the trough of the heavy seas, and she sprang a leak. The big gun threatened to break loose from its lashings, and had to be thoroughly secured by cables. The round shot, which had been built up in pyramids on the deck, got away from their base-frames and were rolling in every direction, while the high waves swept over the bulwarks, deluging the men with water. During the whole of the night and part of the next day the men were kept constantly at the pumps, and by dint of hard work succeeded in keeping the boat afloat until the gale subsided and they entered calmer waters. The crew were pretty well worn out with hunger and fatigue when they reached the mouth of the Detroit River on the evening of the 6th of June. They arrived at Windsor about 8 o'clock on the same night, weary, but none the worse of their experience in a Lake Erie storm, which is said by old sailors to be the worst that can rage on any sea.

As matters looked serious along the Detroit River and Upper Lakes, it was decided to strengthen the naval force at Windsor by equipping another boat for service. Therefore the staunch ferry steamer "Michigan" was chartered and details of British tars from Her Majesty's Ship "Aurora" were brought up from Quebec to form her crew, and also to relieve the Toronto Naval Brigade from duty on the "Rescue." as Capt. McMaster had received orders to transfer his command to the "Magnet" and cruise the lakes. Both the "Michigan" and the "Rescue" were then efficiently armed and equipped for the naval service required, and went into commission under British officers and crews. Each boat had an armament of two Armstrong ship guns (9 and 12-pounders), with full supplies of ammunition, and were manned by one Lieutenant, one Second Lieutenant, and midshipmen, doctors, carpenters, etc., with about 90 seamen, 22 marines and seven other officers, all armed with rifles, cutlasses, revolvers and dirks. Lieut. Fairlie, R.N.., and Lieut. Heron, R.N. (both of the British man-of-war "Aurora"), were placed in command of the "Rescue" and "Michigan," respectively.

On being relieved from duty on the "Rescue" by the British seamen, Capt. McMaster and his men proceeded to Toronto to fit out the steamer "Magnet" for lake service. They had just completed this arduous work and were awaiting sailing instructions, when an order came that their services were not needed for the present. In relieving them from further service they were specially thanked by Gen. Napier for the creditable manner in which they had done their duty, in the following order:

Assistant Adjt.-General's Office.
Toronto, June 10, 1866.

Sir,—I am directed by Maj.-Gen. Napier, C.B., commanding Her Majesty's forces and volunteers, Canada West, to express to you his thanks for the efficient services rendered by the Naval Brigade under your command, particularly recently, when required to take charge of and convert the steamer "Rescue" into a gunboat, in discharging her cargo and getting the necessary armament on board in a very short time and in a highly creditable manner; and, when relieved from the charge of the "Rescue," in performing similar good services when placed in command of the steamer "Magnet." And the Major-General will not fail to again avail himself of the services of the Naval Brigade afloat should an opportunity occur, and will have great pleasure in bringing before the notice of His Excellency the Governor-General the important and valuable services which they have rendered.

I have the honor to be, Sir,
Your obedient servant,

Capt. McMaster,   WM. S. DURIE.
Commanding Naval Brigade, Toronto.   Lt.-Col.. A.A.G.M.

On the St. Lawrence River the necessity for a patrol of gunboats was also very manifest, and the Government fitted out the steamer "Watertown" for such service. She was placed in command of Lieut. French. and was employed in cruising the upper part of the St. Lawrence and the lower portion of Lake Ontario, making her port of rendezvous at Kingston.

The gunboat "St. Andrew," commanded by Lieut. Spencer Smith, R.N., and manned by a detachment of British man-of-warsmen, patrolled the St. Lawrence between Brockville and Gananoque. She carried five guns, and her crew were armed with the usual fighting equipment of seamen in the British navy.

The steamer "Wabuno" was armed and placed in commission to cruise on the Georgian Bay, in which waters her crew performed active and vigilant service on patrol duty for several weeks.

On the Niagara River and Lake Erie the steamer "W. T. Robb" was retained in commission and fitted up for service as a cruiser. In addition to the Dunnville Naval Brigade, a detachment of the St. Catharines Garrison Battery (under command of Lieut. James Wilson) was placed on board with two guns, a 9-pounder and a 12-pound howitzer, and the necessary complement of small arms. The wheel-house and cabins were covered with boiler plates, and the bulwarks strengthened by heavy planking for the protection of her crew. so that she was soon converted into a formidable craft and admirably fitted for the work she was detailed to do. This boat was kept busy patrolling the Niagara River and the lower portion of Lake Erie. and her crew did excellent night and day service during the time she was so employed.

At Montreal the gunboat "Royal" was fitted out and despatched through the St. Lawrence Canals and River. She was armed with an Armstrong 12-pounder and a brass howitzer forward, and a 12-pound Armstrong gun aft. Her batteries around bows and stern were cased with iron for the protection of the men working the guns, and her wheel-house protected with sand-bags, making her secure against rifle fire. The gunboats "Hercules" and "Canada" were also put in commission at Montreal and thoroughly outfitted for service on the lakes and river.

To aid in the protection of Montreal harbor H. M. ship ''Rosario'' (Capt. Versturme) was despatched from Quebec to that point. She was a steam screw sloop of 673 tons and 150 horsepower, with an armament of eleven guns, and had a full complement of British sailors and marines.

At Hamilton and Port Stanley-the Naval Brigades stationed at these points performed shore duty, and did it well. Danger hovered everywhere, and the utmost vigilance was necessary to guard every point. The country was overrun with Fenian spies and emissaries, and arrests of suspicious characters were numerous. Even at home there were traitors who needed watching, as there were some who were ready to give countenance and support to the enemy. Thus the companies who remained at their local headquarters, and the Home Guards who were enrolled for home protection. did remarkably good service along those lines.

CHAPTER XII.

ON THE ST. LAWRENCE AND EASTERN FRONTIERS—MUSTER OF
TROOPS AT KINGSTON, BROCKVILLE, PRESCOTT, CORNWALL
AND OTHER POINTS.

While the sanguinary engagements which have been related
in the preceding pages were in progress on the Niagara frontier, the danger of invasion was just as imminent at many other
points along our border line, and excitement was consequently
as intense. It was felt at the time, and subsequently confirmed
as correct, that the diversion of Gen. O'Neil at Fort Erie was
only a prelude to cover more formidable attacks along the line
of the St. Lawrence, and the frontier of the Eastern Townships
of Quebec.

To guard this lengthy border was the first precaution taken
by the Government, and all troops that were available east of
Toronto were promptly called out for active service. Along the
St. Lawrence River the points most seriously threatened were
Kingston, Brockville, Prescott and Cornwall, and the attention
of the Lieutenant-General Commanding was immediately
directed towards making adequate provision for the protection
of those places.

At Kingston the 14th Battalion of Rifles .the Kingston
Field Battery, the First Frontenac Troop of Cavalry, and the
Garden Island and Portsmouth Infantry Companies, were
assembled and equipped, ready to proceed to any point where
their services might be required. The forts were garrisoned by
regular troops, and the city put in a proper state of defence.
On Sunday, the 3rd of June, just as the garrison was returning
from church parade, Lieut.-Col. John Paton received orders to
proceed at once with the 14th Rifles to Cornwall. The Battalion
started that evening by special train for their destination, amid
tremendous cheering by the patriotic citizens.

The force which was mobilized at Prescott on June 3rd consisted of one division of the Ottawa Field Battery, with two
guns; the Gananoque Battery of Garrison Artillery; three com-

panies of the Prince Consort's Own Rifle Brigade (regulars). under Major Newdegate; the left wing of the 25th King's Own Borderers (regulars) ; the 18th (Hawkesbury) Battalion, under command of Lieut.-Col. John Hamilton; Nos. 1 and 2 Companies of the Ottawa Rifles; the Pakenham and Fitzroy Companies of Infantry; and the 15th (Belleville) Battalion of Infantry, under command of Lieut.-Col. A. A. Campbell. Old Fort Wellington was strengthened and well equipped with three batteries of garrison artillery, and every detail arranged to properly protect the town. All of the danger points were so securely guarded by this efficient garrison (which was under the command of Col. F. T. Atcherly, D.A.G.) that the invaders would have met with an amazingly hot reception had they carried out their threatened intentions to cross the river anywhere in that vicinity.

Lieut.-Col. Crawford had command of the force which was assembled at Brockville, consisting of a battalion composed of the Brockville Rifles, Gananoque Rifles, Brockville Infantry, Perth Rifles, Perth Infantry, Carleton Place Rifles, and Almonte Infantry. These companies were exceedingly efficient, and did great service in guarding the river front and railway communications at Brockville. Col. Crawford and his troops received great praise from the Major-General for the very satisfactory manner in which they did their duty on these trying occasions.

The City of Ottawa was garrisoned by the Civil Service Rifles, Major Ross' Artillery Company, the Bell's Corners Infantry Company, and other companies from the neighborhood. assisted by a strong Home Guard.

The Grand Trunk Railway bridges at Vaudreuil, St. Ann's and Lachine were guarded by the St. Therese, Como and Varennes Infantry Companies. this arduous duty being very accurately and vigilantly performed by the corps mentioned.

At Cornwall the situation was exceedingly serious, as it was known that Gen. Sweeny had particular designs on that place, and was making every preparation to deliver an attack. The possession of the canals was one of his chief desires, and to ward off such an attempt a strong force was quickly mobilized at this point of danger. On the 2nd of June a public meeting of citizens was called and a committee appointed to act in concert with the military commandant in putting the town in a thorough state of defence. A patrol was established for ten miles up and down the river by the local companies, and navigation on the river and through the canal was stopped. Early on the 3rd of June troops began arriving from different points, and by the following morning over 2,000 had been assembled under the command of Col. T. H. Pakenham, of H. M. 30th Regiment. The Canadian force which was mustered at Cornwall was composed of the 14th (Kingston) Battalion, the 25th Regiment (King's Own Borderers), the 11th Argenteuil Rangers, a portion of H. M. 30th Regiment, one division of the Ottawa Field Battery, the 6th Hochelaga Light Infantry, two companies of Ottawa Rifles, and two Cornwall companies.

On the St. John's and Missisquoi frontiers the local companies of Frelighsburg, Philipsburg, Granby and Waterloo were posted, under command of Col. F. R. Elrington, of the P. C. O. Rifle Brigade, and kept a sharp look-out for the appearance of the enemy. They received numerous "alarms," but beyond a general expectancy of a conflict which kept them on the alert, they did not have an opportunity of proving their valor.

Lieut.-Col. W. Osborne Smith, D.A.G., had command of the troops which were assembled on the Huntingdon and Hemmingford frontiers, which consisted of the 1st Prince of Wales Rifles (Lieut.-Col. B. Devlin), of Montreal; the Victoria Rifles, of Montreal; one division of Capt. A. A. Stevenson's Field Battery, of Montreal; the Hemmingford, Roxham and Havelock Infantry Companies, and a detachment of the Montreal Cavalry. With this force he proceeded to Hemmingford, where he halted on the 3rd and sent out scouts to observe the operations of the enemy on the frontier. Learning that an attack was likely to be made on the Huntingdon frontier, Col. Smith left next morning at daybreak with his column for the threatened point. The weather was exceedingly unfavorable, as it rained incessantly all day, and the roads were in a very bad state. Still he pushed on, and covered 37 miles, which his troops accomplished in a splendid manner, and went into camp that night with only two patients reported on the hospital returns as being incapacitated by the fatiguing march. The direct approach to Huntingdon from Malone, where the Fenians were mobilizing, is by the Trout River Road, and across this path Col. Smith constructed a line of breastworks and awaited the approach of the enemy. His position was admirably chosen, and had Gen. Sweeny made an advance down the Chatauguay Valley, he would have met with such a stout resistance that his defeat would have been certain, as the Canadian position was impregnable. For a few days all kinds of rumors were current of an advance being made by the Fenians, and constant vigilance was maintained, but the attack failed to eventuate.

Lieut.-Col. George Browne, D.A.G., with the 1st and 2nd Huntingdon Infantry Companies; the Athelstan, Durham and Rockburn Infantry Companies, and the Hinchinbrook Rifle Company, also assisted to hold the Huntingdon line, and did good service in keeping guard on the frontier.

With the salient points along the Canadian border being thus securely guarded, and every soldier on the *qui vive*, the Fenian troops would most certainly have encountered very strong opposition before they could carry out their designs to conquer Canada.

CHAPTER XIII.

ON THE VERMONT BORDER—FENIANS GATHER IN LARGE NUM-
BERS—THE FIZZLE AT PIGEON HILL—ARREST OF GEN.
SPIER.

During the night of the 31st of May a general movement
of Fenian troops was commenced from different towns and cities
in the New England States towards their point of concentration at St. Albans, Vermont. This force was designated as the
"Right Wing of the Irish Republican Army," and was commanded by Gen. Spier, with Gen. Mahon, of Boston, as his Chief
of Staff. By noon of the 1st of June over 800 men had reported
to Gen. Spier, and during the following twenty-four hours their
number had increased to about 1,800. Like their comrades who
had assembled at Buffalo, they travelled in small squads and
companies, unarmed, and were reticent as to their intentions
while in American territory. They quietly scattered about the
town in groups and made no disorderly demonstrations, as they
seemed to be under some sort of military restraint or orders.
Every train that arrived from the east or the south brought in
fresh contingents, who on arrival received their orders and
silently distributed themselves among the small towns and villages along the Vermont border. For some time previous cases
of arms and ammunition had been shipped to convenient points
where they would be ready for distribution, and staff officers
were busy looking after this war material and getting everything ready for the equipment of the expedition. For a day or
two matters looked very promising for Gen. Spier. Thirteen
thousand troops had been promised to him by Gen. Sweeny,
with an unlimited supply of arms and ammunition, and his
hopes soared high. But alas for human reckoning! The fates
proved unkind, as subsequent developments proved.

On the 4th of June the Boston contingent of Fenians, about
400 in number, arrived at St. Albans, without arms. Of this
command about 200 were sent to Fairfield, Vt., a village eight
miles east of St. Albans, and quite close to the Canadian frontier, where a column was being mobilized to cross the border.

At East Highgate, Vt., the Fenians established a camp and made preparations for an advance into Canadian territory from that point.

All along the border of Missisquoi County, in Quebec, the invaders gathered in groups, companies and regiments, awaiting their arms and orders to move. Finally a sufficient force was equipped to make a forward movement, as the men were getting impatient, and on the 4th of June Gen. Spier led his advance guard across the frontier into St. Armands, where he established his camp and set up his headquarters at Pigeon Hill, from the summit of which he flaunted a large green flag.

There were about 1,000 men in this brigade, which was officered by several old soldiers who had achieved distinction in the American Civil War, among whom were Gen. Mahon, of the 9th Massachusetts, Col. Coutri, and others of prominence.

The only Canadian force in the vicinity of St. Armands was composed of three companies of infantry, consisting of nine officers and about 100 non-commissioned officers and men, the whole being under command of Capt. W. Carter, of H. M. 16th Regiment. These troops were all raw volunteers, who were very deficient in drill or military experience, some of whom had never handled a rifle before, but all were willing and anxious to contest Gen. Spier's advance, and were brave to a fault.

As soon as the Fenians appeared in force at St. Armands, Capt. Carter hastily withdrew his force to the interior, as he said he was under the impression that it was not intended that he should bring on an engagement until he was properly reinforced, as his command was only an outpost. For his action in retiring so early he was severely criticized and reprimanded for his "error in judgment in retreating without sufficient reason," while his troops never forgave him for what they considered an exhibition of cowardice.

The main body of Gen. Spier's forces had advanced about a mile into Canadian territory, and took possession of all the houses and barns in the vicinity for their quarters. Their scouts and pickets were thrown out three or four miles in advance, and for some days they were in complete possession of the country. During this time the Fenians conducted themselves in a most lawless manner, robbing and stealing, and wantonly destroying property. All of the citizens and farmers residing in the neighborhood were the victims of pillage, being robbed of horses, provisions, valuables, etc., while cattle, sheep, poultry and other live stock were confiscated and slaughtered for the use of the raiders.

As the days passed by and the promised arms and reinforcements for Gen. Spier failed to materialize, he became restless and disheartened. The United States authorities had seized all of the arms and ammunition that could be discovered, and the fact was forced on the deluded General's mind that if he did not leave Canada soon a strong force of British troops would be upon him and annihilate his command. Moreover, the demoralization of his whole army was becoming complete, and both officers and men refused to do duty any longer. Desertions were taking place in a wholesale manner, and in several instances Colonels marched off with their entire commands and re-crossed the line. He therefore convened a Council of War to consider the situation. It was of short duration, as the officers were of the unanimous opinion that there was no other course left for them but to retrace their steps and give up the idea of invading Canada. The reinforcements, arms, provisions and munitions of war that had been so liberally promised, had failed to reach them, and weakened as they were by such wholesale desertions to the rear, it was deemed by old soldiers to be nothing but madness to remain where they were, as they would be wholly unable with such a small force to make even a decent show of a fight, should they happen to be attacked, and it was at once determined to give up the intended invasion, leave Canada, and head back for the United States.

Therefore Gen. Spier ordered Col. Coutri and Col. O'Connor to form up their men and march them back to St. Albans to report to Gen. Sweeny. Both of these officers were deeply affected as they proceeded to carry out their orders, as they wanted to stay and fight it out.

The men were formed in companies, but many went off on their own responsibility, and at 9.30 o'clock on the morning of June 9th, all that was left of the grand "Right Wing" were marching back across the border to the United States. The men had a few rounds of ammunition left in their pouches, and immediately commenced firing off their muskets and rifles in a most promiscuous manner. Arms, plunder and everything else that the men could carry off with them on their retreat were lashed upon their backs or packed in satchels, and quite a number of new suits of clothes, hats, shoes and other valuables which they had pilfered were carried off by them. Several horses were also taken across the line by the marauders.

Generals Spier and Mahon marched on foot among their retreating troops, and were very much downcast. Gen. Spier said that he would rather have been shot than have left Canada in the manner he was obliged to, while Gen. Mahon wept with rage at the thought of having to abandon the invasion. Most of the officers expressed themselves as being ashamed of the affair, and would rather never go home. After all their boasting of how easily they would capture Canada and set up their visionary Republic, the disgraceful manner in which the whole campaign terminated, without so much as a slight skirmish having taken place, was more than they could bear. There were many brave yet deluded men who joined the expedition with a determination to fight, but the majority of them were "nothing more or less than an armed mob, roving about wherever they pleased, robbing the houses and insulting and abusing women and children," as stated by a newspaper correspondent.

When the retreating raiders reached United States territory they found detachments of American troops stationed upon all the roads leading to St. Albans, who had received instructions to seize all the arms the Fenians might have in their possession. As the majority of them had thrown away their muskets, sabres and ammunition on their retreat, there was not much left for the United States troops to gather up, but what little there was left was promptly seized.

Upon arrival on the American side of the line Gen. Spier and his staff surrendered to Col. Livingston, of the United States Army, and were taken to St. Albans and placed under heavy bonds to await trial for violation of the neutrality laws.

A portion of Spier's army who were stationed at a point about eight miles from St. Armand when the main body retreated, were charged upon by 40 men of the Montreal Guides.

and in the skirmish several Fenians were killed and sixteen taken prisoners, who were conveyed to Montreal. There were no casualties on the Canadian side.

On the night of the 9th of June a train left St. Albans for the east with nearly 1,000 Fenians bound for their homes, while many others were left skulking around the country in the hope that another raid would soon be organized, whereby they could have an opportunity of securing more booty.

On the 22nd of June a small party of these marauders came on a reconnoitering expedition to Pigeon Hill, and on arriving at the outpost began firing at the Richelieu Light Infantry sentinel who was stationed there. They were in a thick bush off the road, leading across the lines to Franklin County. As soon as they were perceived, the Canadian detachment made an endeavor to get between the Fenians and American territory, for the purpose of intercepting their retreat. But the Fenians fled through a swamp and managed to effect their escape. About twenty shots were fired, but without effect.

This was the last episode of the Pigeon Hill affair, and in another week peace and quietness again prevailed along the Vermont border.

CHAPTER XIV.

FENIAN MOBILIZATION AT MALONE AND ELSEWHERE—GEN. MEADE'S PROMPT ACTION STOPS THE INVASION—ARREST OF GEN. SWEENY AND STAFF.

The principal points of rendezvous for the Fenians who were intended to operate on the St. Lawrence frontier were Ogdensburg. Watertown, Malone and Potsdam, in the State of New York. and at these places large bodies of men began concentrating during the first two or three days in June. General Sweeny was in personal command of the troops of the Irish Republican Army in that department. and had made every arrangement to invade Canada along that line. in accordance with his original plan of campaign. He made his headquarters at Ogdensburg for a time, and from there directed the mobilization of his columns for the contemplated attacks on Prescott. Cornwall and other points on the Canadian border.

Meanwhile Gen. Michael J. Heffernan, Gen. Murphy, and Gen. O'Reilly, were at Malone, N.Y., perfecting the military organization of the column which was intended to attack Cornwall. These officers were all old soldiers, who had held commands in the United States service during the Civil War, and were well posted in the business they had on hand.

While the Fenian leaders were thus employed in getting their forces ready for the movement across the line, Major-General Geo. Meade (the commander of the United States troops) was equally active and vigilant in his determined efforts to stop the promised invasion. He ordered the seizure by the United States officials of all arms and ammunitions of war intended for use by the Fenians that could be located on American territory. and forbade the railways and other transportation companies from carrying further supplies of such material to the frontier. These orders were rigidly complied with, and seizures of arms and ammunition were made at Rouse's Point. Malone. Potsdam, Ogdensburg. Watertown, St. Albans and other places, which considerably disconcerted Gen. Sweeny's plans and thwarted his whole scheme. The presence of United States troops, which had been moved north from various military stations to support Gen. Meade in his efforts to prevent another breach of the Neutrality Act, also had a deterrent effect on the Fenians, and they became disheartened.

On the afternoon of the 4th of June, Major-General Meade ordered the United States Marshal at Watertown, N.Y., to intercept, seize and hold two carloads of Fenian war material which were on the way from Rome to Potsdam Junction and Malone. On arrival of the train at Watertown the Deputy Marshal was in waiting and promptly carried out the instructions. A carload of Fenian soldiers who were on the same train got off the car and angrily remonstrated with the officer when they learned of the seizure, but he was obdurate and retained possession of the two cars, which he had side-tracked. The Fenians remained at Watertown and began plotting for the recapture of the arms and ammunition. Not realizing that any interference with the majesty of the law would be attempted, the Marshal did not deem it necessary to place a strong guard over the two cars, and the Fenians determined to re-possess them. On arrival of the evening express train from the south they gathered around it and captured not only that train, but their two cars of supplies, and taking charge themselves, ran the whole outfit off to De Kalb Junction before they were recaptured. Several other instances of defiance of lawful authority were reported, but Gen. Meade meant *business*, and these infractions of his orders and the laws of the United States only served to make him more determined than ever to strangle the hopes of the Fenians before they had an opportunity of carrying out their designs.

PRESIDENT JOHNSON'S PROCLAMATION.

The tardy proclamation of President Johnson was finally issued on the 6th of June, almost a week after the Fenians under Gen. O'Neil had crossed over the Niagara. Its delay seemed significant to the Canadian people, as the President and his Cabinet were fully aware that the Fenians had been making active preparations for months previously to invade Canada, and made no secret of their intentions. The following is the text of the proclamation:—

By the President of the United States of America—A Proclamation.

Whereas, it has become known to me that certain evil-disposed persons have, within the territory and jurisdiction of the United States, begun and set on foot, and have provided and prepared, and are still engaged in providing and preparing, means for such a military expedition and enterprise to be carried on from territory and jurisdiction of the United States against colonies, districts and people of British North America within the dominions of the United Kingdom of Great Britain and Ireland, with which said colonies, districts, and people, and kingdom, the United States are at peace; and whereas, the proceedings aforesaid constitute a high misdemeanor, forbidden by the laws of the United States as well as by the laws of nations;

Now, therefore, for the purpose of preventing the carrying on of the unlawful expedition and enterprise aforesaid from the territory and jurisdiction of the United States, and to maintain the public peace, as well as the national honor, and enforce obedience and respect to the laws of the United States;

I, Andrew Johnson, President of the United States, do admonish and warn all good citizens of the United States against taking part in or in anywise aiding, countenancing or abetting such unlawful proceedings; and I do exhort all judges, magistrates, marshals and officers in the service of the United States to employ all their lawful authority and power to prevent and defeat the aforesaid unlawful proceedings, and to arrest and bring to justice all persons who may be engaged therein, and in pursuance to the Act of Congress in such cases made and provided.

I do further authorize and empower Major-General G. G. Meade, Commander of the Military Division of the Atlantic, to employ the land and naval forces of the United States, and militia thereof, to arrest and prevent the setting on foot and carrying on the expedition and enterprise aforesaid.

In testimony whereof, I have hereunto set my hand and caused the seal of the United States to be affixed.

Done in the City of Washington the sixth day of June, in the year of our Lord 1866, and in the independence of the United States the 90th.

ANDREW JOHNSON.

By the President,

WM. H. SEWARD, Secretary of State.

Although President Johnson did not issue his neutrality proclamation until the 6th of June, orders had previously been issued to United States officers to stop further invasions, and Gen. Meade exhibited great energy and promptness in carrying out instructions so far as his Department was concerned. Fenians were gathering in thousands, with the understanding that their equipment would be at the border on their arrival, but the bulk of the coveted armament was prevented from falling into their hands owing to the watchfulness of Gen. Meade's staff of officials. This action on the part of the United States authorities deeply incensed the Fenian leaders, and they were disposed to resent any interference with their plans. During an interview between Gen. Meade and the Fenian Generals Heffernan and Murphy, at Malone, the former complained of the interference of the United States Government, and bitterly remarked: "We have been lured on by the Cabinet, and used for the purpose of Mr. Seward. They encouraged us on to this thing. We bought our rifles from your arsenals, and were given to understand that you would not interfere. But this thing is not dead yet. We will succeed. We have our orders from General Sweeny, and we can and will perform them. If we get arms we will cross into Canada. We shall fight your regulars if they oppose us." General Meade replied: "I have got orders, too, and I shall fight you to enforce the neutrality laws."

In the performance of his duty Gen. Meade was inflexible, and would not stand any bluff or bluster from the Fenian leaders. On the contrary, he became very aggressive in compelling them to respect the laws and authority of the United States, and largely through his firmness and stern efforts the whole Fenian campaign was abandoned.

ARREST OF PRESIDENT ROBERTS.

On the 8th of June the United States Government caused the arrest of Col. W. R. Roberts, President of the Irish Republic, on a charge of conspiracy and violation of the Neutrality Act. He was brought before United States Commissioner Betts, at New York, and committed to jail pending a hearing of his case. From the quiet precincts of his contracted quarters he issued several proclamations, which teemed with gasconade and valiant promises, of which the following is a sample:

Ludlow St. Jail, New York, June 11, 1866.
To the Fenian Brotherhood and Irishmen of America:

Friends and Countrymen,—The Irish people of America are again united in the cause of Irish independence and universal freedom. The cheer which arose from the Irish soldiers at Limestone Ridge as the English foe went fleeing before their avenging steel, has found a responsive echo in every Irish heart and made us one in love, purpose and resolve. We see, after ages of your oppression, the unquenchable desire for Irish independence blaze forth anew, and as it sweeps along the cities and prairies of this vast continent it gathers within its magic influence five millions of Irish hearts and twice five millions of friends of freedom and foes of despotism! Arise, then, my countrymen! Nerve yourselves for the struggle so nobly commenced. Cast aside every consideration that would darken the bright hopes of your enslaved countrymen. Be true to liberty, your country, and your God; and your native land, instead of being a lazar-house of slavery, will soon be the garden of freedom. Stand by the cause! Be not dismayed by obstacles you meet; you must surmount them, and you will. Let cowardice and ignorance desert and denounce you—what of that? The true men are still with us, and the struggle must not be abandoned, even though our soldiers should be compelled through the over-zeal of United States officers to abandon the present campaign. There is no turning back for us, my countrymen. Our movement must and will advance. Retrogression would entail certain infamy and bring a deeper stain upon your country and race, and it is as legitimate for you to attack English power in Canada as it was for England to attack France there, or France and America England. Remember, in union there is strength, and that Union which has been cemented by the blood of our gallant brothers must be eternal, and let that man be anathemized and banned who with lying lip or evil heart would dare to weaken or dissolve it. Be true to Ireland—steadfast in the right and undismayed by obstacles, and remember that—

> "Freedom's battle once begun—
> Bequeathed from bleeding sire to son—
> Though baffled oft, is ever won!"

I remain, with unchanged determination and regard, your countryman,.

WM. R. ROBERTS,

President Fenian Brotherhood.

While President Roberts was busy in penning his proclamations and exhorting his deluded followers to stand by the cause and "keep their powder dry" for a future attempt, the Revolutionary Committee of the Irish Republic were also sending out appeals to all lovers of Republican liberty, invoking further aid, from one of which circulars the following is an extract:

Let the Irish citizens in particular send in commissary stores, such as bread, meat, coffee, sugar, etc., just what each one would like at home. We want all the money you can raise for other purposes—what purposes the people can guess. Let no person imagine that the cause is defeated or that the men who have sworn to free their native land or die, will abandon their cause. A few over-zealous officials have placed some obstacles in our way. The voice of the great American people is at last heard in her halls of Congress, not from a single individual, but from the representatives of thirty millions, and true to her natural instincts, they raise their voices for the oppressed. God bless them! They will raise many an anxious spirit through the world and make tyrants tremble on their thrones as the cry goes forth, "America is the defender of liberty." Let the people take heart throughout the land. Call meetings, pass resolutions, pledge support to the men who inscribe on their banner universal liberty. Be patient, but work! work! Collect money. Have your men ready, and when the cry of fight goes forth, let them come as individuals if they cannot come as companies or regiments.

As a large number of Fenians had gathered at Malone with very hostile intentions, Gen. Meade gave particular attention to the marauders who had mustered there. They had taken possession of the old military barracks at Malone. and were running the town to suit their own inclinations. As the days wore on and the prospects of their receiving arms and supplies to equip the invaders became more and more remote, the leaders chafed, fumed and fretted alternately, and finally became absolutely discouraged. Their fondest hopes were blasted, and they bitterly berated the United States Government in blasphemous language for stopping their expeditions. While the officers were in this frame of mind, their soldiers were worse. They were living on short rations, and their promise of a pleasant sojourn in ''The Land of Plenty,'' where they hoped to revel in all the luxuries of life (when they captured it), was likely to prove but an empty dream. They were becoming turbulent and demonstrative, and it was finally found necessary to invoke the majesty of military power to keep them in subjection. Desertions were now frequent, and they had become a disorganized mob rather than a disciplined army. As this state of affairs was a menace to the public safety of the citizens of Malone. Gen. Meade took a firm grasp of the situation and issued the following order:

MALONE, N.Y., June 9th, 1866.

All persons assembled at this place in connection with, and in aid of the Fenian organization for the purpose of invading Canada, are hereby ordered, in compliance with the President's proclamation, to desist from their enterprise and disband. The men of the expeditionary force will, on application to the officer in command of the United States forces, on giving their names and residences, and satisfying him that they are unable to provide their own transportation, be provided with transportation to their homes; and all officers below the rank of field officers who are unable to provide their own transportation, on giving their parole to abandon the enterprise, will be allowed to return to their homes; officers above the rank of field officers will be required to give such bonds as may be satisfactory to the civil authorities; it being the determination of the United States Government to preserve neutrality, and the most stringent measures having been taken to prevent all accessions of men and material, the Commanding General trusts that these liberal offers will have the effect of causing the expedition, now hopeless, to be quietly and peaceably abandoned; and he confidently expects that all those who have any respect for the authority of the United States will conform to the requirements of the President's proclamation; and of this, which if not promptly obeyed. a sufficient force will be brought to bear to compel obedience.

(Signed) GEORGE G. MEADE,

Major-General, U.S.A.

In compliance with this order, the majority of the men immediately gave their paroles, and for the next day or two trains were filled with the discomfitted warriors returning to their homes. All thoughts of the capture of Canada had vanished, and peace reigned once more on the border line.

The day previous, while Gen. Sweeny and Col. Meehan were actively engaged in mobilizing troops and directing operations on the Vermont frontier, warrants were served upon them by the United States authorities for violation of the Neutrality Act. They were arraigned before the United States Commissioner at Burlington, Vt., when they waived examination, and bail was fixed for Sweeny at $20,000 and Meehan at $5,000, to appear for trial at the July term of the United States District Court. Meanwhile other prominent leaders were being arrested at other points. With the President, the Secretary of War, and other members of the Irish Republican Cabinet under arrest, and many others of lesser note being "wanted" by American officers for infractions of the law, the hopes of the invaders sank below zero, and their warlike zeal vanished away.

FENIANISM IN CONGRESS.

As nearly all of the prominent Fenian leaders had been placed under arrest for transgression of United States laws, and quite a number of their deluded followers who were captured in Canada were confined in Canadian prisons awaiting trial, the seriousness of their offences began to dawn upon the minds of those implicated in the movement. The good offices of the United States Government were then eagerly sought by their friends and supporters to get them out of the meshes of the net, and earnest appeals were made to the State Department for some action along these lines. Every possible pressure was brought to bear on Congress and the United States Senate to secure the influence of those two important legislative bodies in taking up the Fenian cause. But it was a delicate question to handle, and although there were some Congressmen who introduced the matter into the

House of Representatives, and made fiery speeches in support of their resolutions, the majority failed to concur, as they rightly conjectured that if the United States gave the Fenians the recognition and liberty of action they desired, it might end in embroiling them in war with Great Britain, for which they were not prepared.

On June 11th, 1866, Congressman Ancona, of Pennsylvania, offered the following preamble and resolution in the United States Congress:

Whereas, the Irish people and their brothers and friends in this country are moved by a patriotic purpose to assist the independence and re-establish the nationality of Ireland, and whereas the active sympathies of the people of the United States are naturally with all men who struggle to achieve such ends, more especially when those engaged therein are the known friends of our Government, as are the people of the Irish race, they having shed their blood in defence of our flag in every battle of every war in which the Republic has been engaged; and whereas the British Government against which they are struggling is entitled to no other or greater consideration from us, a nation, than that demanded by the strict letter of international law, for the reason that during our late Civil War that Government did in effect, by its conduct repeal its neutrality laws; and whereas when reparation is demanded for damages to our commerce, resulting from the wilful neglect of Great Britain to enforce the same, she arrogantly denies all responsibility, and claims to be the judge in her own cause; and whereas the existence of the neutrality law of 1818 compels the executive department of this Government to discriminate most harshly against those who have ever been, and are now, our friends, in favor of those who have been faithless, not only to the general principles of comity which should exist between friendly States, but also to the written law of their own nation on this subject; therefore, be it resolved, that the Committee on Foreign Affairs be instructed to report a bill repealing an Act approved April 20th. 1818. it being the neutrality law, under the terms of which the President's proclamation against the Fenians was issued.''

It is needless to say that the good sense of Congress prevailed. and the resolution was consigned to the morgue which is the receptacle for all undesirable resolutions.

CHAPTER XV.

THE FENIAN PRISONERS—CORRESPONDENCE BETWEEN SECRETARY SEWARD AND THE BRITISH MINISTER.

The question of the ultimate fate of the Fenian prisoners who had fallen into our hands was one which received considerable thought and discussion. While the temper of the Canadian people was not favorable to any leniency being shown to them in those sad days in June when they viewed the death and desolation that had been caused by the raiders, yet all felt constrained to give them the full benefit of British justice—fair trials and an opportunity to separate the guilty from the innocent. The authorities further resolved to be not too hasty in bringing the unfortunates before the tribunal, as in the excited state of the public mind such action might prove disastrous to the accused. This policy was a wise and just one, and met with general approval.

While these Irish-Americans were penned up in Canadian prisons their friends across the line were using every effort to effect their release by supplicating President Johnson and Secretary Seward to interpose in their behalf, and at last succeeded in getting some resolutions put through Congress with this object in view.

Secretary Seward took the question up in an official way with Sir Frederick W. A. Bruce, the British Minister at Washington, who forwarded the documents relating to the matter to the British and Canadian Governments, and no doubt this friendly interposition had some effect in influencing the authorities to adopt the humane policy which subsequently prevailed.

During the month of June the Fenian prisoners who had been captured at Fort Erie and vicinity and lodged in the jails at Brantford and elsewhere, were removed to Toronto Jail and placed under special guard until their cases could receive due consideration by the authorities. At a preliminary investigation a large number of these men were discharged for want of sufficient evidence to convict, and were deported from the country.

About forty were held for trial. Some of these were British subjects, while the remainder claimed American citizenship. The former were charged with high treason, the penalty for which is death. Those claiming to be aliens, and citizens of the United States, were indicted under an old statute which was enacted during the period of the Canadian Rebellion of 1837, which provided that subjects of a foreign state who entered Canada for the purpose of levying war rendered themselves liable, on conviction, to the death penalty.

On the 26th of July, 1866, President Andrew Johnson sent to the United States Congress the following documents from the Department of State, in reply to two resolutions of the House of Representatives, the first requesting him to urge upon the Canadian authorities, and also upon the British Government, the release of the Fenian prisoners captured in Canada; and the second requesting him to cause the prosecutions instituted in the United States against the Fenians to be discontinued. if not incompatible with the public interest:—

DEPARTMENT OF STATE, WASHINGTON, July 26, 1866.

To the President:—

The Secretary of State, to whom was referred two resolutions of the House of Representatives, passed on the 23rd of July, instant, in the following words, respectively:—

"Resolved, that the House of Representatives respectfully request the President of the United States to urge upon the Canadian authorities, and also the British Government, the release of the Fenian prisoners recently captured in Canada.

"Resolved, that the House respectfully request the President to cause the prosecutions instituted in the United States courts against the Fenians, to be discontinued, if compatible with the public interests."

Has the honor to report, in regard to the first resolution, that the Government of the United States holds no correspondence directly upon any subject with the Canadian authorities mentioned in the said resolution, or with the authorities of any colony, province or dependency of any other sovereign state; and that, on the contrary, all its correspondence concerning questions which arise in, or effect, or relate to such colonies, provinces or dependencies, is always conducted exclusively with such foreign governments.

On the 11th of June last a note was addressed by this department to the Honorable Sir Frederick W. A. Bruce, Her Majesty's Minister Plenipotentiary residing in the United States, of which a copy is hereunto annexed. It is proper to say, in relation to that note, first, that the reports mentioned therein to the effect that prisoners had been taken on the soil of the United States and conveyed to Canada, and threatened by Canadian agents with immediate execution without legal trial. were found on examination to be untrue and without foundation in fact. It is due to the British Government to say, in the second place, that the representations made in the said note have been received by the British Government and by the Canadian authorities in a friendly manner.

The resolution of the House of Representatives first recited, harmonizing, as it does, with the spirit of the aforesaid note, will be brought to the attention of Her Majesty's Government and of the Canadian authorities, with the expression of a belief on the part of the President that affairs upon the frontier have happily come to a condition in which the clemency requested by Congress may be extended without danger to the public peace, and with advantage to the interests of peace and harmony between the two nations.

I have already received your directions that the second of said resolutions be taken into consideration by the proper departments of the Government, with a desire that it may be found practicable to reconcile the humane policy recommended with the maintenance of law and order, the safety of the public peace, and the good faith and honor of the United States.

Respectfully submitted,

WILLIAM H. SEWARD.

DEPARTMENT OF STATE, WASHINGTON, June 11, 1866.

Sir,—The Secretary of War has laid before the President several despatches which were received yesterday and to-day from Major-Gen. Meade, who is commanding the United States forces on the Canadian frontier. These communications warrant the President in believing that the so-called Fenian expedition is now entirely at an end, and that order and tranquility may be expected to prevail henceforth on that border. I regret, however, that I am obliged to connect with this gratifying information the further statement that reports have reached Major-Gen. Meade to the effect that some of the Canadian or British troops have crossed the line and entered within the territory and jurisdiction of the United States. It is even said that this entry took place after the disturbers of the peace under the command of the leader Spear had relinquished their forbidden enterprise and withdrawn within the boundary line of the United States. The reports go so far as to say that prisoners have been taken on the soil of the United States and conveyed to Canada, and that the Canadian agents have threatened that these prisoners, together with such stragglers as may now be found within the Canadian lines, will be executed without legal trial. It is believed that these reports are exaggerated. Care has been taken by Major-Gen. Meade to have them promptly investigated.

In the meantime I am instructed by the President to represent to you, and through you to the British and Canadian authorities, that this Government would not look without serious concern upon the practice of any retaliation or other illegal proceedings upon the persons of such of the offenders as have fallen, or shall hereafter fall, into the hands of the Canadian authorities. I respectfully invite your attention to the subject, with the confident expectation that no proceedings that are not authorized and in conformity with law, will be taken against persons of that class, and in the hope that even the customary administration of the law will be tempered with special forbearance and clemency. In view of the effective proceedings which this Government has adopted in regard to the disturbances now so fortunately ended, these representations would have been made by me without waiting to be moved from any other quarter. They are now made, however, with the approval of Major-Gen. Meade, and I believe that they will receive the concurrence of the Congress and people of the United States.

    I have the honor to be, sir,
        Your obedient servant,

                    WILLIAM H. SEWARD.

The Hon. Frederick W. A. Bruce.

TRIALS OF THE FENIAN PRISONERS.

    The Fall Assizes of the Court of Oyer and Terminer and General Jail Delivery for the United Counties of York and Peel, opened at Toronto on October 8th, 1866, His Lordship the Hon. Justice John Wilson being named in the commission to preside over the Court of Justice which was to decide the fate of the Fenian prisoners. The indictments were read, and after an able and exhaustive address to the Grand Jury by Judge Wilson, in which he went fully into every phase of the case, and explained the statute under which the prisoners were to be tried, the documents were handed over to the Grand Jury for their consideration.

    When the Court resumed its sitting on October 17th for the trial of the accused, the Grand Jury presented true bills against three of the most prominent prisoners in custody, viz., Robert Blosse Lynch, of Louisville, Ky. (said to be a colonel in the Fenian forces at Fort Erie and Lime Ridge) ; David F. Lumsden, who claimed to be an Episcopalian clergyman, from Nunda, N.Y., and John McMahon, who stated that he was a Roman Catholic priest, from Anderson, Indiana. Lynch was first placed in the dock, and the indictment read, to which he pleaded "not guilty." Lumsden and McMahon were next charged, and also entered the same plea. The prisoners not being ready to proceed with their trials, they were remanded until October 24th, when the Court re-opened and the trials proceeded with. The counsel for the Crown were Hon. John Hillyard Cameron, Q.C. (Solicitor-General for Upper Canada), Messrs. Robert A. Harrison, John McNab, James Paterson and John Paterson.

    The first prisoner placed in the dock was Col. Robert B. Lynch, who stated that he had no connection with the Fenian Army, but had accompanied the expedition as a reporter for the Louisville *Courier*. A large number of Canadian residents of

Fort Erie and vicinity, however, testified that they had seen him wearing a sword and in command of a body of Fenian troops at that place. The evidence of his guilt was so overwhelming that the jury returned a verdict of guilty, and Colonel Lynch was sentenced to be hanged on the 13th of December. He received the sentence with composure and was removed back to the jail.

Rev. John McMahon was then placed on trial. He claimed that he had only went with the Fenians in a spiritual capacity, and to look after the wounded and dying. He said he was at Lime Ridge and attended to both Fenians and Canadians alike while there. His statements did not accord with the evidence given by other reliable witnesses who saw him giving aid and encouragement to Fenian soldiers at Fort Erie, and after a fair and impartial trial he was found guilty and sentenced to be executed with Lynch on December 13th.

Pending appeal proceedings these executions were deferred.

David F. Lumsden was brought up for trial on November 3rd. He was formerly rector of Trinity Church at Syracuse, N.Y., where he had a reputation of being too fond of drink, rendering himself subject to discipline for intemperance, and had been cited to appear before Bishop Coxe (Bishop of the Episcopal Church in the Western Diocese of New York), who sent him to Nunda, N.Y., in the hope that he might redeem himself. But he had again fallen from grace and was on a big spree in Buffalo when he drifted over to Fort Erie, and was arrested on suspicion of being implicated with the Fenians. After hearing all the evidence, which was in favor of the prisoner, the jury retired and brought in a verdict of "not guilty," and he was discharged.

True bills were then rendered by the Grand Jury in the cases of the other prisoners who were held in custody.

On Nov. 7th, William Slavin was found guilty and sentenced to death. On the same date Benjamin Parry (a lad 16 years of age, from Cincinnati), was discharged.

On Nov. 9th, Daniel Drummond, who was arrested at Fort Erie, was discharged, as there was not sufficient evidence to convict.

On Nov. 10th, William Hayden was found guilty and sentenced to death, while William Duggan was discharged.

On Nov. 14th, Daniel Whalen and John Quinn were both found guilty and sentenced to be hanged.

On Nov. 15th, Thomas School was found guilty and received the death sentence, while Patrick Donohue was discharged.

On Jan. 11th, 1867, Timothy Kiely (who was found wounded in a hay-loft at Major Canty's house near Fort Erie, on June 3rd, and who had been engaged in the battle at Lime Ridge), was found guilty and sentenced to death. On the same day John Smith proved his innocence and was discharged.

On Jan. 12th, Patrick O'Neil and Patrick McGrath were found guilty of high treason, and on the day following Thomas H. Maxwell was convicted for the same crime. Those three men were British subjects, and each received the death sentence.

On Jan. 14th James Burke and Patrick Norton were found guilty and sentence deferred. On Jan. 15th John O'Connor, Daniel Quinn and John Rogan were found guilty, while Patrick Keating, James Spaulding and Wm. Baxter escaped conviction, owing to lack of sufficient evidence.

On Jan. 18th, Peter Paul Ledwith was found guilty and James Macdonough discharged.

On Jan. 21st, Thomas Cooney (who was present at Lime Ridge) was found guilty, and George J. Matthews (who was arrested at Thorold in September, 1866, by some troopers of the Governor-General's Body Guard, for having stated that he had been sent out from Buffalo as a scout by the Fenians, who contemplated another raid) was acquitted for want of evidence.

On Jan. 22nd Michael Purtell was found guilty of high treason, and remanded for sentence. Owen Kennedy, an American who was arrested at Fort Erie, was found guilty with a recommendation to mercy.

On Jan. 24th John Gallagher, of Cincinnati, was found guilty and remanded for sentence, while Thomas King, an American, was discharged.

On Jan. 25th Barney Dunn was convicted, while Wm. Orr, John Hughes, Frederick Fry and James Diamond were acquitted for lack of sufficient evidence. On Jan. 29th John Grace and John Cooney were also acquitted.

This disposed of all the Fenian cases on the calendar.

The Court re-opened on Jan. 30th, His Lordship Mr. Justice Morrison presiding, for the purpose of finally disposing of the cases of eleven of the prisoners who had been convicted but not yet sentenced. After the usual Court preliminaries had been concluded, and the prisoners placed in the dock, Hon. Mr. Cameron moved that the sentence of the Court be passed upon the following prisoners:—Patrick Norton, Thos. H. Maxwell, Patrick O'Neil, James Burke, Daniel Quinn, Peter Ledwith, John O'Connor, John Rogers, Owen Kennedy, Barney Dunn and John Gallagher.

His Lordship then sentenced all of the above named to be hanged on the 5th of March..

Appeals were made to higher Courts in several of the cases, but all were disallowed, and it seemed for a time as if a wholesale execution of the prisoners on the gibbet would be the result. But the better feelings of the Canadian people prevailed, and by appeals for clemency, in the cause of humanity, our country was relieved from the gruesome spectacle of witnessing over a score of these unfortunate dupes dangling from the gallows in expiation of their crimes. That they deserved such a fate is undoubted. They entered our peaceful country with murder in their hearts, and carried out a portion of their programme of butchery, but their leaders escaped, and it would have been poor satisfaction to exact the extreme penalty on those deluded followers who happened to fall into our hands. Therefore all of their lives were spared.

The sentences imposed were commuted to imprisonment in the Provincial Penitentiary at Kingston for various terms, according to the degree of guilt of the accused, and a few years afterward the last of them was released from the grasp of Canadian justice.

CHAPTER XVI.

The Canadian Volunteers Released from Duty at the Front and Returned to Their Homes—They Earned the Gratitude of Their Country and Received it.

After about three weeks of active service, the Canadian volunteers who were on duty at the front were relieved and sent home. Although matters were still in an unsettled state among the Fenians in the United States, and threats were constantly being made of more trouble, yet the occasion was not considered of sufficient serious importance to require the services of the force posted on the frontier for a longer period. The Government was well aware that when occasion demanded the same troops would again take up arms as promptly and cheerfully as on previous occasions, and relied on their patriotic service being immediately available whenever required. In relieving the troops from further duty, the Commander-in-Chief promulgated the following order:—

OTTAWA, June 23rd, 1866.

In relieving the volunteers, for the present, from active duty, the Commander-in-Chief desires to make known to the officers and non-commissioned officers and men of the force, the pride and satisfaction with which he has witnessed the patriotism and energy displayed by them in their instantaneous response to the call to arms. The Commander-in-Chief wishes to express his admiration of the promptitude with which, on the only occasion when an opportunity was afforded them of meeting the enemy, the volunteers went under fire, and his deep sympathy with the friends and relations of those who there met a soldier's death. The discipline and good conduct of the force while on service has secured the approbation of their military commanders, and has been most favorably reported on to the Commander-in-Chief. The Commander-in-Chief wishes to impress on the minds of the volunteers that, though the late attack on the Province has proved a failure, the organization by means of which it was attempted still exists, and that its leaders do not hesitate to declare publicly that they meditate a renewal of the invasion. Under these circumstances, the Commander-in-Chief trusts that the volunteer force generally will continue at all convenient times to perfect themselves in drill and discipline, so that they may be able successfully to repel any future aggression that may be attempted.

MAJOR-GENERAL NAPIER'S ORDER.

Major-Gen. Napier, who commanded the troops in Canada West, returned thanks, in appreciation of their services, by issuing the following:—

BRIGADE OFFICE, TORONTO, June 18th, 1866.

Major-General Napier, C.B., Commanding the First Military District, Canada West, cannot allow the volunteers under his command to return home without tendering them his best thanks for the patriotic way they responded to the Governor-General's call for further services, as well as for their general good conduct whilst in the field. Although only a few were fortunate enough to be engaged with the enemy, the whole force were equally ready and anxious to meet him. The Major-General feels sure that should their services be again required, they will show the same fine spirit, and turn out to a man in the defence of their country. The Major-General, in bidding them farewell for the present, trusts that they will keep up their present efficient state, which can only be done by constantly attending to their drill whenever they have an opportunity of doing so.

By order.

(Signed) H. NANGLE,
Captain and Brigade Major.

MAJOR-GENERAL LINDSAY'S ORDER.

Major-Gen. Lindsay also commended the volunteers for their prompt response to the call of duty, and their valued and faithful service in the field, in the language contained in the following order:—

BRIGADE OFFICE, MONTREAL, 23rd June, 1866.

DISTRICT ORDER.

The emergency which has caused the Volunteer Militia Force of Canada to spring to arms, having passed by, the Major-General commanding the District acknowledges the important services they have rendered.

The patriotic spirit, exhibited both by employers and the employed, placed at the service of the Crown, in a few hours, a force of upwards of 22,000 men in the two Canadas, which, if the occasion had been of more serious character, could have been augmented to such numbers as the Government might have required.

The various corps sent out to the front have shown a zeal and aptitude in the performance of their duties as soldiers, which is calculated to inspire the greatest confidence; while some of the battalions have had severe and difficult marches to perform, all have undergone considerable hardships in most unfavourable weather.

While the good faith and firmness of the General Commanding the U. S. troops on the frontier had the effect of preventing larger assemblies of armed men, and while in the end the long-threatened attempt at invasion proved a miserable failure, the Major-General feels confident that the volunteer force have only one regret, that they have not had the opportunity of driving from the soil of Canada those misguided men, who, under the flimsy veil of so-called patriotic feeling, would have carried war into a country with which they have no pretence of quarrel.

The Major-General feels convinced that, shoulder to shoulder with the regular troops of Her Majesty, the volunteer militia force of this Province would, if they had been brought in contact with an enemy, have proved themselves worthy of the approbation of their fellow-countrymen, and that they would, as their predecessors had done in times long past, have successfully defended their country, and kept it against all aggressors.

While anxious for peace, Canada is showing herself prepared for war; and the Major-General is gratified in bearing his testimony to the noble and independent spirit, which proves that Canada has reason to be proud of her citizen soldiers.

By order,

R. C. HEALEY,
Major of Brigade.

SPECIAL THANKS TO THE QUEEN'S OWN.

The splendid services of the Queen's Own Rifles in the campaign were officially recognized by the General Commanding in the promulgation of the following order:—

ASSIST. ADJ.-GENERAL'S OFFICE, TORONTO, June 8, 1860.

Sir,—I am directed by Major-General Napier, C.B., commanding 1st Military Division, C.W., to acknowledge the receipt of a copy of your despatch dated Stratford, June 6th, 1866, addressed to Lieut.-Col. Lowry, 47th Regiment, detailing the operations of the Volunteer force on the morning of the 2nd, in which the Queen's Own were engaged with the enemy.

It is now my gratifying duty to convey to you not only the approbation but the very great pleasure the Major-General experienced in hearing from you of the good conduct of the officers, non-commissioned officers and men of the regiment under your command on that occasion.

That they fully confirmed and justified the good opinion that the Major-General always entertained of them, by their conduct in meeting for the first time the enemies of their Queen and country.

The Major-General feels quite sure that the regiment will always cherish and sustain the character now so nobly won by the Queen's Own.

I have also to express to you, by the Major-General's desire, his entire approbation of the very able and gallant manner in which you commanded the Queen's Own under very trying circumstances, and it will give him much pleasure in bringing before His Excellency the Commander-in-Chief, the gallant service rendered by the Queen's Own on the occasion, which you will be good enough to convey to the officers, non-commissioned officers and men of the regiment under your command.

I have the honor to be, Sir,

Your most obedient servant,

W. S. DURIE,
Lieut.-Col., A.A.G.M.

Major Charles T. Gilmor, Queen's Own Rifles.

CANADIAN PATRIOTISM.

Lord Monck's communication to the Imperial Secretary of State may also be quoted as showing his views concerning the patriotic conduct of Canadians who were at the time residing in the United States:—

OTTAWA, June 14, 1866.

Sir,—I have had the satisfaction in other communications to report to you the excellent spirit evinced by the resident population of Canada in connection with the late Fenian attack on the Province. There has been in addition an exhibition of patriotism and devotion on the part of Canadians who happened to be domiciled at the time of the disturbance outside of the Province, which deserves, I think, special mention and praise. Immediately after the news of the inroad on the Province reached Chicago, sixty young Canadians who were resident there engaged in various employments gave up their situations and repaired by railroad to Canada to give their aid in defending the land of their birth. These young men have been formed into a Volunteer Company and are now doing duty at Toronto.

I had also a communication from Her Majesty's Consul at New York to the effect that a large number of Canadians, resident there, were prepared to abandon their occupations and come to assist in the repulse of the invaders of Canada if I considered their services necessary. I informed Mr. Archibald by telegraph that I did not require their aid, but begged him to express to them my gratitude for the exhibition of their loyalty. Such conduct speaks for itself, and I would not weaken the effect of the bare relation of the facts by any attempts at eulogy on my part. I have, etc.

(Signed)   MONCK.

The Right Hon. Edward Cardwell, Secretary of State.

FROM THE IMPERIAL GOVERNMENT.

The following General Order, contained in a letter communicated through the regular official channel to His Excellency the Governor-General and Commander-in-Chief (Right Hon. Viscount Monck), was duly promulgated through the Department of Militia of Canada:—

HORSE GUARDS, July 21st, 1866.

The Under-Secretary of State for War:—

Sir,—With reference to the several reports which have been received from the General Officer Commanding in Canada relative to the Fenian movement in that Province, and to the measures taken by the colonists for repelling any Fenian attack, I am directed by the Field Marshal Commanding-in-Chief to request that you will acquaint the Secretary of State for War that His Royal Highness, having observed the alacrity, loyalty and zeal shown by the volunteers and militia forces of Canada in having come forward for the defence of the colony on the late trying occasion, in support of the troops, is very desirous of expressing to the force his full appreciation of their gallant and energetic behavior, and the very great gratification and satisfaction he has thereby experienced. And His Royal Highness trusts, therefore, that Lieut.-General Peel will see no objection to the necessary communication being made by him to the Colonial

Office,. with the view to His Royal Highness' sentiments, as above expressed, being made known through the proper channel to the volunteers and militia of Canada, lately employed against the Fenians.

I am, etc.,

W. F. FOSTER.

LORD MONCK'S ACKNOWLEDGMENT OF AMERICAN INTERVENTION.

In acknowledgment of the service rendered by the United States Government in checking the invasion, Lord Monck, the Governor-General of Canada, sent the following despatch to Sir Frederick Bruce, the British Minister at Washington, for presentation to Secretary of State Seward:—

OTTAWA, June 11th, 1866.

SIR,—I have learned from the public press the terms of the Proclamation which the President of the United States of America has promulgated against the hostile designs of the Fenians on the Province, the Government of which I have the honor to administer. I have also, by the same means, been made acquainted with the orders issued by the Attorney-General of the United States and other officers of the Administration of that country for the apprehension of the persons of Fenian conspirators and the stoppage and seizure of arms and other supplies intended to be used by them against Canada. As these proceedings of the Government of the United States have materially tended to defeat the hostile purposes of the Fenians against this Province, I shall feel much obliged if you will convey to the Secretary of State for the United States my acknowledgments of the course which has been adopted by that Government in reference to this matter.

I have, etc.,

(Signed) MONCK.

LORD MONCK'S REPORT TO THE IMPERIAL GOVERNMENT.

In presenting his report to the Right Hon. E. Cardwell, Secretary of State of the British Government, Lord Monck sent the following dispatch, which was accompanied by the reports of the Lieutenant-General and other officers who were in command of troops during the campaign:—

OTTAWA, June 14th, 1866.

SIR,—I have the honor to transmit for your information, the reports to the Lieutenant-General commanding Her Majesty's forces of the several officers, relating to the proceedings connected with the late Fenian invasion at Fort Erie, Canada West. I think these documents substantially corroborate the account which I gave you from telegraphic and other information in my despatches of the 1st, 4th and 8th instant.

From all the information I have received, I am now satisfied that a very large and comprehensive plan of attack had been arranged by the party which is popularly known as the Sweeny-Roberts section of the Fenian Brotherhood.

The plan of invasion, in addition to the attempt on the Niagara frontier—the only one which actually occurred—appears to have embraced attacks on the line of the Richelieu and Lake Champlain, and also on the frontier in the neighborhood of Prescott and Cornwall, where I have reason to think the principal demonstration was intended.

For the latter object, large bodies of men, sent by railroad from almost all parts of the United States, were assembled at a place called Malone, in the State of New York, and at Potsdam, also in the State of New York, and with a view to the former, St. Albans and its neighborhood in the State of Vermont was selected as the place of asemblage.

Large supplies of arms, accoutrements and ammunition were also attempted to be forwarded by railroad to these points, but owing to the active intervention of the authorities of the United States—as soon as it became apparent that a breach of international law had been committed by these persons—a very large portion of these supplies never reached their destination.

It is not easy to arrive at a trustworthy estimate of the number of men who actually arrived at their different points of rendezvous. It has been reported at times that there were at Potsdam, Malone, and the intervening country, as many as ten thousand men, and similar rumors have been from time to time circulated of the force at St. Albans and its neighborhood. From the best opinion I can form, however, I shall be inclined to think that the number of Fenians in the vicinity of St. Albans never exceeded two thousand men, and that three thousand would be a fair allowance for those assembled at Potsdam, Malone, and the surrounding counties. The men have been represented to me as having, many of them, served in the late Civil War in the United States—to have had a considerable amount of small arms of a good and efficient description. I have not heard of their possessing any artillery, and I am informed that they were deficient in the supplies of ammunition and totally destitute of all the other equipments of an organized force, They appear to have relied very much on assistance from the inhabitants of the Province, as the force which invaded Fort Erie brought with them—as I am told—a large quantity of spare arms to put in the hands of their sympathizers whom they expected to join them. I have in my former despatches noticed the measures which were adopted by the Provincial Government in order to place at the disposal of the Lieutenant-General commanding Her Majesty's forces, the Provincial resources available for defence, both by land and water. The reports of the officers of the army and volunteers, which I transmit, will acquaint you with the manner in which these means were used by the officers in command. I am happy to be able to bear my tribute to the energy and good faith exhibited by the American Government and its officials in checking all infractions of international obligations on the part of any portion of its citizens from the moment that it became evident that an invasion of the Province by the Fenians had actually taken place. The determination of the Government of the United States to stop the transportation of men and supplies to the places of assembly, rendered even the temporary success on the part of the Fenians impossible; while the large forces which the Lieutenant-General commanding was able to concentrate at each of the points threatened, had the effect of deterring from an attack the portion of the conspirators who had already arrived at their places of rendezvous. No invasion in force occurred except at Fort Erie.

A slight incursion took place at a place called St. Armand, about thirteen miles from St. John's, on the borders of the County of Missisquoi, which ended in the capture of about sixteen prisoners, without any loss on our side.

The latest accounts I have received announced that the men who had congregated at the different points of assembly were being transmitted to their homes at the expense of the Government of the United States, most of the leaders having been arrested and held to bail to answer for their conduct.

Although I deplore the loss which the Volunteer Force suffered when engaged on the 2nd of June at Lime Ridge, amounting to six killed and thirty-one wounded, I think it is a matter for congratulation that a movement which might have been so formidable has collapsed with so small an amount of loss, either of life or property. I think it is also a source of satisfaction that such strong proofs have been afforded of the spirit which animates the Canadian people, of their loyalty to the throne, of their appreciation of the free institutions under which they live, and of their readiness at all times to prove their sense of the value of these institutions by incurring expense and personal risk in the defence of them. The period of the year at which the people have been called on to make these sacrifices of timely serving in the volunteer ranks has been the most inconvenient that could have been selected, yet I have never heard a murmur from any quarter at the necessity of suspending industrial occupation involving the risk of a whole year's production, while I have received information of a good deal of discontent on the part of those who were anxious to give their services, but whose presence in the ranks was not considered necessary.

I have to express my very high sense of the services performed by Lieutenant-General Sir J. Michel and the officers under his command in the able disposition of troops, both regulars and volunteers. The officers of the Royal Navy stationed at Quebec and Montreal deserve the highest credit for the rapidity with which they extemporized gunboats for the defence of the St. Lawrence and the Lakes. I have already spoken of the admirable spirit displayed by the Volunteer Force, both officers and men. I have every reason to believe that their conduct as regards discipline and order has entitled them to as much commendation as does their spirit of patriotism and self-reliance.

I desire particularly to bring before your notice the ability and energy exhibited by Colonel Macdougall, A.G.M., with a view to having his services specially mentioned to His Royal Highness, the Commander-in-Chief. This officer has not yet been one year in Canada, yet so admirable is the system of organization which he has established that he is able within a few hours to assemble on any given point over a line of more than 1,000 miles, masses of volunteers who at the time the order was given were scattered over the country pursuing their ordinary avocations. While I attribute full credit to the excellent spirit of the people for its share in this effect, I think the administrative ability which has given practical operation to this good feeling of the population ought to have its meed of praise and in the interests of the public service on some possible future emergency ought not to be left without official record.

There are prisoners in our hands to the number of about one hundred and fifty. (I have not yet received official returns of them), whose trial will be proceeded with at an early day.

I confidently expect within a few days to be able to dismiss to their homes the great majority of the Volunteers, and my firm conviction is, that this disturbance will produce beneficial effects by discrediting Fenian enterprises, exhibiting the futility of any attempt at invasion of the Province, and showing the absence of all disaffection amongst any portion of the people of Canada.

I have, etc.,

(Signed)   MONCK.

The Right Honorable E. Cardwell.

WELLAND COUNTY HONORS THE BRAVE.

The services of the officers and men of the Welland Canal Field Battery and the Dunnville Naval Brigade—for their gallantry in the fight at Fort Erie—were recognized by the Municipal Council of the County of Welland by the public presentation to each of them of a handsome silver medal, commemorative of the occasion. In addition, Capt. King and Capt. McCallum were each presented with handsome swords of honor by the County Council, as special marks of appreciation of their bravery by the people of the county. To each of the wounded a grant of 100 acres of the lands owned by the county in the Cranberry Marsh was given. In addition to the above honors the Corporation of the Village of Fort Erie presented Capt. King with a valuable sword as a testimonial of their recognition of his services at that place on the 2nd of June.

CHAPTER XVII.

A RETROSPECT OF EVENTS—A COMBINATION OF UNFORTUNATE
CIRCUMSTANCES INVOLVE LEADING OFFICERS.

That the campaign on the Niagara frontier might have been
conducted on lines which would have proved much more satisfactory for the success of the Canadian forces, is admitted. It
seemed to be a combination of errors and omissions from the
beginning, which furnished food for unfavorable criticism and
condemnation by journalistic and arm-chair critics which created
impressions on the public mind that exist even at the present
day. Of course each critic would have done different—this plan
or that plan "should have been" adopted, regardless of all military rules. The trite saying that "nothing succeeds like success" should be supplemented by adding, "and nothing more
reprehensible than failure." In military operations success or
defeat are in the scales, and the least little occurrence is liable
to outbalance the other. No matter how carefully a commanding
officer may lay his plans, or how minutely he may explain them
to his staff and subordinates, if one does not do his part in
promptly carrying out instructions at the proper moment, the
whole machinery is thrown out of gear, and failure is the inevit-
able result.

In the first place, while Gen. Napier's plan of campaign was
excellent in itself, there were several very important things
omitted that were essential to its success. That of the greatest
importance was the lack of proper provision being made for
obtaining information of the exact position and movements of
the enemy, such as a corps of competent scouts could have given.
That omission is fatal to the success of any military movement.
Again, those who were in command of columns on the 2nd of
June do not seem to have had an intelligent idea of the country
they were about to move over, and had to rely on whatever chance
information they could obtain, much of which, in the excited
state of the minds of the people, was unreliable. To condemn
any particular officer for an unlooked-for disaster is a serious

matter, unless such defeat is clearly the result of his own negligence, or some movement of which he had personal control. Therefore critics should always be careful to put the saddle of blame on the right horse.

As Col. Peacocke had been assigned to the immediate command of the troops operating on the Niagara frontier by Gen. Napier, it will be noted (as related in a former chapter) that he arrived at Chippawa on the evening of June 1st, with a considerable number of regular troops and a complete battery of field guns, manned by experienced gunners of the Royal Artillery. His reinforcements from Toronto and St. Catharines were closely following, and quickly available. That night he sent Capt. Akers across the country with definite orders to Lieut.-Col. Booker to move eastward to Ridgeway by rail at 5 o'clock the next morning, and effect a junction with his (Col. Peacocke's) column at Stevensville at 10 o'clock. These instructions stated that Col. Peacocke would leave Chippawa at 6 a.m., and in accordance with this programme Lieut.-Col. Booker proceeded to carry out his orders. On the other hand, it was nearly 8 o'clock before Col. Peacocke left Chippawa, which threw the whole programme out of joint by nearly two hours. Various excuses were made for the delay, but some of them were not very tenable. The regulars had had a good night's rest, and the volunteers (who were all on the ground at Chippawa before 4.30 a.m.) were eager and willing to proceed. Why he did not leave Chippawa by at least 6 o'clock (in the cool hours of the morning) is not sufficiently clear. A pilot engine was sent up the line of the Erie & Niagara Railway early in the morning, upon which were Lieut.-Col. John Hillyard Cameron and a detail of riflemen from the St. Catharines Battery of Artillery. They made a reconnaisance nearly as far as Black Creek, and returned with the report that they had not observed any signs of the enemy between Chippawa and that point. This was before Col. Peacocke started on his march. Why could it not have been possible for him to have moved a portion of his advance up by train as far as Black Creek, was a question that was prevalent at the time. But Col. Peacocke was not apparently taking any chances. He appears to have been overly cautious, and was disposed to adopt the old-time method of plodding along the beaten trail.

Here again he made a mistake in taking "the longest way around" to reach Stevensville, while the intense heat and dust began to tell on his troops, which compelled him to halt at New Germany about 11 o'clock. Before reaching there he was informed of the disaster at Ridgeway by parties who had arrived from the battle-field. Why, then, did he not push on in search of the enemy, instead of remaining at New Germany until 5.30 p.m.? is another question. Excuses are easily framed and plausibly given in reports, but the country generally, and his soldiers particularly, have always thought that he might have managed to have got into a conflict with the enemy in some way. Col. Peacocke was a very fine gentleman, and had the reputation of being a skilfull military officer, but his extreme caution in this campaign spoiled all chances of any success in winning the renown that might have been his portion had he acted with snap and celerity of movement in battering the Fenian army before they left Canada. He had the opportunity, the men and the guns, but he let his golden chances slip by while he idly passed away the time "resting" at Chippawa and New Germany.

Capt. Akers was another officer whose action in consenting with the ideas of Lieut.-Col. Dennis to change the plans of their commanding officer is inexplicable. Why these two officers should have dared to assume such responsibility is beyond all comprehension. A soldier's first duty is obedience to orders, and as these had been definitely issued by Col. Peacocke, it was manifestly not their business to change them, but to see that they were rigidly carried out. For that purpose Capt. Akers had been specially dispatched from Chippawa to Port Colborne; but in less than half an hour after his arrival he was busily engaged with Lieut.-Col. Dennis and Lieut.-Col. Booker in concocting a new plan of campaign. After deciding on what they intended to do, they condescendingly notified Col. Peacocke of the change in his own plans, and without waiting for a reply they started off for Fort Erie on the steamer "W. T. Robb" to put them in execution. Such assumption was certainly astounding, and no doubt Col. Peacocke had a choleric fit when he was apprised of it. This was another mistake, which contributed largely to the defeat of Col. Peacocke's purposes, and left a cloud on the military prestige of both Lieut.-Col. Dennis and Capt. Akers.

As Lieut.-Col. Booker had also been persuaded to join in the new plan, he was making his arrangements to do so when he received an imperative order by telegraph from Col. Peacocke to adhere to his original instructions.

As Lieut.-Col. Dennis and Capt. Akers sailed away in high hope from Port Colborne, they probably built the fairy air castles which were doomed to totter and fall before night. It did not seem to occur to them that Col. Peacocke's sanction to, and co-operation in, their change of plan would be necessary to ensure success. Therefore their disappointment must have been great when they found that Lieut.-Col. Booker failed to arrive at Fort Erie at 7 o'clock, as provided in their new arrangement. At this hour Lieut.-Col. Booker was leaving Ridgeway (in pursuance of his latest orders) on his march for Stevensville, and soon after had the misfortune to strike the enemy in force. And thereby hangs another tale of a grave mistake, which brought considerable censure to that officer. The story of the battle is told elsewhere, and need not be repeated.

In the light of official reports and the testimony of officers and men who were engaged in the battle of Lime Ridge, the disaster which occurred to Lieut.-Col. Booker's column (almost in the moment of victory) can be attributed wholly to a fatal order being given at the most critical time in the progress of the fight. Lieut.-Col. Booker had up to that eventful moment displayed singular sagacity and wisdom in the handling of his troops, and had correctly followed the usual military rules which would be applicable to the occasion. But somebody appears to have originated the report that the enemy were about to make a cavalry charge, and at this crisis, when the troops were ordered to "Form square," the demon of disaster suddenly appeared. It was the proper order to have given had there really been a cavalry force advancing, but as the alarm originated in the imagination of others, for which there was no valid reason, the movement proved a mistake which turned the tide of battle and caused the dire disaster for which Lieut.-Col. Booker was, and is to this day, most unjustly blamed. A little reflection on the part of his critics might have tended to tone down their asperity and given him some credit for what he did do, both before and after the unfortunate order was given. But some person had to take the blame, and Lieut.-Col. Booker was made the victim of circumstances.   Here was a volunteer Colonel (who had never previously commanded a brigade) suddenly placed in command of the whole column because he happened to be the senior officer present, and ordered to advance across the path of the enemy to make a junction with Col. Peacocke's forces at Stevensville.   His orders were to leave Port Colborne at a certain hour, which he did—exactly on time.   He was handicapped in many ways, yet he did his duty and carried out the orders he received to the letter.   He had neither cavalry, artillery or scouts with his column, so that his position was not a very enviable one.   Had Capt. Akers remained with Col. Booker instead of going off on an excursion with Lieut.-Col. Dennis on the tug "Robb," his presence might have made some difference in the fortunes of the battle at Lime Ridge.   Lieut.-Col. Booker had no staff officer to assist him, and in this position Capt. Akers might have been of some service, and won more glory than he did in the campaign. As to Lieut.-Col. Booker's conduct on the field at Lime Ridge (which was so unfavorably commented upon by the public press and carping critics who accepted the multitude of erroneous rumors that were prevalent during that period of excitement), it may be stated that the whole affair was fully investigated by a Military Court of Inquiry, composed of three competent officers of high and honorable standing, who took the sworn testimony of a large number of officers and men who were engaged in the battle.   As the whole evidence, and a full report of the proceedings of the Court, are published as an appendix to this book, it will prove very interesting to the reader, and serve to give an intelligent idea of the events narrated, from which you can draw your own conclusions as to whether Lieut.-Col. Booker was unjustly censured or not.

Another officer who was roundly condemned by the officers and men under his command, and by the public generally, for his singular conduct during the engagement at Fort Erie, was Lieut.-Col. J. S. Dennis, who was in command of the expedition on the steamer "W. T. Robb."   Grave charges were filed against this officer, which resulted in a Court of Inquiry being appointed to investigate the case.   As the charges made and the finding of the Court will be found in the latter portion of the appendix of this book, the writer will not discuss them here. Suffice it to say that the officers and men of the force which he landed on the dock at Fort Erie on the 2nd of June, and placed in great jeopardy and peril, were not at all satisfied with the opinion of the Court, which they considered in the nature of a "white-wash" for Lieut.-Col. Dennis (and a thin coat at that), as the President of the Court dissented from the finding of his two colleagues on two charges, but was over-ruled by them.

CHAPTER XVIII.

DANGERS WHICH EXISTED PREVIOUS TO CONFEDERATION OF THE
PROVINCES—PROPOSALS OF ANNEXATION TO THE UNITED
STATES—LESSONS LEARNED BY THE FENIAN RAID.

Forty-four years have elapsed since the perilous events
recorded in the preceding pages occurred. A new generation
has come and grown into middle life, while the second generation is now budding forth into manhood and womanhood. How
many of these are conversant with the history of their own country? Beyond a very vague knowledge of what has been taught
to them in a superficial manner in our schools and colleges, and
the fragmentary reminiscences that may have been recounted to
them by their sires and grandsires who passed through these
troublous times, it is doubtful whether even one-tenth of our
present population have any idea of just how near Canada came
to being absorbed by the United States in that critical period.

At that time Canada was in a peculiar position, which may
be described as "a house divided within itself," as there was
no cohesion among the scattered Provinces, each regulating its
own affairs, with the exception of Canada East and Canada
West (now Quebec and Ontario) who were governed by the
same Parliament. The situation was certainly a dark and
serious one. We had subtle traitors at home and scheming
enemies abroad who labored assiduously to bring about annexation, but the stern spirit of loyalty to the British Crown which
pervaded the hearts of the people as a whole, and the wise
statesmanship of that noble group of patriots whose names will
go ringing down through the corridors of time in the existence
of our nation as "The Fathers of Confederation," saved the
situation, and made Canada what it is to-day, a heritage of which
our sons and daughters may well feel proud.

It was during the year 1866 that the apostles of Confederation were busy educating the people of the different Provinces
in the creed of that very desirable proposition. While they met
serious opposition in some portions of what is now our grand

Dominion, yet in others the proposal was received favorably, while one or two of the Provinces expressed an antipathy to the movement. But just at this time two important events occurred which had a material bearing on the question, and had an effect in bringing about the Union. The first was the sudden abrogation by the United States of the Reciprocity Treaty which for some years had existed between the Canadian Provinces and that country, and the second the Fenian Raid. Each of these events sent a thrill through the Canadian people which fired their hearts and settled the project of Confederation. The necessity of united action in defence, and co-operation in other matters for the benefit of the whole, was heartily admitted, and forthwith the Provinces joined hands and hearts in bringing about its early consummation. The full meaning of the motto, "United we Stand—Divided we Fall," was realized by the majority, and the necessary legislation was carried through the several Provincial Parliaments that year, which received Imperial sanction, and resulted in the birth of the Dominion of Canada on July 1st, 1867.

While the campaign for Confederation was in progress, and its stalwart advocates were using their best endeavors throughout the country to bring the project to fruition, considerable opposition was manifested by a certain section who favored annexation to the United States. These men were backed up by American influences, and went so far as to secure the assistance of several prominent United States Congressmen to draft a proposal whereby the Provinces of Canada might become annexed and made certain States of the Union. The subject was discussed seriously by a large section of the American press, while statesmen and others who were eager to acquire our territory lost no opportunity to present their views in that respect.

While the annexation pot was boiling, and the Fenians were still threatening another raid, the question was brought before the American people in a tangible form. On the 2nd of July, 1866, the following bill was reported to the United States Congress by Representative Banks, and recommitted to the Committee on Foreign Affairs. As viewed in the light of the present day, its provisions contain very interesting reading:—

A Bill for the admission of the States of Nova Scotia, New Brunswick, Canada East and Canada West, and for the organization of the Territories of Selkirk, Saskatchewan and Columbia.

SEC. 1. *Be it enacted by the Senate and House of Representatives of the United States of America in Congress assembled,* That the President of the United States is hereby authorized and directed, whenever notice shall be deposited in the Department of State, that the Governments of Great Britain and the Provinces of New Brunswick, Nova Scotia, Prince Edward Island, Newfoundland, Canada, British Columbia, and Vancouver's Island, have accepted the proposition hereinafter made by the United States, to publish by proclamation that, from the date thereof, the States of Nova Scotia, New Brunswick, Canada East and Canada West, and the Territories of Selkirk, Saskatchewan, and Columbia, with limits and rights as by this Act defined, are constituted and admitted as States and Territories of the United States of America.

SEC. 2. *Be it further enacted, etc.,* That the following articles are hereby proposed, and from the date of the proclamation of the President of the United States shall take effect, as irrevocable conditions of the admission of the States of Nova Scotia, New Brunswick, Canada East and Canada West, and the future States of Selkirk. Saskatchewan and Columbia, to wit:

Article I. All public lands not sold or granted; canals, public harbours, lighthouses and piers; river and lake improvements; railways, mortgages and other debts due by railway companies to the Provinces; custom houses and post offices shall vest in the United States; but all other public works and property shall belong to the State Governments respectively, hereby constituted, together with all sums due from purchasers or lessees of lands, mines, or minerals at the time of the union.

Article II. In consideration of public lands, works, and property vested as aforesaid in the United States, the United States will assume and discharge the funded debt and contingent liabilities of the late Provinces at rates of interest not exceeding five per centum, to the amount of $85,-700,000, apportioned as follows: To Canada West, $36,500,000; to Canada East, $29,000,000; to Nova Scotia, $8,000,000; to New Brunswick, $7,000,000; to Newfoundland, $3,200,000; and to Prince Edward Island, $2,000,000; and in further consideration of the transfer by said Provinces to the United States of the power to levy import and export duties, the United States will make an annual grant of $1,646,000 in aid of local expenditures, to be apportioned as follows: To Canada West, $700,000; to Canada East, $550,000; to Nova Scotia, $165,000; to Newfoundland, $65,000; to Prince Edward Island, $40,000.

Article III. For all purposes of State organization and representation in the Congress of the United States, Newfoundland shall be a part of Canada East, and Prince Edward Island shall be a part of Nova Scotia, except that each shall always be a separate representative district, and entitled to elect at least one member of the House of Representatives, and except also that the municipal authorities of Newfoundland and Prince Edward Island shall receive the indemnities agreed to be paid by the United States in Article II.

Article IV. Territorial divisions are established as follows: (1) New Brunswick, with its present limits; (2) Nova Scotia, with the addition of Prince Edward Island; (3) Canada East, with the addition of Newfoundland and all territory east of longitude 80 deg. and south of Hudson Straits; (4) Canada West, with the addition of territory south of Hudson's Bay, and between longitude 80 and 90 deg.; (5) Selkirk Territory, bounded east by longitude 90 deg., south by the late boundary of the United States, west by longitude 105 deg., and north by the Arctic Circle; (6) Saskatchewan Territory, bounded east by longitude 105 deg., south by latitude 49 deg., west by the Rocky Mountains, and north by latitude 70 deg.; (7) Columbia Territory, including Vancouver's Island and Queen Charlotte's Island, and bounded east and north by the Rocky Mountains, south by latitude 40 deg., and west by the Pacific Ocean and Russian America. But Congress reserves the right of changing the limits and subdividing the areas of the western territories at discretion.

Article V. Until the next decennial revision, representation in the House of Representatives shall be as follows: Canada West, 12 members; Canada East, including Newfoundland, 11 members; New Brunswick, 2 members; Nova Scotia, including Prince Edward Island, 4 memberes.

Article VI. The Congress of the United States shall enact, in favour of the proposed Territories of Selkirk, Saskatchewan and Columbia, all the provisions of the Act organizing the Territory of Montana, so far as they can be made applicable.

Article VII. The United States, by the construction of new canals, of the enlargement of existing canals, and by the improvement of shoals, will so aid the navigation of the St. Lawrence River and the Great Lakes that vessels of fifteen hundred tons burden shall pass from the Gulf of St. Lawrence to Lakes Superior and Michigan; *Provided* that the expenditure under this Article shall not exceed $50,000,000.

Article VIII. The United States will appropriate and pay to "The European and North American Railway Company of Maine" the sum of $2,000,000 upon the construction of a continuous line of railroad from Bangor, in Maine, to St. John, in New Brunswick; *Provided* said "The European and North American Railway Company of Maine" shall release the Government of the United States from all claims held by its assignees of the States of Maine and Massachusetts.

Article IX. To aid the construction of a railway from Truro, in Nova Scotia, to Riviere du Loup, in Canada East, and a railway from the city of Ottawa, by way of Sault Ste. Marie, Bayfield and Superior, in Wisconsin, Pembina and Fort Garry, on the Red River of the North, and the Valley of North Saskatchewan River, to some point on the Pacific Ocean north of latitude 49 degrees, the United States will grant lands along the lines of said roads to the amount of twenty sections, or 12,800 acres, per mile, to be selected and sold in the manner prescribed in the Act, to aid the construction of the Northern Pacific Railroad, approved July 2, 1862, and Acts amendatory thereof; and, in addition to said grants of land, the United States will further guarantee dividends of five per cent. upon the stock of the company or companies which may be authorized by Congress to undertake the construction of said railways; *Provided* that such guarantee of stock shall not exceed the sum of $30,000 per mile, and Congress shall regulate the securities for advances on account thereof.

Article X. The public lands in the late Provinces, as far as practicable, shall be surveyed according to the rectangular system of the General Land Office of the United States; and in the territories west of longitude 90 degrees, or western boundary of Canada West, Sections sixteen and thirty-six shall be granted for the encouragement of schools, and after the organization of the territories into the States, 5 per centum of the net proceeds of sales of public lands shall be paid into their treasurers as a fund for the improvement of roads and rivers.

Article XI. The United States will pay $10,000,000 to the Hudson Bay Company in full discharge of all claims to territory or jurisdiction in North America, whether founded on the charter of the company or any treaty, law or usage.

Article XII. It shall be devolved upon the Legislatures of New Brunswick, Nova Scotia, Canada East and Canada West, to conjoin the tenure of office and the local institutions of said States to the Constitution and laws of the United States, subject to revision by Congress.

SEC. 3. *Be it further enacted, etc.,* If Prince Edward Island or Newfoundland, or either of those Provinces, shall decline union with the United States, and the remaining Provinces, with the consent of Great Britain, shall accept the proposition of the United States, the foregoing stipulations in favor of Prince Edward Island and Newfoundland, or either of them, will be omitted; but in all other respects the United States will give full effect to the plan of union. If Prince Edward Island, Newfoundland, Nova Scotia, and New Brunswick shall decline the proposition, but Canada, British Columbia and Vancouver Island shall, with the consent of Great Britain, accept the same, the construction of a railway from Truro to Riviere du Loup, with all stipulations relating to the Maritime Provinces, will form no part of the proposed plan of union, but the same will be consummated in all other respects. If Canada shall decline the proposition, then the stipulations in regard to the St. Lawrence canals and a railway from Ottawa to Sault Ste. Marie, with the Canadian clause of debt and revenue indemnity, will be relinquished. If the plan of union shall only be accepted in regard to the north-western territory and the Pacific Provinces, the United States will aid the construction, on the terms named, of a railway from the western extremity of Lake Superior, in the State of Minnesota, by way of Pembina, Fort Garry and the Valley of the Saskatchewan, to the Pacific Coast, north of latitude 49 deg., besides securing all the rights and privileges of an American territory to the proposed Territories of Selkirk, Saskatchewan and Columbia.

The "generosity" of the above proposal was very kind of our neighbors, but it had no avail. The abrogation of the Reciprocity Treaty and encouragement of the Fenian Raids by the American people had put the Canadians on their mettle and stiffened their backbone, so that neither retaliatory threats or honeyed allurements had any effect in changing their minds from carving out their own destiny under the broad folds of the Union Jack. How well this has been done by the earnest efforts and honest toil of our people, guided by the wisdom and sagacity of those statesmen who laid the foundation of our Dominion as it exists at present, is for other nations and other people to judge. Canada enjoys a prominent position in the estimation of the world to-day, and under the blessings of the Most High we will continue on in the march of progress and development of our bountiful resources.

The Fenian Raid, although it cost Canada sacrifices in precious lives and the expenditure of millions of money, proved of benefit to our young country in several ways. In the first place, it demonstrated the fact that the Canadians were loyal and patriotic to their heart's last drop in preserving British connection, and were true to their Flag and the freedom it symbolized. Again, the invasion enlightened the Fenian foemen and all other schemers who cast covetous eyes in our direction, that the Canadians were capable of protecting themselves, and were ready at all times to do their duty on the field of battle in defence of their native land and its institutions. Finally, it taught our people a lasting lesson in self-reliance, which should be instilled into the hearts and minds of our future generations, so that they too may always be found prepared to accept their share of responsibility in defending their country in times of peril and danger.

The Fenian Raid of 1870

CHAPTER I.

GEN. O'NEIL PREPARES FOR ANOTHER RAID ON CANADA—SECRET SHIPMENT OF ARMS TO THE FRONTIER.

In the early spring of 1870, the irrepressible General O'Neil (who was then President of the Fenian Brotherhood) decided that another diversion should be made on the Canadian frontier, and actively began making preparations to mass his forces for the invasion.

During the fall and winter of 1869 and 1870 all of the "circles" and existing military organizations were busy raising the necessary funds and gathering together the war equipment. The utmost secrecy was observed on this occasion, as the Fenian leaders were very careful to avoid a repetition of the intervention of the United States authorities in thwarting their plans to cross the border, as was the case in 1866. So they worked unceasingly and enthusiastically in maturing their plans, while they maintained absolute silence as to their intentions. The boasting bombast which had been so largely indulged in previous to the Raid of 1866 was not manifested on this occasion, consequently little interest was taken by the general public in Fenian affairs.

During the month of December, 1869, the Ninth Annual Convention of the Fenian Brotherhood was held in New York City. At this convocation there was a large gathering of delegates, every State in the Union being represented. All wore an air of confidence and suppressed emotion. While enthusiastic and determined at heart, they were careful to conceal their feelings, so as to avoid betrayal, by the least sign or word, of the result of their deliberations or the designs of their leaders.

At this meeting the Fenian Senate announced that complete arrangements had been secretly made for the second invasion of Canada, and asked that the delegates should ratify the programme. The announcement was hailed with great satisfaction by all present, and for some moments a regular pandemonium of cheers and yells of approval prevailed.

After order had been restored, Gen. O'Neil and others vehemently addressed the delegates, and worked up their patriotic feelings to such a hot pitch that each and every man present pledged himself to assist in the enterprise to the fullest extent of his power, even unto death.

A Council of War was then held, when it was resolved to begin active operations as early in the spring of 1870 as the roads would permit of the movement of troops. Brigadier-General M. Kerwin was then the Fenian Secretary of War, and during the next few months was very busy with his staff, getting everything in readiness. His orders and addresses to the Irish Republican Army were of such a patriotic and inspiring character that the officers and men of the various commands were constantly kept in a state of warlike excitement, which they controlled with marvelous secrecy. The months of January and February were spent in quiet preparation, and in March Gen. Kerwin issued a mandate that all military organizations of the Fenian Brotherhood should hold themselves in readiness to move forward to the Canadian frontier as soon as the final orders were issued. Meanwhile cases of arms, ammunition and other war material were being secretly shipped to different points along the border under various guises, and trusted officers were at the designated points to receive them and store them away in secluded hiding places until they were required. Everything was going along very satisfactory to the Fenian leaders, and it seemed to them as if Uncle Sam and the Canadian Government would both be caught napping.

During the first week in April Gen. O'Neil and some of his staff arrived at a point on the Vermont border to inspect the munitions of war and see that his directions were being properly carried out. Fifteen thousand stands of arms, and almost three million rounds of ammunition, had been actually received and carefully stored at various places along the frontier between Ogdensburg and St. Albans. Several thousands of these arms were breech-loading rifles of heavy calibre, for which there was an unlimited amount of cartridges.

Malone, N.Y., and St. Albans, Vermont, were again selected as bases of operations by Gen. O'Neil, and these towns were to be his principal places of muster. When he had concluded his examination of "affairs at the front," the valiant General was in high spirits, occasioned by the belief that he would steal a march on the Canadian Government and again be over the border before his intention was observed. He had taken great pains to have every preliminary preparation minutely made, and the fact that he had already smuggled an armament for fully 15,000 men to the frontier without exciting the suspicion of the usually vigilant officials of the United States, gave him considerable satisfaction and confidence. His plan of campaign was to rush the Fenian troops across the border without delay, and to intrench themselves at points where reinforcements could rally around them as supports when they had obtained a foot-hold. Malone and Franklin were chosen as the points from which the raiders were to make their forays, his chief object being, as before, to destroy the canal systems, and by cutting the railroad communication between Montreal and the West, hamper the movement of Canadian troops and cause consternation among the people.

CHAPTER II.

ANOTHER CALL TO ARMS—FENIANS AGAIN THREATEN AN INVA-
SION—GALLANT RESPONSE BY THE CANADIAN VOLUNTEERS.

Early in the month of April the Government was apprised
by its secret service agents that Fenian trouble was again brew-
ing on the frontier, and from details of the plot given, the
Vermont border was specially designated as the quarter from
which an invasion was extremely probable. Prompt measures
were at once taken by Sir George E. Cartier, the Minister of
Militia and Defence, to prepare for such an emergency, and
complete arrangements were made to guard our entire frontier
whenever necessary.

Notwithstanding their great secrecy, and the surreptitious
methods the Fenians employed to smuggle their arms, ammunition and war supplies to the border during the winter months,
the Government was kept fully informed of every movement by
reliable officials, who had special means of getting inside information.

As matters became more threatening, and acting on additional information received, the Government considered it advisable to call out a force of 5,000 men for active service on the
frontier of the Province of Quebec, the whole to be under the
chief command of the Lieutenant-General commanding Her
Majesty's regular troops in Canada, with Col. W. Osborne
Smith, D.A.G. of Military District, No. 5, in command of the
troops operating on the south-eastern frontier.

On April 11th the call to arms was made, and the different
battalions and companies responded with their usual promptitude and alacrity, so that within 48 hours all were assembled at
their posts on the frontier to which they had been assigned,
ready for action.

The Cookshire Troop of Cavalry, under command of Lieut.
Taylor, was stationed at Frelighsburg, with pickets at Pigeon
Hill and Abbott's Corners. The 52nd Battalion, under com-

mand of Lieut.-Col. P. Miller, was posted at Frelighsburg, with detachments stationed as pickets at Mansonville, Abercorn and Cook's Corners.

The 60th Battalion, under Lieut.-Col. B. Chamberlin, had its headquarters at Pigeon Hill, with detachments at St. Armand and Philipsburg.

On the Huntingdon frontier the troops were posted as follows:

At Huntingdon—No. 1 Troop, Montreal Cavalry, in command of Capt. Muir, with videttes at Franklin and Hemmingford; the 50th Battalion, commanded by Lieut.-Col. McEachren; and the 51st Battalion, under command of Lieut.-Col. Rogers, with detachments at Franklin and Havelock.

At Beauharnois—The Beauharnois Battalion, under Lieut.-Col. Rodin, with a detachment at Valleyfield, guarded the canals.

While the above forces thoroughly covered the exposed points on the frontier, the following troops were held in reserve at Montreal, ready to go at a moment's notice to any point where their services might be urgently required: Montreal Garrison Artillery, two companies of Engineers, 1st Battalion (Prince of Wales Rifles), 3rd Battalion (Victoria Rifles), 5th Battalion (Royal Light Infantry), 6th Battalion (Hochelaga Light Infantry), First Provisional Battalion, Second Provisional Battalion, 65th Battalion (Mount Royal Rifles), 4th Battalion (Chasseurs Canadiens)—a total of all ranks of 1,940.

At Quebec a force of 1,617 officers and men of the Sixth Military District were concentrated, ready for duty anywhere.

On the 12th of April a further call was made for troops to guard the St. Clair River frontier, in Western Ontario, which was completed as follows:

At Sarnia—The London Field Battery, with two field guns (manned and horsed by 35 gunners and drivers), and two companies of the 7th Battalion of London, under command of Lieut.-Col. Shanly.

At Windsor—The Windsor and Leamington Companies of Infantry (each 55 strong), with Major Walker, of the 7th Battalion, in command.

In addition to the above troops, companies of the Grand Trunk Railway Brigade were judiciously posted at certain vulnerable points along the line of that railway by its commander, Lieut.-Col. C. J. Brydges, so that in all a force of fully 6,000 men were stationed on duty where required within a very short period.

These troops remained on active service until the 21st of April, when it was considered advisable to release all from duty with the exception of the 50th, 51st, 52nd, 60th and Beauharnois Battalions, and the two troops of cavalry originally placed on the south-eastern frontier, who remained on duty until the 29th of April, when they were also withdrawn. The Government was confident of the fact that the services of the volunteers would be cheerfully and promptly given whenever they would again be called upon, and in relieving them from duty, thanked them warmly for their service, and reminded them that it might be necessary to rally again to the colors almost any day, and to be ready to respond to the call.

CHAPTER III.

Gen. O'Neil Again Invades Canada—A Raid Made from Vermont Promptly Repulsed by a Handful of Canadians.

About the middle of May orders went forth from Gen. O'Neil for the Fenian forces to again take the field, and a week later they began to assemble in the border cities, towns and villages of the United States, ready for another campaign against Canada. The rallying points were the same as those designated in Gen. Sweeny's plan of campaign in 1866. Gen. O'Neil seems to have considered that his chances of success would be better on the eastern frontier than by again attempting the invasion of the Niagara District, although his plan was to muster a strong force in Buffalo, as before, and, if opportunity offered, and he was successful in the east, to again attempt the passage of the Niagara. Consequently he gave his personal attention to the troops that were gathering on the Northern New York and Vermont frontiers, and directed the mobilization of the divisions at Malone and St. Albans, with the intention of following out Sweeny's old programme of conquest, while several officers of experience would lead in the attacks on other points.

The 24th of May (Queen's Birthday) was the date selected for the invasion, and the night previous every train bound north from New York, Boston, and the New England States, carried contingents of Fenian soldiers on their way to the appointed rendezvous on the border. Gen. O'Neil established his headquarters at Franklin, Vermont, where his staff were energetically at work equipping the troops as they arrived. O'Neil fully expected that from 2,000 to 3,000 Fenians would have assembled at Franklin on the 24th, but through some delay in transportation the bulk of the forces failed to appear. Only about 800 had reported themselves, and the tardiness of movement of the remainder of the army threatened a fatal ending to the enterprise. O'Neil chafed under his disappointment, and sent urgent telegrams and messengers to hurry up the laggards.

but the morning of the 25th dawned without the arrival of the expected soldiers. Gen. O'Neil then became so impatient that he could bear the suspense no longer. He was fearful of the interposition of the United States authorities, and resolved to immediately advance into Canada with the force present under his command, and leave his reinforcements to follow.

The Fenian camp was located at Hubbard's Farm (about half a mile from Franklin), and the officers were busy there distributing arms, ammunition and equipment. They had collected armament for about 3,000 men, and the cases were opened and scattered along the road to facilitate the quick issue of rifles and cartridges to the reinforcements as soon as they arrived.

On the 24th of May President U. S. Grant had issued his proclamation forbidding a breach of the Neutrality Act, and the United States officials were prompt in their endeavors to stop the raid. Gen. George P. Foster (United States Marshal) called on Gen. O'Neil at Franklin, and after reading to him President Grant's proclamation, endeavored to dissuade him from advancing over the line. But the Fenian General refused to comply with his advice, and expressed his contempt for the President in language more forcible and profane than polite. As Gen. Foster had no troops at his command to compel obedience by the Fenian leaders, he crossed over the line and informed the Canadian commander (Col. Chamberlain) of O'Neil's designs and his inability to stop the raiders.

About 11 o'clock on May 25th Gen. O'Neil mounted his horse and rode down from Franklin to the Fenian camp. He realized that if he did not move quickly there was a probability of the arrival of United States troops to stop the expedition; therefore he gave immediate orders to his men to "fall in" for the advance across the border. When the troops were formed up, he addressed them as follows:—

"Soldiers! This is the advance guard of the Irish-American army for the liberation of Ireland from the yoke of the oppressor. For your own country you enter that of the enemy. The eyes of your countrymen are upon you. Forward—March!''

At the word of command the column moved promptly, with Gen. O'Neil and Gen. Donnelly (his Chief-of-Staff) at the head, and the green flag of the Irish Republic flapping in the wind. The Fenian column was formed in three divisions, consisting of an advance guard of skirmishers, a strong support of about 200 men, and the balance of their troops in reserve. They had only a short distance to go before they reached the boundary line. Some eight rods north of the line (on the Canadian side) is a gully through which runs a small brook known locally as "Chickabiddy Creek," over which the road is bridged, and beyond which are the rocky heights of Eccles' Hill, where a small Canadian force was entrenched among the rocks and trees awaiting the approach of the invaders.

The house of Alva Richards, about ten rods south of the border line, on the road from Franklin to Cook's Corners, was chosen by Gen. O'Neil as his headquarters. From the Richards house to the Canadian position was a distance of only about a quarter of a mile.

Immediately after crossing the boundary, the Burlington (Vermont) Company of Fenians (about fifty men), under command of Capt. Cronan, dashed down the hill to form a skirmish line across the brook. Just as they did so the Canadians opened fire. At the first volley Private John Rowe was instantly killed, and Lieut. John Hallinan received a flesh wound in the arm. The company wavered, and receiving no support, fell back to the shelter of the Richards house and outbuildings. The next company (under Capt. Carey) joined Capt. Cronan in the rear of the house, and commenced firing. Soon afterwards Private James Keenan ventured out too far and received a ball in the leg, near the ankle. This hot reception, and the sharp fire of the Canadians, caused a stampede, and Gen. O'Neil endeavored to rally his troops by the following address:—

"Men of Ireland! I am ashamed of you. You have acted disgracefully, but you will have another chance of showing whether you are cravens or not. Comrades, we must not, *we dare not*, go back now, with the stain of cowardice upon us. Comrades, I will lead you again, and if you will not follow me, I will go on with my officers and die in your front. I leave you now under command of Gen. Boyle O'Reilly."

After this brave utterance, Gen. O'Neil (who had been across the border on an eminence opposite the Canadian position, watching events) retired to an attic window in the Richards house, from which point he intended to observe the fortunes of the day.   But the Canadian riflemen having discovered his presence there, directed their fire upon him, and Mr. Richards ordered O'Neil to leave his residence, which was getting seriously damaged by bullets.   Just as he went out of the house, General Foster (United States Marshal), with a couple of his officers, stepped forward and arrested O'Neil for breach of the Neutrality Act.   At first the Fenial General was very wrathy, and threatened to use force if he was not released, but on Gen. Foster placing a revolver at his head and intimating that he would shoot if he did not submit, O'Neil's courage quailed, and he surrendered.   He was shoved into a covered carriage and driven off to St. Albans under guard of two men, very much dejected.

By this time a contingent of about 500 Fenians had arrived from St. Albans, and were being armed and equipped at the Fenian camp for the purpose of making another dash.   As O'Neil had been so unceremoniously whisked away by Gen. Foster, the Fenian army was now without a leader.   So a Council of War was held, all of the leading Fenian officers in the field being present.   Reinforcements were now arriving hourly, and strong efforts were made to induce Gen. John Boyle O'Reilly (a noted Irish patriot) to take command and again lead them on to glory.   The Council convened in an open glade near the Fenian camp, where, surrounded by their troops, the leaders pleaded with Gen. O'Reilly to assume command, but he could not be prevailed upon to accept the risk, and the spirits of the raiders sank as they began to realize the hopelessness of their position.

Early next morning Gen. Spier arrived at St. Albans and endeavored to bring order out of chaos, and continue O'Neil's plan of invasion.   But by this time the golden opportunity had slipped by, and all chances of success had vanished.   A strong force of Canadians had arrived at the frontier, determined to resist every foot of advance into Canadian territory, while a body of United States troops appeared in the rear of the Fenian army for the purpose of making arrests for breach of the neutrality laws. Being caught between two fires, they thought discretion was the better part of valor, and fled in dismay. And thus the grand "Army of the Irish Republic" melted away in disorganized mobs.

At Malone similar conditions existed, and the large number of Fenians assembled there were quickly dissolved by the United States troops and all their war material seized by the United States authorities.

A description of the fight at Eccles' Hill, as viewed from the Canadian side, is given in the succeeding chapter.

CHAPTER IV.

OPERATIONS ON THE MISSISQUOI FRONTIER—THE BATTLE OF
ECCLES' HILL—COMPLETE DEFEAT OF THE FENIAN ARMY.

On the morning of the 24th of May Lieut.-Col. W. Osborne
Smith, Deputy Adjutant-General of the Fifth Military District,
at Montreal, received advices from trustworthy sources that the
Fenians were again assembling on the Vermont border, and that
telegraph wires had been cut in several places by them. He at
once notified the authorities at Ottawa by wire of these events,
and asked for instructions in regard to calling out the forces
under his command for active service.

As was customary, the whole of the Montreal Garrison had
been assembled that day for the usual parade and review in
honor of Her Majesty's birthday. As the hours wore on and
no reply had been received from Ottawa by Col. Smith in answer
to his telegrams, he promptly took the extreme responsibility
permitted by the 60th Section of the Militia Act, and called out
for service a large portion of the troops of his district, including all the frontier and Montreal corps. He reported his action
to the Lieutenant-General Commanding, who approved of his
action and his suggestions as to the disposal of the troops instantly required on the frontier, and further ordered that he
should personally assume command at the threatened point of
attack in the neighborhood of Frelighsburg.

He then addressed the men on parade, informing them that
the Fenians were on the frontier with warlike intentions, and
that from that moment they were on active service; moreover,
that he required five companies at once to proceed to the frontier under his command. The entire brigade responded with
great enthusiasm, and was ready there and then to move off
to the border to meet the enemy. As the whole force was not
required, Col. Smith made his selections and left for the front
within a few hours, taking with him the Montreal Troop of
Cavalry, and companies from the 1st Prince of Wales Rifles,
3rd Victoria Rifles, 5th Royals, 6th Battalion Hochelaga Light

Infantry, together with one officer and 20 men of the Montreal Garrison Artillery. The latter contingent was detailed to reinforce Isle aux Noix, while the remainder of the force proceeded on to St. John's. On arrival there the Montreal troops (with the exception of the cavalry and the company of Victoria Rifles) were left to garrison St. John's, together with the 21st Battalion and the St. John's Garrison Battery of Artillery. Lieut.-Col. Fletcher was left in command at St. John's, with instructions to secure the safety of that place from a sudden dash by the enemy, and on the following morning proceed to the Huntingdon frontier and assume command of the troops assembled there. A party of the 21st Battalion (Richelieu Light Infantry) was detached at Malmaison to guard the bridge over the Pike River at that place.

About midnight Col. Smith arrived at Stanbridge Station with the Montreal Cavalry Troop and the one company of the Victoria Rifles. After detraining the troops he at once started on his march to Stanbridge (about eight miles distant). The roads were deep and miry from heavy rain, and the night intensely dark, but the men, who had been under arms and with little refreshment since early morning, performed the march uncomplainingly, and were eager to press on to the front.

At Stanbridge the 60th Missisquoi Battalion, under command of Lieut.-Col. Brown Chamberlin, were assembling, and on arrival there Col. Smith learned that a Fenian force had gathered near Franklin, Vermont, and were preparing to make a dash across the border in the vicinity of Eccles' Hill.

During the previous night about thirty farmers of the neighborhood (who had armed and enrolled themselves as a Home Guard, under the leadership of Mr. Asa Westover, of Dunham) occupied Eccles' Hill, a strong position on the frontier, with the determined intention to keep the Fenians in check until the arrival of the regular volunteer force. On Lieut.-Col. Chamberlin's arrival at Stanbridge on the night of the 24th he found No. 3 Company of the 60th Battalion assembled, and was informed by Capt. Kemp, his Adjutant, of the state of affairs at the front. He was quick to act, and sent forward a picket to Cook's Corners, in support of the party occupying Eccles' Hill, with instructions to move forward at daylight and reinforce it. Another detachment of 24 men, under Capt. Bockus, of No. 5 Company of the 60th, were ordered to move up as supports to Cook's Corners at daylight, and later to reinforce the men in their position at the Hill. In the early hours of the morning two prisoners were captured by the farmers near their position, one of whom was a Fenian captain named Murphy, and the other one of his men. They were sent under guard of a corporal and two men to Stanbridge. This left Lieut.-Col. Chamberlin's total force at the front three officers and 46 men of the 60th Battalion, and 35 farmers.

Lieut.-Col. Chamberlin made his dispositions by placing a picket of one officer and ten men on his right rear, and the remainder of the volunteers (two officers and 36 men) were posted among the rocks and trees, and behind the fences stretching from the road to the crest of the hill, while the right flank was protected by the 35 farmers, most of whom were sharpshooters. Thus Lieut.-Col. Chamberlin's combined force to resist an attack was two officers and 71 men.

On a hill about 300 yards distant, across the American border, the sentries of the advanced guard of the enemy were visible, while a short distance beyond their main body were preparing for an advance on to Canadian soil.

Shortly before 12 o'clock (noon), General Foster, the United States Marshal for the Northern District of Vermont, drove over to the Canadian lines and had an interview with Lieut.-Col. Chamberlin. He said that he desired to offer assurances that his Government and himself personally were doing all that was possible to prevent a raid, and that the United States troops were being moved up to assist him in the discharge of his duty and enforcement of the neutrality laws as fast as they could be transported. He also stated that he was charged with a message from Gen. O'Neil, to say that those under his command would not make war upon women or children, nor be permitted to plunder peaceable inhabitants, but would conduct their war in the manner approved among civilized nations.

Col. Chamberlin replied that he would receive no message from men who were mere pirates and marauders, and it was scarcely satisfactory to those whom they intended to murder.

because they were in arms for the defence of their Government and country, that their piracy would not be attended with unusual barbarities.

While they were still in conversation, the head of the Fenian column began to advance. Lieut.-Col. Chamberlin called Gen. Foster's attention to the fact, who replied, "I thought they intended to attack you soon, but not so soon as this." He then drove away in the direction of, and past the advancing Fenian column.

Lieut.-Col. Chamberlin then hastily made such disposition of his small force as seemed most advantageous, with Capt. Bockus on the left of the skirmish line, which rested on the main road.

The enemy advanced in close column, about 200 strong, with an advance guard about 100 yards ahead of the main body. On its approach to the boundary line it was ordered to move at the double, and the advance guard rushed across. As soon as it was on Canadian soil, Lieut.-Col. Chamberlin's men opened fire on the advance guard. The fire was returned from the main column of attack, which was still within United States territory. The conflict then became general. Upon the first volley from the Canadians one man in the leading section of the Fenian advance guard was shot dead and others wounded. The remaining men comprising it then sought refuge behind the neighboring barns and under a bridge near at hand. The main body halted, wavered, partially rallied again, and then, being galled by the well-directed fire of the Canadians, broke and ran for cover behind the houses and stone fences along the road, or made their way to a wood which crowned the summit of the hill opposite to our position on the western side of the road, another man being killed and several more wounded while seeking this shelter. From this time a desultory fire was kept up from behind trees and fences.

Col. Smith was on the way to Stanbridge for the purpose of ordering up reinforcements to strengthen the position at Eccles' Hill, when he was overtaken by a mounted messenger sent by Lieut.-Col. Chamberlin, stating that the Fenians were on the point of attack. He therefore ordered his aide (Capt.

Gascoigne) to hasten on to Stanbridge and bring up every available man, and at once rode back to Eccles' Hill. On arrival there he found that the first attack had been bravely repulsed by Lieut.-Col. Chamberlin's men, and assumed command of the future operations. The total force of the Fenians had not yet been brought into action, their reserve of 350 or 400 men being still on the American side of the border line. A possible attack being feared from this force, Col. Smith took every precaution to hold his own until reinforcements arrived. About 2.30 p.m. the Montreal Troop of Cavalry, a company of the Victoria Rifles, and another detachment of 20 men of the 60th Battalion, reached the Canadian position from Stanbridge. With this additional force Col. Smith was enabled to strengthen his skirmish line, and better secure the right flank of his position. Firing was kept up until about 5 o'clock, when the Fenian fire began to slacken, with the exception of a few dropping shots from the enemy, who had taken shelter in the houses along the road. These riflemen were carefully marked by the Canadian skirmishers, and searched for by a shower of bullets whenever a shot was fired.

About 6 o'clock the Fenians were busy getting a field gun in position, and had it placed about 1,200 yards in front of the Canadian line. But before it was fired Col. Smith ordered an advance of his force, the detachment of the 60th Battalion and the Home Guards advancing in skirmishing order, and the company of Victoria Rifles covering their advance from the slope of the hill. This movement was well executed, and had the effect of driving the Fenians from their cover in all directions, in full flight. Not over a dozen shots were fired by them against the Canadians in their retreat. They threw away their arms, accoutrements and clothing as they ran, and did not stop until they were far over the American border.

At nightfall three shots were fired by the Fenians from their field gun, but their aim was faulty, and the shots did no damage to our men. During the whole engagement not one of the Canadians was even wounded.

The Fenian loss was four or five killed and 15 or 18 wounded. Three of their dead were at one time plainly in view from our lines, while another was reported as lying dead in a brook at the foot of the hill. Among the wounded was the Fenian General Donnelly. During the night lights were seen moving over the fields in search of the Fenian dead and wounded, who were removed to the United States by civilians. After his defeat the repulsed General O'Neil took refuge in a brick house, from which he was turned out by the owner. He then hastened to the rear, and on arrival on American territory was arrested by Gen. Foster, the United States Marshal, for breach of the neutrality laws.

The Canadian troops held their position and laid on their arms all night, expecting another attack, but the enemy had seen enough of Canadian valor, and did not make the attempt again to renew the combat.

On the following morning the Fenians abandoned their camp at Hubbard's Farm, leaving large quantities of arms, ammunition and clothing, which were seized by the United States Government. Their rifles were the best obtainable at that time, being breech-loading Springfields and Spencers of the latest pattern. Their field-piece (which was a breech-loading rifled steel gun) was captured on Canadian soil, and is one of the trophies held by the Missisquoi Home Guard in memory of O'Neil's dismal failure to capture Canada in 1870.

CHAPTER V.

The Ontario Frontier Vigilantly Guarded—Volunteers on Service at Danger Points all Along the Line.

On the frontier of the Province of Ontario the danger of invasion was just as imminent as in the East, as Fenians were assembling at all points with definite objects in view. The invasion was well planned, but its execution was very poorly managed. It was not the intention of the Fenian leaders to bring on battles at either Eccles' Hill or Trout River unless success was well assured. These were only intended to be feints to draw the attention of the Canadians, while the main attacks were to be made at Cornwall and Prescott, with another heavy attack on the Niagara frontier if opportunity offered. Their object (as in 1866) was to destroy the St. Lawrence and Welland Canals and cut railway communication wherever practicable, thus preventing rapid concentration of Canadian troops while they proceeded to occupy the country. In conformity with their plans the Fenian troops gathered at convenient places to make their raids on the objective points in Ontario they had in view.

Owing to the extreme probability of an attack being made on Cornwall by the Fenians who had gathered at Malone, N.Y., it was deemed advisable by the Government to assemble a large force for the defence of that place as speedily as possible. Therefore orders were wired at 2 p.m. on May 24th to Lieut.-Col. F. T. Atcherly, Deputy Adjutant-General of the 4th Military District, to call out the militia force at Brockville and Prescott forthwith for active service. This was immediately accomplished, and guards posted for the protection of these towns. On the following day he received instructions to proceed at once to Cornwall and assume command of the force there. He arrived at Cornwall that night with the Iroquois Battery of Garrison Artillery, and in conjunction with Lieut.-Col. Bergin, commanding the 59th Battalion, made all the necessary dispositions of guards for the protection of the town and the locks and bridges on the Cornwall Canal. In the meantime the entire 59th Battalion had been mustered, and on the following day his force was strengthened by the arrival of a demi-battery of the Ottawa Field Artillery, with two guns and 23 horses, under command of Capt. Forsyth, and also the Ottawa Brigade of Garrison Artillery, under Lieut.-Col. Forrest. About the same time the 18th Battalion began to arrive from L'Original, having been conveyed the whole distance in waggons. During the afternoon the 41st Battalion, under command of Lieut.-Col. Crawford, arrived by steamer from Brockville. In addition to this force, a corps of mounted scouts of about 60 men had been organized by Lieut.-Col. Bergin, and placed under command of Capt. Mattice. This company did most excellent service at night, patrolling along the banks of the canal from the guard lock at Dickinson's Landing to the village of Summerstown, a distance of about 21 miles. Strong pickets were posted every night to guard the culverts in the canal at various places. At the guard lock at the head of the canal, No. 5 Company of the 59th Battalion, under command of Capt. Bredin, was stationed, and did very excellent service. The town of Cornwall and the lower locks of the canal were so efficiently guarded and the surrounding country so thoroughly patrolled, that had an attack been made the invaders would certainly have met with a decidedly hot reception by Col. Atcherley's force.

While the land forces were so arduously performing their duties, the steamer "Prince Alfred" was employed in patrolling the river. She was manned by a detachment of artillerymen and sharp-shooters, who were unceasing in their vigilance to overhaul any craft that looked suspicious.

Lieut.-Col. W. H. Jackson, Brigade Major of the 8th Brigade Division, was in command of the force which assembled at Prescott, and performed the arduous duties required of him most efficiently. On the departure of Lieut.-Col. F. T. Atcherly to take command of the force at Cornwall, Lieut.-Col. Jackson was instructed to assume command of the forces which were concentrating at Prescott. A large body of Fenians had gathered at Ogdensburg, just across the river, and rumors were rife that they intended making a crossing. He accordingly took prompt precautions to place that important point in a state of defence. The troops at his command were one division of the

Ottawa Field Battery, with two guns; the Ottawa Rifle Company (Capt. Mowat), the 43rd Carleton Battalion (Lieut.-Col. Bearman), and the 56th Battalion Lisgar Rifles (Lieut.-Col. Jessup). In addition he had two companies of Railway Guards. making his total force about 750 officers and men. With this command he thoroughly guarded, picketed and patrolled every important point east, west and north, and so keen was his vigilance that the enemy across the river could find no loop-hole for an attack and abandoned their intention. This force was kept on duty until the 3rd of June, when the danger having passed, they were relieved from further service.

The situation at Brockville was as grave as at other points along the frontier, owing to its close contiguity to the American shore. It was the headquarters of the 42nd Battalion, which was speedily mustered under command of Lieut.-Col. J. D. Buell. Several of the companies of this corps were located many miles from headquarters, but on receiving the call for active service they moved with remarkable activity, and arrived at the frontier within 24 hours after the summons had been sent forth. No. 4 Company (Capt. Allan Fraser), from Fitzroy, had about 80 miles to travel, partly by waggon and partly by rail. They quickly mustered at Kinburn and moved with such celerity that they reported at Brockville early the next morning. Such, indeed, was the spirit that prevailed among the volunteers everywhere, and to their promptness is due the defeat of the enemy's plans. The Forty-second did very great service in protecting the railway docks and other points of landing at Brockville, besides patrolling the river banks as far east as Maitland. thus keeping up a chain of communication with the garrison at Prescott. Several "scares" occurred during the time they were on service, which caused sleepless nights, but by their vigilance the Fenians were deterred from making an attack. All were prompt, willing and eager to obey every command. and were warmly commended for the soldierly manner in which they performed their duty.

For the protection of the Niagara frontier, all available troops in the immediate vicinity were called out for active service on the 24th of May. The Nineteenth Lincoln Battalion, under command of Lieut.-Col. J. G. Currie, the St. Catharines Troop of Cavalry under Capt. Gregory, and the St. Catharines Battery of Garrison Artillery, were quickly assembled and placed on active service. One company of the 19th was detached to guard the Suspension Bridge at Clifton, in conjunction with three companies of the 44th Welland Battalion. The remainder of the 19th Battalion were posted as follows:—Two companies (with regimental staff) consisting of 12 officers and 87 men, at St. Catharines and Port Dalhousie; one company (Capt. Upper) with three officers and 42 men at Niagara; three officers and 42 men at Port Robinson, three officers and 42 men at Welland, and three officers and 42 men at Allanburg.

The St. Catharines Troop of Cavalry (Capt. Gregory) was dispatched to Chippawa to patrol the River Road between that point and Fort Erie—one officer and 13 troopers being stationed at Chippawa; one officer and 13 men at Black Creek, and one officer and 14 men at Fort Erie. This command maintained a complete system of patrols along the upper Niagara River. Two companies of the 44th Battalion were also stationed at Chippawa to guard the bridges and approaches to that place.

The St. Catharines Battery of Garrison Artillery (Capt. Thomas Oswald) was attached to the 19th Battalion, a portion of the Battery, under Lieut. J. G. Holmes, doing duty in guarding the locks on the Welland Canal at Allanburg, and the remainder being placed on board the tug "Clara Carter" with two field guns, which boat was employed to cruise Lake Erie and the Niagara River.

The Queenston Mounted Infantry, under command of Capt. Robert Currie, maintained an efficient patrol of the lower Niagara frontier, with two officers and 18 men at Niagara, and one officer and 18 men at Queenston.

The 37th Haldimand Battalion was ordered to Port Colborne, and also the Welland Canal Field Battery, where they maintained a vigilant guard on the entrance to the Welland Canal, which was threatened by an Fenien attack.

The United States gunboat "Michigan" was at Port Colborne on the 24th, and left on a cruise along the shores of Lake Erie with positive orders from the American Government to sink any piratical craft that might attempt to make a crossing. The Fenians assembled at Buffalo were anxious to get over into

Canada, but could not get any ship owners willing to take the risk in face of such orders.

With the Niagara frontier thus protected and the remainder of the Active Militia in Toronto, Hamilton, Brantford and all other points in the Second Military District under orders to be prepared to move whenever their services might be required, the danger was averted, and the alarm of the people of that section soon subsided.   The total strength of the force on active service on the Niagara frontier at that time (under command of Lieut.-Col. Durie, D.A.G.) amounted to 1,159, consisting of 93 officers and 966 men, with 147 horses and four guns.

To guard the St. Clair River frontier, a sufficient force was placed on active service to keep in check any raiders that might attempt a crossing from the State of Michigan, while all of the troops in the First Military District were warned to be ready to move to the front when summoned.   The troops called out were posted as follows:—

At Sarnia—London Field Battery, with two guns, three officers, 30 men and 25 horses, Lieut.-Col. Shanly commanding; Mooretown Mounted Infantry, three officers, 39 men and 42 horses, Capt. Stewart commanding; 27th Battalion of Infantry, 24 officers and 224 men, Lieut.-Col. Davis commanding.

At Windsor—St. Thomas Cavalry Troop (Capt. Borbridge), six officers, 42 men and 45 horses; Leamington Infantry Company (Capt. Wilkinson), three officers and 45 men; Windsor Infantry Company (Capt. Richards), three officers and 42 men; Bothwell Infantry Company (Capt. Chambers), three officers and 40 men; Lobo Infantry Company (Capt. Stevenson), three officers and 47 men.

Ceaseless vigilance was in evidence everywhere among the volunteers who guarded the points above mentioned, and the troops on duty were fully prepared for any invading force that might set foot on our soil.   But fortunately the Province of Ontario was spared a repetition of the events of 1866, although it was not the fault of the enemy, who made strenuous efforts to get over the border.   In 1870 President Grant took prompt measures to prevent unlawful expeditions from leaving the United States, and through the watchfulness of the American Government the designs of the Fenian leaders were defeated. Generals O'Neil, Starr, Gleason, O'Reilly. Donnelly and others had been promptly arrested by the United States authorities, and the rank and file soon abandoned their campaigns and returned to their homes.

PERSONAL REMINISCENCES.

While perusing the fyles of the Toronto *Globe* in the Public Reference Library recently, my eye caught the following item in the issue of that journal dated June 1st, 1870, which brought back to memory personal reminiscences which may be of interest:

"The St. Catharines *Journal* says that three young Canadians in Corry, Pa., named respectively John A. and George Macdonald, of St. Catharines, and Thomas Kennedy, of Niagara, hearing that the Fenians were on Canadian soil, determined to be on hand in the hour of danger, and at once took train for home, arriving at St. Catharines last Wednesday night (May 25th). It is no small thing for a working man to throw up a situation and sacrifice all for their love of country, and Canada should be proud of such sons.''

At the time the Fenians were getting ready to make their second invasion of Canada in 1870, the writer of this book was employed as a newspaper reporter in a town in Pennsylvania where Fenianism was rampant, and in the course of my daily duties had rare opportunities for gleaning information as to the intentions of "the Brotherhood." I noticed that preparations were being made with the utmost secrecy possible, and that those who were engaged in organizing the movement were men of the most determined and desperate character. I chanced to know some of them personally, and by a careful process of reportorial "interviewing," learned that a sudden dash on Canadian territory was to be made within a few days. The chief desire of the leaders was to keep their intentions from the knowledge of the United States authorities, and they were very averse to giving the least publicity as to their movements.

However, in a casual way I received information from a reliable source that large numbers of men were on their way from the southern part of Pennsylvania, Ohio. Indiana, Kentucky, Tennessee and other places. travelling as ordinary passengers, and that they would rendezvous at Erie, Dunkirk. Buffalo, Niagara Falls and other places along the border, where they were to receive their equipment. This news I duly communicated to my friends at home (St. Catharines) and gave them notice that trouble was impending.

The next day (25th of May) things were looking more serious. About 9 o'clock in the morning I went down to the rail-. way depot on my quest for "news items," and found that two trains had just arrived—one from Pittsburg and the other from Central Ohio, on which were an unusually large number of men, who were bound for Buffalo. They were swarming on the station platforms and patronizing nearby saloons and restaurants freely while waiting for train connections. I wanted more information, and mingled with them with the intention of getting it. Most of them were very reticent, but I finally found out, by judicious pumping of a burly fellow from Pittsburg, that they were Fenians on their way to Canada. I instantly made up my mind that it was time for me to go home. I had previously written to the Captain of my old corps (in which I had served at Fort Erie in 1866) giving him "pointers" as to what the Fenians were doing, and notifying him that I would be home to fill my place in the ranks when occasion required. I considered that the time had now arrived for prompt action on my part, and as the train was due to leave within an hour, I hurried over to my employer and explained matters, resigned my situation, got my salary, secured my valise (which I had already packed), and was ready to leave in less than half an hour. My brother (George M. Macdonald), who was also employed on the same paper as myself, did likewise, and when we were leaving the office our employer very cordially commended our action and bade us "God speed" on our journey, at the same time handing us a roll of money "for present use," as he expressed it, and adding that when the trouble was over and we were ready to return, our situations would be open for us. Such generous kindness, and the warm words of appreciation of our services which accompanied the genial "good-by" of our employer, touched us both deeply, and have remained in my memory ever since as one of the bright spots in my life. On our way to the station we met another Canadian (Thomas Kennedy), whose old home was at Niagara, where he belonged to No. 1 Company of the 19th Battalion. He was greatly "worked up" when he saw the Fenian contingent getting ready to start, and when we informed him of our intentions, he resolutely remarked, "Boys, I'm going home, too; and as I haven't got time to go down to my boardinghouse for my clothes, I'll go just as I am. We'll be in uniform in Canada to-morrow." So he came with us. By this time the train was ready to leave, and we managed to get a double seat in one end of the car. The coach we were in was soon filled with Fenians, and the vacant seat beside me was taken by a sturdy-looking fellow who confidentially told us that he was a Sergeant in a company from Cincinnati, and that a large force of "the byes" were proceeding to the frontier. From this soldier we got considerable valuable information as to the strength and composition of the troops on the train, and also those following, which was carefully stored in our memories and afterwards duly reported to the Canadian authorities. Two or three times this Sergeant inquired what company of Fenians we belonged to, but we artfully managed to evade a direct answer to his questions, and switched the conversation in another direction. Had he realized or became aware of the fact that we were Canadians on our way home to take up arms against him and his comrades, there is no doubt but that we would have had a very unpleasant experience on that car. Quite a number of the Fenians on board were under the influence of liquor, and as they pushed around their bottles of whiskey several of them forgot the lessons of caution that had been impressed upon them by their officers, and became very talkative as to their organization and intentions. Our ears were strained to catch every syllable, and we gathered considerable desired information that otherwise would not have leaked out. On arrival at Dunkirk our travelling companion (the Fenian Sergeant) left the train with about twenty men, bidding us a friendly farewell and saying that perhaps we might soon meet again, "in the camp or in the field." We hoped the latter, but did not consider it necessary to explain our thoughts. We were much pleased to lose this gentleman's company, as he had again began to persistently ask us awkward questions as to what Irish Republican Regiment we were in, and who were our officers; also what Fenian "circle" we belonged to, and who was the "Centre" of it. Such queries were so very pointed and direct that we were obliged to use all sorts of evasions and diplomacy to throw our interlocutor off his guard. Before we reached Buffalo another chap approached us, and began asking a series of vexing questions, but fortunately the conductor just then happened to come through the car, and we disposed of the inquisitive Fenian by halting the train official and asking him a lot of questions about railway connections for points east, and other matters, of which we knew as much as he did. The Fenian stood by for a while listening, until a comrade in the centre of the car called him to partake of some liquid refreshments. He promptly responded to the summons, and after a liberal libation from the neck of a bottle he seemed to forget all about us, for which we were duly thankful. A few moments afterward our Fenian friend broke forth into song in stentorian tones, in which the rest of his comrades joined in the rendition of "The Wearin' o' the Green." This diversion drew their attention from our direction until the train finally rolled into the Exchange Street Depot at Buffalo. We quietly slipped off the rear platform of the car, and were obliged to elbow our way through a throng of Fenians who had gathered to meet the new arrivals. On reaching the street we quickly proceeded across to the Erie Street Station, where we caught the evening train for Suspension Bridge. This train also was pretty well filled with Fenians, but we were not bothered by any of them on the way. Soon after we crossed the Niagara River and were on Canadian soil. To express our gratification and pleasure to be once more at home in our native land, cannot be fully expressed in words, so I will leave the feeling to be imagined by the reader.

That night at 9 o'clock my brother and myself reported to Capt. Thomas Oswald in the Drill Shed at St. Catharines. The old St. Catharines Battery of Garrison Artillery was on parade, and when we made our appearance we received such a hearty reception and ovation that the ringing cheers of my old comrades and their spontaneous greetings still haunt my memory. We were immediately ushered into the Armory by the Quartermaster-Sergeant, who issued to us our uniforms and equipments, and in half an hour we were again in the ranks, ready for service in defence of Canada.

Both my brother George and Comrade Tom Kennedy have long since passed away to eternal rest, and as an affectionate tribute to their memory and worth, and in remembrance of their loyal devotion to Queen and country, I deem it fitting to here put on record this evidence of the high spirit of patriotism which inspired these noble boys to respond to the call of duty when danger threatened their native land.

CHAPTER VI.

FENIANS GATHER ON THE HUNTINGDON BORDER—SKIRMISH AT
TROUT RIVER—THE ENEMY ROUTED BY THE CANADIAN
TROOPS.

Simultaneous with Gen. O'Neil's raid into Canada at
Eccles' Hill on May 25th, an invasion took place on the Huntingdon border, when a strong force of Fenians under command
of Generals Starr and Gleason advanced about a mile and a half
into the Province of Quebec, on the line of the Trout River. On
arrival at a chosen position which possessed great advantages
for a successful defence, they began throwing up entrenchments, and prepared to make a determined stand. A whole day
was spent in the work of constructing rifle pits and breastworks, but being no doubt discouraged by the news of O'Neil's
defeat at Eccles' Hill, they abandoned their position on the 26th
and returned to their camp on the American side of the line.
While there they evidently received some encouragement and
reinforcements, as they returned to their entrenchments in
Canada early on the morning of Friday, the 27th of May, and
re-occupied their works, which they busily began to strengthen.
Their rifle pits were dug in front of some hop-fields, defended
by stockades, with a stout barricade across the road. The line
of entrenchments rested on the river on one side and a dense
wood on the other, while their centre was strongly protected
by a forest of hop-poles, through which their retreat, in case of
necessity, would be comparatively safe. The whole position was
chosen with considerable skill, and was so strong that 500 men
could easily have held off several thousands for a considerable
length of time, had they been properly directed.

The Canadian force chosen to operate against this column
of the enemy was composed of H. M. 69th Regiment, the 50th
Battalion (Huntingdon Borderers), and the Montreal Garrison Artillery, the whole under command of Col. Bagot. At 3
o'clock in the morning of the 27th, the Montreal Garrison
Artillery and the Huntingdon Borderers were ordered on the

march from Huntingdon Village, where they had arrived the previous night. In less than two hours the whole force was on the move along the road leading to Holbrook's Corners. At 8 o'clock the entire column had reached Hendersonville, which is two miles from Holbrook's, and there one company of the Montreal Garrison Artillery (under Capt. Rose) was ordered to proceed along the concession road to the west in order to flank the enemy, whose glittering bayonets were plainly visible in the sunlight as they were drilling in a field about a mile and a half distant.

The advance guard of the Fenians were posted behind a very strong entrenchment, with their right flank resting on the river and their left covered by the woods. Their skirmishers were about 150 in number, and their supports and reserves (amounting to about 300 or 400 more) were stationed a short distance in the rear.

The Huntingdon Borderers formed the Canadian advance guard, and as soon as they had approached within about 300 yards of the Fenian position, were deployed in skirmishing order, and advanced with great gallantry. The centre support was composed of one company of the 69th Regiment, under Capt. Mansfield and Lieut. Atcheson. The remainder of the 69th, under Major Smythe, was drawn up in quarter distance column as a reserve. One company of the Montreal Garrison Artillery (under Capt. Doucet) marched across the bridge and along the road on the left, and afterwards took part in the engagement with those who had been sent in the opposite direction further back, to prevent a flanking movement from either side. The remainder of the Artillery and Engineers, under Capt. Hall, marched to the front as a reserve, but afterwards returned to Holbrook Bridge, which it was feared the Fenians might attempt to capture, and advance along the south side of the river. The skirmish line advanced with great steadiness against the enemy behind the entrenchments. The Fenians fired three volleys as they advanced, the fire being promptly returned by our men as they gallantly moved forward. When the Canadians came within 100 yards of the entrenchments, the Fenians fell back through the hop-field, firing as they retreated, and when they got beyond its protection, ran for the buildings further back, where it was thought they would make a stand. Col. Bagot then ordered Capt. Mansfield's company of the 69th to fix bayonets and charge, which was done in grand style, amid loud cheering, and resulted in the complete rout of the Fenians. Capt. Hall's Battery of the Montreal Garrison Artillery, directed by Lieut. Fitzgeorge, cleared the wood on the left in a very thorough manner, and soon the whole Fenian army were in a helter-skelter race out of Canada and back to American territory. When the Canadian troops reached the boundary Col. Bagot had great difficulty in restraining them from crossing into the United States after the fugitives, so eager were they to effect the capture of the marauders. The Fenians were so swift in their retreat that only one was captured, but three men were killed and several wounded during the fight. No losses occurred among the Canadians.

The Fenians were utterly dispirited and completeely demoralized, and when their commanders (Gen. Starr and Gen. Gleason) were arrested at St. Albans by the United States authorities on the following day, they abandoned all further thoughts of invading Canada, and left for their homes thoroughly sick of their experience on their excursion to Trout River.

At Buffalo, Detroit, Ogdensburg, and other points where Fenians had gathered for the purpose of invading Canada, the news of the fizzles at Eccles' Hill and Trout River caused consternation and depression among their ranks, and the fact that Gen. O'Neil and several others of their military leaders were in jail on serious charges, served to put an end to all thoughts of continuing the movement, and they hastily dispersed and returned to their homes.

Gen. O'Neil was brought to trial some time after by the United States Government, on a charge of violation of the Neutrality Laws, and was sentenced to six months' imprisonment. This was a hard blow to the Fenian organization, and it gradually went to pieces.

But the warlike spirit had not died out in O'Neil, and he began to plan new ideas. His hatred of British institutions appears to have been so deep-seated that he was willing to sacrifice not only his liberty, but life itself, to undertake any scheme that had for its object their overthrow, and it was not long before he was again implicated in a plot against the Dominion of Canada.

Shortly after his release from prison in 1870, he entered into a conspiracy with emissaries of the rebel Louis Riel to assist in a great uprising in the Canadian Northwest, in which the Indians and half-breeds were to be utilized. O'Neil was ready for anything, and consented to invoke Fenian aid in conjunction with Riel's rebellious plans, by participating in an invasion of Manitoba. He managed to obtain a few hundred stands of breech-loading rifles and a quantity of ammunition that had escaped seizure by the United States authorities at the time of the Fenian Raid of 1870, and with the assistance of Gen. J. J. Donnelly, he fitted out an expedition on the Minnesota frontier. He started from Port Pembina, Minn., on October 5th, 1871, to invade Manitoba and raise his standard, but had barely crossed over the boundary line when he was arrested, with his troops. All of their armament was seized and they were marched back as prisoners to Pembina and handed over to the United States authorities. They were indicted on charges of breach of the Neutrality Laws, but at the trial were acquitted on some slight technicality.

This ended Gen. O'Neil's career as a fillibuster, and becoming disheartened and discouraged by his failures. he began drinking heavily, and soon became a wreck, subsequently dying alone and miserable as the result of his excesses. "unwept. unhonored and unsung."

CHAPTER VII

THE DAWN OF PEACE—THE VOLUNTEERS RELIEVED FROM
FURTHER SERVICE—THANKED BY THE GOVERNMENT AND
THE LIEUTENANT-GENERAL COMMANDING.

The active militia of the Dominion which was called out for
active service remained on duty wherever posted until all signs
of danger had disappeared, and were then withdrawn by degrees, until on the 3rd of June all were released from duty and
directed to return to their homes.

The Honorable Minister of Militia, in his report of the
military operations, paid the following tribute to the gallantry
of the volunteer militia force on this occasion:—

"Although the honor and satisfaction of repelling these
lawless invaders had fallen to the lot of a few gallant men of
the active militia, the desire evinced by the whole force called
out to be afforded a similar opportunity of inflicting well-merited
punishment on those daring to invade Canadian soil, was uni-
versally and ardently longed for; and, doubtless, had any
attempt been made in force by the enemy to penetrate into the
country, they would have met with heavier punishment than
they experienced in this futile attempt—all classes in the
Dominion (both French as well as English-speaking Canadians)
having turned out manfully in so good a cause; and when it is
considered that a great majority of the militia men called out
are farmers, that the call made upon them was in the midst of
their sowing season, that at the first sound of danger they gave
up their work, abandoning their fields and their families, risk-
ing, perhaps, the loss of a whole year's crop, and the manifest
distress which such would have entailed, it is not too much to
say that they have well-earned the gratitude and admiration of
their Queen and country for the self-sacrifice they exhibited,
and the courage and loyalty they displayed.

"As an interesting proof of the loyalty and patriotism displayed by Canadians who at this period (as in 1866) were resident in the United States. many of them came home at the first

note of alarm to take their places in the ranks of the active
militia force to assist in defence of their country, for which
they received the special thanks of the Government.''

The Lieutenant-General in command of Her Majesty's
troops in Canada, who was in supreme control of the active
militia force of Canada, also recognized their faithful service
by issuing the following order:—

HEADQUARTERS, MONTREAL, 4th June, 1870.

GENERAL ORDERS No. 1.

Canada has once more been invaded by a body of Fenians, who are
citizens of the United States, and who have again taken advantage of the
institutions of that country to move without disguise large numbers of men
and warlike stores to the Missisquoi and Huntingdon frontiers, for the
purpose of levying war upon a peaceful community.

From both these points the invading forces have been instantly driven
with loss and in confusion, throwing away their arms, ammunition and
clothing, and seeking shelter within the United States. Acting with a
scrupulous regard for the inviolability of a neighboring territory, the troops
were ordered to the halt, even though in pursuit, upon the border.

The result of the whole affair is mainly due to the promptitude with
which the militia responded to the call to arms, and to the rapidity with
which their movements to the front were carried out, and the self-reliance
and steadiness shown by this force, as well as by the armed inhabitants on
the frontier. The regular troops were kept in support, except on the Huntingdon frontier, where one company took part in the skirmish.

The proclamation of the President, and the arrival of the Federal
troops at St. Albans and Malone, were too late to prevent the collection
and transport of warlike stores, or an inroad into Canada.

The reproach of invaded British territory, and the dread of insult
and robbery, have thus been removed by a handful of Canadians, and the
Lieutenant-General does not doubt that such services will receive the recognition of the Imperial Government.

The Lieutenant-General congratulates the militia upon this exhibition
of their promptness, discipline and training, and in dismissing the men
to their homes, he bids them carry with them the assurance that their
manly spirit is a guarantee for the defence of Canada.

By order,

J. E. THACKWELL, D.A.G.

In consideration of their services at Eccles' Hill and on the
Huntingdon frontier, Her Majesty the Queen was graciously
pleased to bestow the Order of St. Michael and St. George
(third class) upon the following officers: Lieut.-Col. Osborne
Smith, Commandant Military District No. 5; Lieut.-Col.
Fletcher, Brigade Major, Second Brigade, Military District No.

5; Lieut.-Col. Brown Chamberlin, commanding 60th (Missisquoi) Battalion. and Lieut.-Col. McEachern, commanding the 50th (Huntingdon) Battalion.

MEDALS GRANTED BY THE QUEEN.

In 1899 the services of the survivors of the Fenian Raids of 1866 and 1870, and the Red River Rebellion, were recognized by Her Majesty Queen Victoria in the bestowal upon each of them of a General Service Medal, for the loyalty and patriotism they displayed in assisting to defend their country and flag in those times of danger. The medals are of the standard pattern adopted by the British Government for military service. Each medal bears the name and rank of the recipient stamped upon the edge. A clasp bearing the words "Fenian Raid, 1866" (crossing a scarlet and white ribbon) surmounts the medalion bearing the vignette of Queen Victoria on one side, and on the obverse a design emblematic of the Dominion of Canada. For those who served in 1870 the same medal was granted, with lettering to correspond, while to the volunteers who were on duty on both occasions, an extra clasp was issued, to denote service in both 1866 and 1870. These medals are highly prized by the veterans of the Fenian Raids, as they are commemorative of a time in the history of Canada which they will never forget.

It is possible that a large proportion of the recipients of the medals are not aware of how and where the idea originated which finally resulted in their obtaining these special marks of the Queen's favor. Therefore it may be as well to present the facts here. On the occasion of the celebration of the Queen's Jubilee in 1897, a large committee of loyal citizens of Toronto was organized for the purpose of arranging for a proper observance of the event, and among the members of that committee were quite a number of military men. At one of the meetings, held in the City Hall, Toronto, the following resolution was presented and unanimously adopted:—

"Moved by Capt. S. Bruce Harman, seconded by Lieut. R. E. Kingsford, That the following Committee be appointed to report the necessary steps to obtain a Medal, or other suitable Decoration, to be awarded to the Canadian Militia who took part in the campaigns of 1837, 1866 and 1870, viz.: Lieut.-Col. G. D. Dawson, Lieut.-Col. Vance Graveley, Lieut.-Col.

Orlando Dunn, Major Frederick E. Dixon, Major R. Y. Ellis, Major Frederick Manley, Capt. S. Bruce Harman, Capt. Wm. Fahey and Lieut. R. E. Kingsford.''

This committee went earnestly to work, and after deciding on the mode of procedure, issued a large number of blank petitions, which were sent out through the country. It is needless to say that these were very numerously signed and returned to the committee, who forwarded their petition in a handsomely bound volume to Her Majesty Queen Victoria through the proper channels. The Dominion Government acquiesced in the request. and the result was that the petition was granted, and the issue of the medals authorized, the veterans of the Red River Rebellion also being honored with the decoration.

GRANTS OF CROWN LANDS FROM THE PROVINCE OF ONTARIO.

The Province of Ontario also generously recognized the service of those who defended the Provincial domain by giving a grant of 160 acres of Crown lands to each of the veterans of the Fenian Raids who were on active service in Ontario during those periods.

RECOGNITION BY THE DOMINION OF CANADA.

Up to the present date the Dominion Government has not moved in the matter of recognizing the services of the Veterans of the Fenian Raids. Deputations have waited upon the Premier and the Government. and petitions have been presented asking for grants of land, but beyond specious promises of ''consideration of their requests'' no progress has been made in this respect. This is hardly fair or just to the men who stood on the ramparts of the country with their rifles in hand in times of peril and danger, and made it possible that the Dominion Government should now have any land to bestow. Had it not been for the patriotism of the ''Men of '66'' it is just a question whether the Dominion of Canada as now constituted would be in existence to-day. Therefore these surviving veterans deserve all the recognition that a grateful country can give. We have millions of acres of vacant lands in our Northwest which need development, and who is better fitted for settlers than the resourceful Canadians themselves? We have sons and grandsons who have the will. the knowledge, the mettle and the courage to break the prairie sod and bring the virgin soil to successful fruition, and assist in developing our country's resources. They will be glad to do this, and take particular pride in the patrimony of their military ancestors. Then why not do justice to the Veterans of 1866 and 1870 by putting them on the same footing as the Dominion Government accorded to the soldiers of other campaigns? The volunteers who went to Manitoba on the Red River expedition in 1870 received land grants of 160 acres each. Those who served in the Northwest Rebellion in 1885 were given scrip to the same value, while those who went out of Canada to serve in the South African War were granted 320 acres of Crown lands each. That was quite proper, but why should our paternal Government make any invidious distinctions? Surely those who helped to make the Dominion, and bravely guarded her shores in times of danger, are at least entitled to justice in the matter of receiving due recognition for their services. Emigrants have been assisted into Canada from all parts of Europe and given slices of our public domain, while the bone and sinew of our own people have been "passed by on the other side." This is not right—it is not patriotic, neither is it good public policy. Let justice prevail in all things, and our country will prosper and flourish. One by one the old Veterans of 1866 and 1870 are being finally "mustered out," and in a few years the last of them will have "crossed the bar." While they are still living the Government should bestow upon them that tardy recognition which they have a right to expect, and it is to be hoped that in its wisdom and sense of justice this act will not be long delayed. Let it never be said of Canada that

> When war clouds break, and danger is nigh.
> "God and the soldiers" is the people's cry.
> But when war is o'er and all things righted.
> God is forgot and the soldiers slighted.

Not a single volunteer ever thought for one moment of a monetary or other reward for his services when he shouldered his rifle and went forth in defence of his country when the bugles sounded. All were moved by a common patriotic impulse, and unselfishly and faithfully did their duty. At that time the Government appreciated their service, and was profuse in thanks, and there the national gratitude seems to have ended so far as the Fenian Raid Veterans are concerned. But, perhaps, they may yet be accorded fair play. Let us hope so, for the honor of our country.

CHAPTER VIII.

The Red River Rebellion—Brutal Murder of Thomas Scott —Organization of a Military Expedition to Quell Riel's Revolt.

Almost at the same moment that we had Fenian troubles at home, and threatened invasions of our Quebec and Ontario frontiers, the standard of revolt had been raised in Manitoba by the turbulent rebel Louis Riel and his band of half-breeds.

Arrangements had been completed between the Dominion Government and the Imperial Government with the Hudson's Bay Company, whereby the rights of the latter to lands in the Northwest Territories were to be transferred to the Dominion, subject to certain reservations. It was made an express agreement that the rights of the Indians and half-breeds in certain territory were to be respected by the Dominion Government. The arrangement was sanctioned by Parliament, and the sum of £300,000 sterling was appropriated for the purchase of the Hudson's Bay Company's titles as specified. In the preceding year Lieut.-Colonel Dennis (of Fort Erie fame) was sent to the Red River country by the Dominion Government to institute a system of public surveys. When he appeared among the half-breeds, and they learned his intention, they strenuously objected, as they believed by the inauguration of a new system of survey their titles to the lands which they held might be jeopardized. Moreover, they thought that they should have been consulted when the purchase and transfer of the territory was made. The French half-breeds were especially fearful that the Dominion Government might dispute their titles to the lands, and gave Colonel Dennis to understand that trouble might result if he attempted to carry out his plans of survey. In the meantime Hon. Wm. Macdougall had been appointed Lieutenant-Governor of the Northwest Territory, and started west for the purpose of assuming office. He had been warned by Col. Dennis of the unfriendly feeling which prevailed among the half-breeds in respect to himself and the Dominion Government, and on arriving at Pembina (Minnesota), he was more forcibly notified of

the disaffection which existed when he was forbidden by them
to cross the border into the territory. He was determined to
go ahead, however, and advanced about two miles over the line
with his party, when he received news from Col. Dennis that
rebellion was rife, and that the insurgents, under the leadership
of Louis Riel, were determined to prevent his further progress.
Riel had posted armed guards at various points along the trails
leading from Pembina to Fort Garry for the purpose of resisting
the advance of Lieutenant-Governor Macdougall, and as there
was not a sufficient force available to overcome the rebels, he was
obliged to remain where he was. Then Riel became emboldened,
and seized Fort Garry, where he set up a "Provisional Government," and organized a force to hold the territory. During the
fall and winter of 1869 and 1870 he held high revels at Fort
Garry, and amused himself by arresting and imprisoning all
loyal Canadians he could lay hands on. Several prominent citizens were confined in the fort by Riel's order and subjected to
insults and indignities, while their wordly possessions were pillaged and destroyed. Among those who especially fell under
Riel's displeasure was a loyal Canadian named Thomas Scott.
He was a bold and fearless young man, and his sturdy patriotism
to his country and his determined manner of expressing his
views, angered Riel, who ordered him under arrest. He was
taken to Fort Garry and confined in a cell, but made his escape.
He was soon recaptured, and Riel at once convened a court-
martial and sentenced Scott to be shot at 10 o'clock the next
morning. The unfortunate prisoner was not allowed to make any
defence. Riel's word was law, and to gratify his angry passions
he ordered the execution to take place the following morning.
Therefore on the 4th of March, 1870, poor Scott was led outside
of the walls of the fort by a party of six rebels under command
of Ambrose Lepine and brutally murdered. When the news of
this inhuman butchery reached Ontario the people of the Province were filled with feelings of intense indignation, and the
public and press demanded the Government to take immediate
action in organizing a force to stamp out the rebellion and effect
the arrest and punishment of the perpetrators of the crime.

The Government promptly heeded the appeals of the people,
and on the 16th of April, 1870, an Order-in-Council was passed

by the Cabinet authorizing the organization of a military contingent for service in the new Province of Manitoba, the principal object being to quell the Riel Rebellion, arrest the leaders, and establish law and order in that territory. In accordance with this resolution two battalions of riflemen were organized, which were designated as the First (Ontario) Battalion, and the Second (Quebec) Battalion of Rifles. Each battalion consisted of seven companies, with an establishment of three officers and 50 non-commissioned officers and men to each company. The staff of each battalion consisted of one Lieutenant-Colonel, one Major, one Adjutant (with rank of Captain), one Paymaster, one Surgeon, one Quartermaster-sergeant, one Hospital Sergeant, one Sergeant-Major, one Armorer-Sergeant, and one Paymaster's Clerk, making the total strength of each battalion 375 of all ranks. These battalions were composed of volunteers from existing corps of the Active Militia in the seven Military Districts of the Provinces of Ontario and Quebec, and the terms of enlistment were for one year, or longer if their services were required. The enrolling of the men to form these organizations commenced on the 1st of May, and the ranks were quickly filled. The various companies were concentrated at Toronto, where they were clothed and equipped, and placed under the orders of Colonel Fielden, of Her Majesty's 60th Royal Rifles. All of the field and line officers were duly appointed, gazetted, and joined their respective corps in due time, and in a few weeks the expeditionary force was in excellent condition for active service.

The following is a roster of the officers who were on active service, in command of the volunteer corps named, on the Red River Expedition:—

FIRST (ONTARIO) RIFLES.

Lieut.-Col. Samuel P. Jarvis, commanding officer; Major Griffiths Wainwright.

Captains—Thomas Scott, Thomas Macklem, William M. Herchmer, William Smith, Alex. R. Macdonald, Daniel H. McMillan and Henry Cook.

Lieutenants—Donald A. Macdonald, David M. Walker, William N. Kennedy, Andrew McBride, William J. McMurty, Samuel B. Harman and James Benson.

Ensigns—A. J. Z. Peebles, Stewart Mulvey. Josiah J. Bell, Samuel Hamilton, John Biggar, William H. Nash and Hugh John Macdonald.

Paymaster—Capt. J. F. B. Morrice.
Adjutant—Capt. Wm. J. B. Parsons.
Quartermaster—Edward Armstrong.
Surgeon—Alfred Codd, M.D.

SECOND (QUEBEC) RIFLES.

Lieut.-Col. Louis Adolphe Casault, commanding officer; Major Acheson G. Irvine.

Captains—Z. C. A. L. de Bellefeuille, Allan Macdonald, Jacques Labranche, Samuel Macdonald, Jean Baptiste Amyot, John Fraser, Wm. J. Barrett.

Lieutenants—J. W. Vaughan, John P. Fletcher, Edward T. H. F. Patterson, Oscar Prevost, Maurice E. B. Duchesnay, Henri Bouthillier, Leonidas de Salaberry.

Ensigns—Ed. S. Bernard, John Allan, George Simard, Gabriel L. Des Georges, Alphonse de M. H. D'Eschambault, William W. Ross, Alphonse Tetu.

Paymaster—Lieut. Thos. Howard.
Adjutant—Capt. F. D. Gagnier.
Quartermaster—F. Villiers.

The following officers were appointed to positions on the Brigade Staff in connection with the expedition:—

Assistant Brigade Major—Major James F. McLeod.
Assistant Control Officer—Capt. A. Peebles.
Orderly Officer on Staff of Commanding Officer—Lieut. Frederick C. Denison.

The total strength of the expeditionary force amounted to about 1,200, which was composed of about 350 officers and men of H. M. 60th Royal Rifles, detachments of Royal Artillery and Engineers, the First and Second Rifles above mentioned, and a contingent of Canadian voyageurs.

The whole expedition was in command of that gallant soldier Colonel Garnet S. Wolseley (who afterwards won honor and fame in foreign campaigns, and became a Field Marshal of the British Army). The troops left Toronto in May on their long trip to Fort Garry, going by steamboat to Prince Arthur's Landing (now Port Arthur), from which point they took the old "Dawson route" to their destination. It was a most difficult undertaking, but the undaunted courage of the officers and men and their determination to overcome all obstacles triumphed, as they forced their way through rivers, lakes, swamps, muskegs and forest until they reached the prairie land of Manitoba. They were about three months on the way, arriving at Fort Garry on the 24th of August. During this time it became necessary for the men to cut trails through brake and bramble, construct corduroy roads, build boats, ascend dangerous rapids, portage stores and supplies over almost insurmountable places, meanwhile fighting mosquitoes and black flies, and encountering countless dangers, all of which they cheerfully performed with their characteristic bravery until the whole expedition was successfully landed on Manitoba soil without serious mishap.

Their approach to Fort Garry was made so quietly and quickly that Riel and his followers had barely time to get out of the fort and scatter in all directions before the troops arrived, and therefore they did not have an opportunity of using force to quell the rebellion. Unfortunately Riel and his lieutenants succeeded in making their escape. Fort Garry was at once occupied by the column and the Union Jack hoisted on the flag-staff, amid ringing cheers for the Queen, while the artillery fired a royal salute.

The arrival of Col. Wolseley's troops was hailed with delight by the loyal residents of what is now the flourishing city of Winnipeg, as they had suffered severe persecutions by the rebels during the period that Riel and his lieutenant Ambrose Lepine held sway in their career of rebellion. Lawful authority was quickly established, and all fragments of the revolt being stamped out by Col. Wolseley, the loyal citizens took up the work of temporary organization of the necessary civil institutions for the proper government of the Province, pending the arrival of Hon. Mr. Archibald, who had been appointed Lieutenant-Governor of the new domain. In this work Mr. Donald A. Smith (now Lord Strathcona) proved a tower of strength, and with the assistance of Dr. John Schultz and other loyal residents of the Province, matters were soon shaped into a state of peace, progress and prosperity.

Lieutenant-Governor Archibald arrived at Fort Garry on Sept. 2nd, and a few days later assumed the duties of his office. When it became absolutely certain that all of the embers of the rebellion had been extinguished, Colonel Wolseley returned to the east with the regular troops, leaving the Canadian volunteers still on duty in Manitoba. They remained at Fort Garry until the following spring, when their services being no longer required they were ordered home for "muster out."

That the Canadian volunteers and voyageurs acquitted themselves creditably on the occasion of the Red River Rebellion is a matter of history, and that their services were highly appreciated by Colonel Wolseley is evidenced by the fact that when he was put in command of the British troops operating in the Egyptian campaign, and desired a method of transporting his troops and stores up the River Nile, he remembered his Red River experience, and promptly asked for a contingent of Canadian voyageurs to handle his system of transport by the great water route, and got them. That they did their duty in the Land of the Pharoahs as thoroughly as they did on previous occasions at home, will always stand to their credit in the annals of the British Army.

Appendix.

APPENDIX

CHAPTER I.

THE BOOKER INVESTIGATION—RESULT OF THE FINDING OF THE
COURT OF INQUIRY REGARDING THE CAUSE OF THE RETREAT
AT RIDGEWAY.

The following is a report of the proceedings of the Court
of Inquiry held at Hamilton on Tuesday, July 3rd, 1866, by
order of His Excellency the Commander-in-Chief, on the application of Lieut.-Col. Booker, to examine and report on the circumstances connected with the engagement at Lime Ridge (or
Ridgeway) on June 2nd:

The following officers composed the Court: President, Col.
George T. Denison, Commandant Volunteer Militia, Toronto;
members—Lieut.-Col. James Shanly, London; Lieut.-Col. G. K.
Chisholm, Commanding Oakville Rifle Company, Oakville.

The letter of instructions from Col. P. L. Macdougall, the
Adjutant-General of Militia, for the guidance of the Court,
addressed to Col. Denison (the President), and also the letter
from Lieut.-Col. Durie, by the authority of the Adjutant-General. on the same subject (also addressed to the President) were
both read and duly considered by the Court previous to their
entering upon the subject of inquiry.

Lieut.-Col. Booker having previously received due notice
of the sitting of the Court and of the object of the inquiry,
was permitted to be present, and he desired liberty of the Court
to put in a written narrative of events as they occurred from
the time he left Hamilton until he returned from Lime Ridge
to Port Colborne.

The orders for the assembling of the Court were then produced and read, as follows:—

GOVERNMENT ORDERS.

On application of Lieut.-Col. Booker, the Commander-in-Chief directs
the assembly of a Court of Inquiry at Hamilton, on Tuesday, the 3rd of

July, 1866, to examine witnesses and report on the circumstances connected
with the late engagement at Lime Ridge. President, Col. G. T. Denison;
members, Lieut.-Col. James Shanly, and Lieut.-Col. G. K. Chisholm.
                      (Signed) P. L. MACDOUGALL,
                              Colonel, A.G.M.
                          WM. L. DURIE,
                              Lieut.-Col., A.A.G.M.
          OTTAWA, 24th June, 1866.
[A true copy].

                                          TORONTO, 2nd July, 1866.
     Sir,—In reply to your inquiries on Saturday last, I am directed to
inform you that "the Court of Inquiry is to be closed," and that Col.
Booker can produce any evidence he thinks proper. If the Court requires
further evidence it may produce witnesses.
     I beg to remain,
               Yours truly,
                              WM. L. DURIE,
                                  Lieut.-Col., D.A.G.M.
          COL. DENISON, President Court of Inquiry.

                                          OTTAWA, June 23rd, 1866.
     Sir,—I have the honor to instruct you that the Court of Inquiry of
which you are named President, is ordered on the application of Lieut.-
Col. Booker, in order to give that officer the opportunity of disproving the
unfavorable imputations which have been cast upon him in the public
prints. You will therefore be pleased to take all evidence which may be
produced before the Court by Lieut.-Col. Booker, and you will also endeavor
to procure all other evidence which may tend to elucidate the truth.
     The opinion of the Court of Inquiry must, of course, be based on and
sustained by such evidence only as is embodied in the written proceedings.
     I have the honor to be, sir,
          Your very obedient servant,
                              P. L. MACDOUGALL,
                                  Colonel, A.G.M.
          COL. G. T. DENISON, President Court of Inquiry, Toronto.

     The Court then considered the application of Lieut.-Col.
Booker to put in his narrative, and after due deliberation came
to the conclusion that they should comply with his request, and
accordingly gave him permission to put in his written statement.

     Lieut.-Col. Booker then read and afterwards handed in to
the Court the following statement of his connection with the
operations of the troops under his command in the engagement
at Lime Ridge:

                              NARRATIVE.

     On the morning of the 1st of June, 1866, at the hour of
5.30, I received the following telegraphic message from Lieut.-
Col. Durie, A.A.G.M.:

TORONTO, June 1st, 1866.

To Lieut.-Col. Booker, Commandant:

Call out your regiment for active service at once, and proceed by special train to Dunnville *via* Paris immediately. Complete your men to sixty rounds per man. Take spare ammunition with you. Ascertain enemy's position as you progress, who are reported to have landed at Fort Erie. In proceeding to Dunnville stop at Caledonia Station and take command of two volunteer companies (Caledonia and York) in readiness there. Better take cars with you for their transport.

If Port Colborne is occupied by the enemy, secure yourself at Dunnville and report to me.

By Order,

(Signed) WM. L. DURIE,

Lieut.-Col., A.A.G.M.

And I proceeded to warn the Thirteenth Battalion, under my command, for immediate active service. The members mustered rapidly at the rendezvous, but as many came without overcoats or breakfasts, I caused them to return home for breakfast and report again within the hour, instructing them to bring their overcoats, and those who had them, their haversacks with food. I cautioned them that I could not tell when nor where they would have the next opportunity for a meal.

At about 7 a.m. the Commandant (Col. Peacocke) informed me that he also was under orders to leave. Shortly afterwards the manager of the Great Western Railway notified me that the cars were ready for transport.

The 13th Battalion, say 265 of all ranks, embarked at 9.30 a.m., and proceeded by way of Paris to Dunnville, taking up the York and Caledonia Companies (Captains Davis and Jackson), who reported 95 of all ranks.

On arrival at Dunnville, where we expected to remain during the night, we were met by the Reeve of the town, who provided the men with billets, and I reported our arrival to

Col. Peacocke by telegraph. We were at dinner when I received the following telegram:

By Telegraph from Clifton, June 1st.

To Commander Hamilton Volunteers, Dunnville:

Go on to Port Colborne at once.

(Signed) G. Peacocke.

A few minutes sufficed to see all on the cars (which had been retained at Dunnville for orders) *en route* for our destination, which we reached at about 11 o'clock p.m. We found the Queen's Own of Toronto had preceded us during the afternoon (say 480 of all ranks). The Queen's Own had secured all the billets, and the command with me endeavored to settle themselves as best they could in the cars for the night.

During the night, at my request, Major Skinner endeavored to secure a bread ration for the men. Some biscuits and bread were obtained, and that officer reported to me that the baker would prepare a batch of bread to be ready at 3 a.m. of the 2nd June.

I may now mention that, being the senior officer present, the entire command of the force at Port Colborne devolved on me. About midnight I received the following despatch by telegraph:

By Telegraph from Chippawa, 2nd June. 1866.

To Officer Commanding at Port Colborne:

I have sent Captain Akers to communicate with you. He will be with you at about half-past one. Send back the Great Western cars, if, after seeing Captain Akers, you think they are not wanted. If you get the ferry boat, send a detachment to patrol the river.

(Signed) G. Peacocke, Colonel.

Capt. Akers arrived punctually. On his arrival it appeared that Lieut.-Col. Dennis and myself were in possession of later and more reliable information of the position of the enemy than Colonel Peacocke seemed to have had when Captain Akers had left him at midnight. It then seemed necessary to inquire whether the original plan for a junction at Stevensville, to attack the enemy, supposed to be encamped near Black Creek.

should be adhered to, when it appeared they were encamped much higher up the river, and nearer to Fort Erie.

It was therefore proposed that the tug boat "W. T. Robb," whose Captain had expressed a desire to be of service, should patrol the shore of the lake as far as Fort Erie, and endeavor to communicate with Col. Peacocke's command. It was at the same time suggested that I should take my command down by rail to the railroad buildings at Fort Erie, and occupy and hold them until 7 a.m. If not communicated with before 7 a.m., to proceed to Frenchman's Creek, on the north side of which, it had been reported to me by an officer of Her Majesty's Customs at Fort Erie, that the Fenians were encamped not more than 450 strong; that they had during the day stolen 45 or 50 horses, and were drinking freely.

It was also suggested that in the event of my not being communicated with before 7 a.m. (and then being at Fort Erie), I should proceed to Frenchman's Creek and attack the enemy, if still there. This command, however, was to depend upon the approval of Colonel Peacocke.

In the meantime, and before I had received the telegram (No. 4) Lieut.-Col. Dennis and Captain Akers had left in the tug (in company with the Welland Field Battery, armed with short Enfields, under the command of Captain King) for Fort Erie, Captain Akers, at the last moment, leaving the final arrangement with me, which I took down as follows:

"*Memo.*—Move at not later than 5.30; 5 o'clock if bread be ready. Move to depot at Fort Erie and wait till 7. If not communicated with before 7, move to Frenchman's Creek. If 'No' by telegraph, disembark at Ridgeway and move to Stevensville at 9 to 9.30 a.m. Send pilot engine to communicate with Lieut.-Col. Dennis at Erie and with telegrams."

Soon after their departure I received Col. Peacocke's telegraph. as follows:

BY TELEGRAPH FROM CHIPPAWA, June 2nd, 3.50 a.m.
To Commanding Officer, Port Colborne:

Have received your message of 3 a.m. I do not approve of it. Follow original plan. Acknowledge receipt of this.

(Signed) G. PEACOCKE.

This negatived our proposed change of plan, and left me to follow the instructions which I had received from Colonel Peacocke through Captain Akers, namely:

"Move at not later than 5.30; 5 o'clock if bread be ready. * * * Disembark at Ridgeway and march to Stevensville at 9 to 9.30 a.m."

The bread ration having been secured, the train left Port Colborne soon after 5 a.m. *en route* for Stevensville. The only horse on the cars belonged to Major Skinner, 13th Battalion, who had kindly offered him for my service. I expressed a desire that the field officers of the Queen's Own would take their horses, but was met by the reply that they would be of no use in the woods where we should likely be, and that it was thought best not to take them.

I sent a pilot engine in advance of the train some ten or fifteen minutes, and instructed its driver, if possible, to communicate with Fort Erie. The train with the volunteers proceeded very slowly and cautiously, and arrived at Ridgeway without a sign of obstruction, after more than an hour from its departure from Port Colborne. At Ridgeway we formed battalions in column of companies, right in front.

Means of conveyance for my stores not being at hand, I thought best to distribute as much spare ammunition amongst the men as possible, and requested those who could do so to carry an extra ten rounds in their pockets. At this time it was reported to me that the Caledonia Rifle Company had no percussion caps, and but few rounds of cartridge. I supplied them from the spare ammunition of the 13th Battalion. I endeavored to procure a horse or team for my medical officers' stores, but without success, and failing means of transport, I returned tents and blankets to Port Colborne, relieving the cars from further waiting at Ridgeway.

After a little delay I requested Major Gillmor (as the Queen's Own was the senior battalion) to take the lead of the column, and as one of his companies was armed with the Spencer repeating rifle, that it should form the advance guard.

When the battalions were proved, and before forming the advance guard, I gave the order to the column, "With ball cartridge—load.'' I made inquiries from the inhabitants as to their knowledge of the whereabouts of the enemy. The reports were contradictory and evidently unreliable. To take proper precaution and keep my appointment at Stevensville was my obvious duty.

The column of route was formed as follows: Advance guard of Queen's Own; remainder of the battalion, Major Gillmor commanding; York Rifles, Captain Davis; the 13th Battalion, Major Skinner in command; the Caledonia Rifles (Captain Jackson), forming the rear guard. On the advance I was in the centre of the column, looking out for signs of the enemy. After proceeding about two miles the advance guard signalled indications of men moving in our front. The column (say 840 of all ranks) was hereupon halted on the road. I gave the horse on which I rode to the Orderly, in order that I might carefully examine with my field glass the country over which we were advancing. Soon after I observed loose horses moving about in the woods to our left front, but saw no men.

Before ordering the advance, flanking parties were thrown out to scour the woods, right and left. This duty was performed by companies of the Queen's Own. Proceeding in this order for some distance, a volley was fired upon our advancing men from behind the zig-zag fences in the open. Our volunteers accepted the challenge. The affair had commenced.

The Queen's Own, as skirmishers and supports, slowly advanced, pushing back the enemy. We were gradually changing our front to the right, when Major Gillmor wished me to relieve the Queen's Own and send out the reserves, as his men were falling short of ammunition, and that one company (No. 5) had none for their Spencer rifles. I at once directed the right wing of the reserve to deploy on the rear company to the right and to extend. Major Skinner commanded the 13th Battalion, and acted throughout out very gallantly. The movement was admirably executed. The York Rifles were on the left and No. 1 Company of the 13th Battalion on the right of the line. A hearty cheer was given by the Queen's Own when they saw the 13th advancing, who, with the company named, relieved the Queen's Own, supported by the left wing of the reserve, which was composed of the 13th Battalion. The Queen's Own then became the reserve. The 13th and York Rifles in advance, driving the enemy before them to the woods, cheered heartily and were answered by the yells of the Fenians. I felt anxious about our right flank, as with my glass I noticed the enemy throwing back his right into the woods. I requested Major Gillmor, who was in command of the reserve, to keep a sharp look-out for the cross roads on which the reserve rested, and to send two companies from the reserve to occupy and hold the woods on the hill to our right. He sent the Highland Company of the Queen's Own to perform that duty.

At this time (nearly 9.30 a.m.) two telegrams were brought to me by a gentleman from Port Colborne, one informing me that the column under Col. Peacocke could not move until 7 o'clock, and the other in the following words:

CHIPPAWA, June 2, 5.30 a.m.

To the Officer Commanding, Port Colborne:

Be cautious in feeling your way, for fear obstacles should prevent a junction. If possible open communication with me, and I will do the same.

(Signed) G. PEACOCKE.

At this unexpected information I was much disappointed. Major Gillmor was then with me, and I showed it to him. I at once realized that the force which I had expected about this hour at Stevensville could not now render me assistance, and turning to Detective Armstrong (who had accompanied us from Hamilton and obtained a horse at Ridgeway), I desired him to convey to Col. Peacocke a message I wrote on the telegram I had just received, to the effect that the enemy had attacked us in force at 7.30, three miles south of Stevensville.

Immediately afterwards Major Gillmor reported that the Highland Company had been compelled to leave the woods on our right, as they had found the woods occupied by Fenians. Almost simultaneously cries of "Cavalry" and "Look out for cavalry" came down the road. I then observed men doubling down the hill . In the next few moments events succeeded each other very rapidly. As the cry came down the road, directions were given the reserves on the road to "Form square." At this crisis the fire of the enemy came heavily to our right flank, as well as into the front and rear of our force in advance. I saw nothing to justify the first impression that we were to be attacked by cavalry. I gave the word to "Re-form column," with the view of deploying, when to my surprise I found the rear of the reserve which had formed part of the square had dissipated, and moving down the road. Major Gillmor came and reported to me that the enemy was bringing up his reserves. I asked him how he knew. He replied that he saw them himself. I then inquired, "In what shape?" when he replied, "In column—in mass of column." I then ordered to retire. But the confusion had become a panic. The Thirteenth did all that men could do under the circumstances, and were the last in the retreat. which became general.

Many men were trodden down. I endeavored to rally the retreating mass. and gave orders to hold the woods on either side, and some little distance down the road was assisted by Surgeon Ryall (of the Thirteenth) and several men. but all of no avail. Bugler Clarke (of the Queen's Own) sounded "the halt" at my request several times. The horse was brought to me and I mounted and rode amongst the men. I entreated them to rally. and implored them to halt, but without effect. If I could form at Ridgeway I might regain order. I there found Lieutenant Arthurs, of the Queen's Own, and other officers, attempting to rally and form companies. I called for "coverers" for the men to form. I was answered that the men could not find their officers. I then ordered the men to fall in. so as to show a good front. The attempt was made. but without success, and I ordered the retreat upon Port Colborne. towards which place many had previously turned their steps. I requested a gentleman from Toronto (Mr. George Arthurs). who was present at Ridgeway. and mounted, to ride forward to Port Colborne and report that we were retiring. and to send help down the road for the stragglers. I saw that the colors of the Thirteenth were safe, and I moved off with the column. A short distance from Ridgeway I dismounted and walked with a member of the Queen's Own who was wounded, and kept the road afterwards for some time with him. A volunteer rode the horse into Port Colborne, where we arrived, much fatigued and distressed, at about 3 p.m. Nearly two miles from Port Colborne I was, with others, taken up by the second train which came down the road to meet us. The train took up several officers of the 13th and the Queen's Own.

At Port Colborne, through the kindness of Mr. Pring, the Collector of Customs, I was provided with the requisites for writing my despatches to the Major-General Commanding and to Colonel Peacocke. The drafts were perused by Major Gillmor; and one despatch was copied by Major Cattley of the Thirteenth and the other by a non-commissioned officer of the Queen's Own.

Shortly after returning to Port Colborne I received advice of ten companies of volunteers from Paris. Others arrived during the evening. Among the latter were the Home Guard of St. Catharines, under Lieut.-Col. McGiverin. I beg leave especially to thank that officer for the assistance he afforded, and for very generously dividing with my command the provisions he had brought from St. Catharines with him for his own men.

Prisoners were being brought in in numbers, and every question was referred to me personally. I had no Major of Brigade, no aide, no staff, not even an office clerk of whose services I could at the moment avail myself, while farmers as scouts were coming in with their varied reports. I felt it due to the large force of volunteers under my command to request the Major-General Commanding to relieve me and send a professional soldier (one from whom I might take my orders) to assume the command.

When at Port Colborne I reported that the Thirteenth and Queen's Own were alike tired and hungry, and that if it were possible they should have a day's rest, and that those volunteers who had arrived during the day of the 2nd of June at Port Colborne should be sent forward first.

I pointed out that uncooked rations, which it was intended to serve out to the Queen's Own and the Thirteenth, would not benefit them, as they were without the necessary appliances to cook and make use of them. But it was not by my wish that the Thirteenth were detained at Port Colborne on the morning of the 3rd June, while the Queen's Own were ordered to march on to Fort Erie. I was anxious that both should be thoroughly refreshed, and I felt regret that the companions of the day previous should be separated, as they were equally able to proceed.

Then, either from misunderstanding, or perhaps that I was not sufficiently explicit, I found that I had been relieved from the command of my own battalion, and not of the general command only, as I had expected. I immediately communicated with Majors Skinner and Cattley that I had been relieved.

The history of my connection with the campaign, which resulted in the expulsion of the Fenians from the Niagara District, has now been detailed, from the moment I received orders until I was relieved from command. I submit to those to whom the inquiry of my conduct on the occasion may be entrusted, that the state of affairs which existed at Port Colborne on my arrival at 11 o'clock p.m. on Friday, 1st of June, will be better understood if the communications which previously passed between Colonel Peacocke and the officer commanding at Port Colborne were obtained. I have reason to believe that they will bear materially in explaining the plans proposed and under consideration before Captain Akers' arrival, and the propriety of the modification which, if Colonel Peacocke's approval were obtained, was to have been pursued.

I further submit the official despatches connected with the affair at Lime Ridge, published by authority in the *Canada Gazette* of Saturday, 23rd June, 1866. Upon two points I expect inquiry will be directed, namely, to the capacity and care shown by me for the command entrusted to me, and my personal conduct on the field. On this latter point I ask for the evidence of those who are present.

That every precaution and every consideration for the comfort and advantage of my battalion which the circumstances did permit, I confidently assert were taken.

The volunteer force from Hamilton answered to the call for service with alacrity. The entire force which I had the honor to command was animated with the highest feelings of patriotism and zeal. All personal considerations gave way, all hardships were borne cheerfully and without a murmur. We had but one wish—to meet the enemy; and but one hope, to aid in his discomfiture; and if under the trying circumstances in which we were placed the result was not so triumphant as the devotion and heroism of the volunteers deserved, I trust that as their conduct cannot be impugned, the Court of Inquiry will, on appreciation of the facts, exonerate their commanding officer from the complete want of success of an attack which undoubtedly caused the enemy to abandon their plans of invasion and commence their retreat.

A. BOOKER,
Lieut.-Colonel.

The Court then proceeded to the examination of witnesses.

The first witness called by Lieut.-Col. Booker was Major Chas. T. Gillmor, commanding the Second Battalion, or Queen's Own Rifles.

MAJOR GILLMOR'S EVIDENCE.

Question from Lieut.-Col. Booker—When I relieved the Queen's Own and advanced the Thirteenth, did you report to me that your men were becoming short of ammunition?

Major Gillmor—On some one occasion I mentioned that one or two companies stated to me that they were short of ammunition.

Question from Lieut.-Col. Booker—When the Thirteenth were in action, did you send out the Highland Company, at my request, to hold the woods to our right, and the road, from the reserve?

Answer—I did send out the Highland Company with orders as described, but I cannot say if it was before or after the Thirteenth went out.

Question from Lieut.-Col. Booker—What did they report on their return?

Answer—I don't recollect their return. I believe them to be the last to leave the field.

Question from Lieut.-Col. Booker—Did you hear the cry of "Cavalry"?

Answer—Yes.

Question from Lieut.-Col. Booker—Did you see the Fenian reserves advancing after the cry of "Cavalry"?

Answer—No.

Question from Lieut.-Col. Booker—Did you see that we were outflanked to the right?

Answer—No. I believe it was the reserve. I could not see the extreme right.

Question from the Court—On what do you ground your belief that they were not outflanked on the right?

Answer—Principally on the statements of the officers and men who were out skirmishing on the right.

Question from Lieut.-Col. Booker—Did you notice men coming down the hill to our front at a double, in front of the reserves, crying "Cavalry"?

Answer—No.

Question from the Court—When three companies of the Thirteenth were sent out to relieve the Queen's Own, had the movement been executed before the retreat was sounded?

Answer—No, so far as my knowledge extends. Both lines of skirmishers, Rifles and Thirteenth, came in together.

Question from Lieut.-Col. Booker—Was the endeavor made to bring the men out of square into column?

Answer—Yes. They did re-form column.

Question—Was the rear of the column or square now in retreat?

Answer—No. Not at that time.

Question from Lieut.-Col. Booker—Do you consider there was a panic when the retreat ocmmenced?

Answer—I think the retreat was caused by a panic. After the column was re-formed I ordered the two leading companies again to extend and skirmish. They did so. I ordered the rest of the column, which at that time was composed of Queen's Own and Thirteenth mixed together, to retire, as they were exposed to a heavy fire on the front and right from the enemy's front and left. This order was being obeyed by the men with reasonable steadiness, when as I was standing in rear of the retiring column, I heard them cheer loudly and call out "reinforcements." I then saw some men in red, whom I believe were the left wing of the Thirteenth, and whom these men, I suppose, took to be reinforcements. When these men in red heard the cheer they broke and retired. Then the whole column became disorganized. This was about 9 o'clock a.m. The first shot was fired about half-past seven a.m.

Question from Lieut.-Col. Booker—Did you believe, when you saw my despatches to Col. Peacocke and Gen. Napier, that they were correct, and did you concur in the correctness of them when you were with me in the customs office at Port Colborne?

Answer—Yes, the general tenor of the report was correct, and I assented to it.

Question from the Court—Is there anything in Lieut.-Col. Booker's report, just read to you, that places the Thirteenth Battalion in a false position?

Answer—No.

Question from Lieut.-Col. Booker—Do you think the men could have been rallied after they had commenced the retreat?

Answer—The whole force could not have been, but I could have rallied two or three hundred men around me at any time during the retreat, had I been disposed to do so. Officers of both the Queen's Own and the Thirteenth were frantically exerting themselves to rally their men, but, knowing that I could not be relieved by Col. Peacocke, and fearing that the enemy might pass to our rear, I thought it wiser to conduct the retreat in as orderly a manner as I could.

Question from Lieut.-Col. Booker—Were you satisfied with my conduct on the field?

Answer—Col. Booker asked me the same question in Port Colborne, and I now give him the same answer that I did then, which was, that I could see nothing in his conduct to disapprove of, except with regard to the formation of the squares, which I thought at that time was a mistake, and I think so still.

Question from Lieut.-Col. Booker—As you were not mounted, would you explain the reason why you did not take your horse with you when you left Port Colborne?

Answer—I had my horse at the station at Port Colborne, when Mr. Magrath, the manager, told me that I could not get him off the cars at Ridgeway without breaking his legs, there being no platforms.

EVIDENCE OF CHARLES CLARKE.

The second witness called by Lieut.-Col. Booker was Charles Clarke, a Government detective officer, by commission from Mr. G. McMicken, the stipendary Magistrate at Windsor.

Question from Lieut.-Col. Booker—Were you with the volunteers in the affair at Lime Ridge on the 2nd June?

Answer—Yes.

Question from Lieut.-Col. Booker—Did you see the square disperse?

Answer—Yes. I was with the reserve in the ranks when the square was formed. A number of men, as they were coming in as the reserve, cried out, "Prepare to receive cavalry!" I should say it came from as many as fifty men. I saw the column re-formed. At this time a body of red-coats were coming around a curve in the road about two hundred yards in rear of the square. The Queen's Own and those of the Thirteenth began to cheer, supposing them to belong to the 47th Regiment coming to their relief. As soon as we ascertained that they were not the 47th, we supposed that they were two companies of the Thirteenth who had been driven in by main force, and the result was that we became panic-stricken, and we all broke. I saw several officers belonging to the Queen's Own and the Thirteenth attempting to rally the men. I saw Lieut.-Col. Booker attempting to rally the men, telling them to get into the bush on each side of the road, about four or six hundred yards from where they commenced to retreat. He got the bugler to sound the "halt" several times, and I heard the bugler say he was tired sounding the "halt." The men continued to retreat, except sixteen or seventeen of us, who got over the fence into the bush on our left, but had to leave because the main body continued their retreat towards Ridgeway. At Ridgeway I saw Lieut.-Col. Booker with four officers of the Thirteenth and one of the Queen's Own, each with a revolver in his hand, and Lieut.-Col. Booker had his sword, threatening to shoot the men if they did not stop. They broke through the line of these officers.

Question from the Court—When Lieut.-Col. Booker ordered the battalions that were retreating to get into the woods on each side of the road, what was your impression of his object?

Answer—He wanted to make a stand by getting into the bush to repulse the Fenians, and it was a splendid opportunity, from the country being so open in front of the bush. I served nearly six years in India in the 40th Regiment, and during the affair in Candahar.

Question from the Court—Did you see Lieut.-Col. Booker on the field before and during the retreat?

Answer—Yes, several times.

Question from the Court—Did you observe anything in his conduct which appeared to you like shirking his duties?

Answer—No. On the contrary, I saw him urging on a company of the Thirteenth, which appeared to be dilatory.

Question from Lieut.-Col. Booker—Do you recollect the fact of our force being outflanked to our right?

Answer—Yes.

Question from Lieut.-Col. Booker—Was the firing from the Fenians more rapid than from our men?

Answer—Yes, much more so. Part of the time it was like file firing. I am since aware that they used both the Sharpe and Spencer rifles.

Question from Lieut.-Col. Booker—Did you receive a letter from Major Gillmor and other officers of the Queen's Own, complimenting you for your coolness and conduct at Lime Ridge?

Answer—I did.

EVIDENCE OF GEORGE ARTHURS.

The third witness called by Lieut.-Col. Booker was Mr. George Allan Arthurs.

Question from Lieut.-Col. Booker—Were you at Ridgeway on the 2nd of June, and what did you see there?

Answer—I was there, and was at Ridgeway when the army was retreating. I there saw the bugler come from the field on Lieut.-Col. Booker's horse. My brother (Lieutenant Arthurs, of the Queen's Own) mounted the Colonel's horse and drew his pistol, and threatened to shoot the first man that did not do his duty. Lieut.-Col. Booker came up as my brother was checking the retreat. He mounted his own horse and rode back towards the field to consult with his officers. The retreat was checked so far by my brother that he "told off" a company of men composed of red coats and green coats. I did not see any exhibition on the part of Lieut.-Col. Booker of either cowardice or fear.

EVIDENCE OF JOHN DOUGLAS.

The fourth witness called by Lieut.-Col. Booker was John Douglas, Captain of No. 4 Company of the Queen's Own Rifles.

Question from Lieut.-Col. Booker—Did you, on the 2nd of June last, see me at Lime Ridge?

Answer—Yes, in front of your command, under fire.

Question from the Court—Did his conduct on this occasion attract your attention?

Answer—Yes. It struck me that he was not very careful of his own safety, he being in front of the column of the Queen's Own, and clothed in scarlet. He was directing the movements, with a field-glass in his hands. This was when the Queen's Own were in column, after part of the Thirteenth had gone out in skirmishing order. I saw no hanging back on the part of any officer or man up to that time.

Question from Lieut.-Col. Booker—How did Col. Booker go from Ridgeway to Port Colborne?

Answer—I found Lieut.-Col. Booker on the last train going into Port Colborne. Major Gillmor and several officers of both regiments, with men of both regiments, were in the same train. The great bulk of the force had preceded them.

EVIDENCE OF LIEUTENANT ARTHURS.

The fifth witness called by Lieut.-Col. Booker was Lieut. William Arthurs, of No. 4 Company of the Queen's Own.

Question by Lieut.-Col. Booker—Were you at Ridgeway as Lieut.-Col. Booker arrived there during the retreat on the 2nd of June, and what did you see?

Answer—Yes. I saw Col. Booker on the retreat, and he seemed no way flurried or excited, but quite cool and collected. He spoke to the men. He asked them to form on their coverers. Several companies were formed up and retreated in order.

EVIDENCE OF FRANCIS CLARKE.

The sixth witness called by Lieut.-Col. Booker was Francis Clark, Bugle-Major of the Queen's Own Rifles.

Question from the Court—Did you sound the "halt" on the 2nd of June, by order of Lieut.-Col. Booker during the retreat?

Answer—Yes, repeatedly. He used his best endeavors to halt the men, and then he went forward amongst the men and asked them to halt and front and form. It had no effect, and he said, "Oh, God! what is this?" They still moved on. They retreated, red and green mixed together, as far as I could see, to the turn of the road.

EVIDENCE OF ALEXANDER MUIR.

The seventh witness called by Lieut.-Col. Booker was Alexander Muir, a private in the Highland Company of the Queen's Own, a Lieutenant of Militia, and President of the Highland Company at that time in its civil organization.

Question from Lieut.-Col. Booker—Were you at Lime Ridge on the 2nd of June, and will you recite what you saw there?

Answer—After leaving the cars at Ridgeway, before marching, the whole force received orders, "With ball cartridge—load!" The column then advanced. After proceeding about two and a half miles, I perceived a number of horses (between twelve and fifteen in number) loose in an open near the corner of a bush, about three-quarters of a mile in front of the left side of the road. These having attracted my attention, I also perceived a number of men flitting among the trees, near to the horses. I cried out, "I see the Fenians—there are the Fenians!" My discovery was made known to Col. Booker, who, perhaps, from hearing my cry, came up to me. I was the left hand front rank man of the Highland Company, the rear company of the battalion. He gave the order to halt. He then asked me, "Where?" I pointed out to him where I saw the men and the horses. He had a field-glass which he then used. He tried to use it on horseback, but his horse was so restive that he could not use the glass. He then dismounted by my side. At this moment Major Gillmor came up. I directed him to the proper point to see them. Both Col. Booker and Major Gillmor seemed convinced that all was not right in the bush. The leading company of the column was then sent out to reconnoitre to the left in the direction of these horses, in skirmishing order, supported by the next company. The column remained at the halt. After the skirmishers had advanced to within a short distance of where the horses were, the bugle sounded the "retire" or the "incline" to the skirmishers, and the column was advanced. The near party of the advance guard halted at the same time the column halted, and just after the column was again put in motion, I saw several of them, if not all of them, with their hats on their rifles raised in the air and moving them, indicating thereby that the enemy was in sight. The column was again halted. At that moment a bullet came whistling from the direction of an orchard on our right front. This was the first shot, and came close to Capt. Gardner and myself. Here the Queen's Own were ordered to skirmish, and our company furnished the right company of the line of skirmishers, and in this order we advanced in a northerly direction. The firing commenced opposite the centre of the line of skirmishers immediately upon their advancing. We continued advancing and firing for some distance, perhaps three hundred yards at that time, when the order came for the Queen's Own to fall back on its supports. We had then been under fire for three-quarters of an hour. I distinctly heard Col. Booker's words of command, given with coolness and deliberation, as we were going into action. The Queen's Own were then relieved by the Thirteenth. The Thirteenth advanced in skirmishing order, appearing to take the ground which had previously been occupied by the Queen's Own, the enemy continuing their fire during the advance of the Thirteenth. The enemy had evidently been previously driven back by the Queen's Own. An order from Col. Booker now came to our company, which was then under cover of the school-house, acting in reserve, directing our company to take possession of the road to the right which led in the direction of Fort Erie, because the enemy was manoeuvring to outflank our right. Capt. Gardner was told it was an important position, and he then advanced our company till we came opposite a bush north of the road. He then ordered us to advance in skirmishing order through that bush, which we did. After passing through the bush we came to a wheat-field, on the opposite side of which we found the Fenians thickly posted opposite our front and to our right. When we entered the bush they had evidently been in the same bush at the farther side of it, and had retreated on our advance to the other side of the wheat field. We had reason to know this, because we found quantities of their ammunition, a company sheet roll, and a blank book, a roll book, also a Fenian drill book with the name of "Capt. George Sweeny, Company B, 19th Regiment, Irish Republic Volunteers, Cincinnati, Ohio." The roll book contained about 120 names, with the trades, residences and callings of the men. I have seen the list of Fenian prisoners captured and now in Toronto Jail, and I believe that some of the names are the same as those in the roll book. We commenced firing upon the enemy as soon as we saw them, and they began to retreat. They were about 200 yards from us. We fired here for some time, until an order came to advance from Capt. Gardner, and we leaped over the fence and entered the wheat field. We fired from this wheat field for some time. After entering the wheat field I saw the line of the Thirteenth Battalion to my left, below me, in skirmishing order, advancing towards the enemy. While they were thus advancing I distinctly saw the enemy retreating a long distance before them towards a bush in the rear. Suddenly they seemed to rally, and came down upon the line of the Thirteenth, yelling. At this moment I saw a wavering in the line of the the Thirteenth. The Fenians advanced in a loose manner, but in great strength. Here the Thirteenth retreated at the double, but I did not hear the "retire" sounded for that purpose. As the Fenians rushed upon the Thirteenth, we from our positions gave them two or three volleys, which seemed to check them, and their left swerved inwards from us towards their own centre. While we were here in this position, Sergeant Bain, of our company, called out, "Retire, retire!" We then retired firing. I heard the bugle call to retire. When I came to the school-house I was surprised to see our forces marching back again towards Ridgeway. I turned round and saw the Fenians advancing from the orchard on the road at the same place where I saw our advance guard give the signal before the action commenced. I thought there were as many as 600 or 700 on the road, and more moving out of the orchard. I leaned my rifle over a fence and took my last shot at them with one arm (having previously sustained an injury in my shoulder while getting over a fence). Several of my comrades fired also. This drew fire upon us from them, and it was here that McHardy and White were wounded. On my return to the cross-road at the hotel nine-tenths of our force had passed on towards Ridgeway. I then saw Col. Booker and spoke to him. He was on foot. I heard "Halt! halt!" called, but no one seemed to notice it.

Question by Lieut.-Col. Booker—Are you satisfied we were outflanked on our right?

Answer—Yes.

Question by Lieut.-Col. Booker—Did you see Col. Booker after this?

Answer—I saw him at Ridgeway.

Question from Lieut.-Col. Booker—What was he doing?

Answer—He was standing in conversation with some one on the road.

Question from Lieut.-Col. Booker—Did you see him afterwards, and where?

Answer—I saw him afterwards on the march to Port Colborne, after leaving Ridgeway.

Question—Did you see him afterwards, and where?

Answer—I saw him afterwards on the march to Port Colborne, after leaving Ridgeway. I became weak and exhausted and was taken into a house about 250 yards south by two of my

comrades, where Dr. Neff, assisted by two others, set my left
arm and left me alone. I became insensible, and in that state
had lost all recollection of the fight. After I came to myself
I heard a volley and ran to the door. I saw the Fenians sur-
round the village. I ran to try to catch up to our force, which
had all left, and they fired upon me. I had my arm in a sling,
and my tunic flying from my right shoulder. I overtook the
force after running for some distance (nearly a mile), and
there again I saw Col. Booker in rear of the force. He offered
me his horse. I declined the offer, because I thought it would
pain me more to ride than to walk.   Where the main road
crosses the railway he dismounted and gave his horse to some
one of the Thirteenth, with some orders to take to Port Colborne. He then took my arm and assisted me along the track
until we got into the last train and went into Port Colborne.

Question from Lieut.-Col. Booker—How many rounds of
ammunition had been issued to you previous to the engagement,
and where issued?

Answer—I received five rounds at Toronto before leaving
and thirty at Port Colborne—that was, I had thirty-five rounds.

RONALD M'KINNON'S TESTIMONY.

The eighth witness called by Lieut.-Col. Booker was Ronald
Archibald McKinnon, at that time a cadet in the Military School
at Toronto.

Question—Were you present at Lime Ridge on the 2nd of
June last, and in what capacity did you act?

Answer—I was present at the engagement at Lime Ridge,
and acted as a volunteer officer with the Caledonia Rifle Company, though not regularly attached to that company.

Question—Did you see Lieut. Arthurs mounted on Lieut.-
Col. Booker's horse?

Answer—Yes.

Question—Were you with Lieut. Arthurs, endeavoring to
rally the men near Ridgeway?

Answer—Yes.

Question—Were you there when Lieut.-Col. Booker arrived from the field at Lime Ridge?

Answer—Yes.

Question—Was Lieut.-Col. Booker mounted when he returned from Lime Ridge to Ridgeway?

Answer—Yes.

Question—Were you with the rear guard of the column before the action?

Answer—Yes.

Question—When you saw Lieut. Arthurs mounted on Lieut.-Col. Booker's horse, was it previous to the arrival of Lieut.-Col. Booker mounted on his return from Lime Ridge?

Answer—I cannot say. But I know that after I saw Lieut. Arthurs on Lieut.-Col. Booker's horse I saw Lieut.-Col Booker ride back towards Ridgeway.

ROBERT BENHAM'S TESTIMONY.

Robert Benham, a private in the Thirteenth Battalion (Major Skinner's groom), was the ninth witness called by Lieut.-Col. Booker.

Question—Did Lieut.-Col. Booker's orderly bring you back the horse which Col. Booker rode at Lime Ridge before the firing commenced?

Answer—Yes.

Question—During the retreat what became of the horse?

Answer—I was leading him away to Ridgeway, when Quartermaster Stoneman said, "Get on the horse." I then mounted and rode him to Ridgeway, and there watered him. While I was watering him one of the officers of the Queen's Own Rifles came and asked me who owned the horse. I told him that the horse belonged to Major Skinner, but that Col. Booker had been using him. The officer then took the horse from me and mounted him. I saw him, while mounted, draw a pistol and endeavor to stop the men by threatening to shoot if they did not stop. I saw Col. Booker on the horse afterwards.

CAPT. HENERY'S EVIDENCE.

The tenth witness called by Lieut.-Col. Booker was Capt. Henery, Adjutant of the Thirteenth Battalion (formerly a Sergeant-Major of the Coldstream Guards).

Question—Will you recite what from your own knowledge occurred from the time the Thirteenth were engaged at Lime Ridge until they retired, and how long they were in action?

Answer—At the commencement of the action, or rather just previously to the action, the Queen's Own were thrown out to skirmish, the reserve being composed of the Thirteenth Battalion, with the York and Caledonia Rifle Companies. Soon afterward the action commenced. The whole force continued to advance in this order. The reserve then halted, the skirmishers and supports continuing their advance. We remained halted only about three minutes before an officer of the Queen's Own came up and shouted, "Surgeons to the front." I then saw two officers in green running to the front. I then heard Major Gillmor tell Col. Booker to deploy the right wing of the Thirteenth Battalion and relieve the Queen's Own, because their ammunition had been expended. Col. Booker then gave the command to the Thirteenth Battalion to deploy the right wing on No. 3 Company, which was executed after advancing a few yards to enable them to deploy and avoid an obstacle in its way. This wing was then extended to skirmish and relieve the Queen's Own, from its left towards the right side of the road. The whole wing and supports were on the right side of the road. While this deployment was being executed, several companies of the Queen's Own came and formed in quarter distance column in rear, forming the reserve. The right wing then advanced and relieved the Queen's Own in a very steady manner, their supports being regularly posted. Then I advanced between the supports and skirmishers. I was not mounted. The support laid down after arriving at the orchard, under cover. I then left the supports and joined the skirmishers. They continued firing for some time, receiving the fire of the enemy. There was then a cry of "Cavalry!" from my right rear. I was on the road with the left of No. 2 Company on the line of skirmishers. I looked and saw two or three horses, and cried out that there was no cavalry. I heard no bugle blow the "retire." When I looked around I saw both red and green coats running to the rear from the line of skirmishers, in order, but not firing. I think this retreat was about one hour after the Thirteenth took the field. I think those of the Queen's Own who formed the reserve as we were deploying, came in about ten minutes after the firing commenced.

ROBERT MAUN'S TESTIMONY.

Robert Maun, a private in the 13th Battalion, was the eleventh witness called by Lieut.-Col. Booker.

Question—Will you state what you saw at Lime Ridge on the 2nd of June?

Answer—I was on duty on the field hospital staff. There was a cry for the doctor from one of the companies of the Thirteenth, acting as a support in the orchard. I was sent to find the man, and did so. He had been wounded in the wrist. He was a rifleman, not one of the Thirteenth. I saw no other "green" soldier there. Just as we had finished dressing the man's hand I heard a cry of "Cavalry, cavalry! Look out for cavalry!" coming from the direction of the right of the skirmish line. I saw a company of Rifles in line with the skirmishers of the Thirteenth. I suppose they were the York Rifles. When I heard the cry of "Cavalry!" I was near the support of one of the companies, and then I also heard an order given to the reserve to "Form square!" I suggested to the doctor that we should go to the square formed on the road by the reserve. He came with me toward the square, but I cannot tell whether he got into the square or not. I was too late to get in. I threw myself under the bayonets of the front face of the square. This square was composed of the Queen's Own, and the color party of the Thirteenth was with them. A company of the Thirteenth came up at a steady "double," most of them at "the trail," but some of them at "the slope," and passing the right face of the square formed in rear of the Queen's Own. I then, finding a company of my own corps at hand, jumped up, fixed my bayonet, and joined them. It was then that I saw a few straggling men of the Thirteenth, mixed up with some Rifles, retiring from the direction of the skirmish line towards us. An order was

then given by a voice. which I took to be Col. Booker's. to ''Re-
form column,'' which was done. At this moment a rather too
sharp fire came upon us, but it was rather high to do us much
damage. I then heard an order to ''Deploy on the rear company'' in the same voice, which I took to be that of Col. Booker.
At this time there was a company of the Thirteenth which
formed the rear company of the reserve, the rest of the reserve
being composed of the Queen's Own. When the order to deploy
was given a heavy volley struck the column, and I heard a
sound which I took to be that of men falling. The column
swayed backwards, as I supposed, from the effects of the fire.
The column broke immediately and commenced a retreat down
the road. The main body of the Thirteenth were at this time in
the field, and firing was going on more to the right. I went
down the road with the retreat and felt a heavy fire from a wood
on the left as we retired. I saw several of the enemy jumping
a fence, as if they were intending to pursue the retreating
column. I fired at them, and several others of our men also fired
at them. After I had loaded my rifle I returned from the direction in which we had just come and met Col. Booker with the
Thirteenth following the Queen's Own, or the retreating column.
The Thirteenth were in a confused mass, and I heard several
officers say to Col. Booker, ''Let us stop them,'' or words to
that effect, and prevent a rout. Col. Booker then said he would
go on to the front and stop the men of the retreating column,
and then ran out ''at the double'' and got in front of nearly
all of the Thirteenth. He then faced about and. flashing his
sword about, said, ''For God's sake, men, don't make cow-
ards of yourselves.'' I had followed him in search of the doctor, and so had the opportunity of witnessing this on the part
of Col. Booker. I do not know the names of the officers who
said to Col. Booker, ''Let us try and stop them and prevent a
rout.'' The men seemed to pay no attention to Col. Booker's
entreaties for them to stop, but continued the retreat. A man
of No. 1 Company. of the Thirteenth, who was shot through the
thigh, demanded my attention, and I went to him. Dr. Ryall
was with him attending to him. We got him on a waggon and
took him down the road to Ridgeway. While going with this
man I heard several officers (Col. Booker of the number) urging

the men to stop and take to the woods, as there was good cover there. I think that Adjutant Henery was one of the officers who urged the men to do this. At this time I saw a number of the York Rifles obeying the order to take to the woods. They cried out. "Hurrah for old York! Let us take to the woods and we will give them hell." There was only about a dozen of them. I passed on with the waggon, and saw no more.

Question—Did you hear Lieut.-Col. Booker, when under fire. encouraging the reserves?

Answer—I heard him joking them about their politeness in bowing to the bullets that passed over their heads.

MAJOR GILLMOR RECALLED.

Question from the Court—Major Gillmor, state the companies of the Queen's Own who were first advanced as skirmishers, how armed, and the amount of ammunition issued to each man.

Answer—No. 5 Company were the entire skirmishers. There were about forty of them armed with Spencer rifles. and had under thirty rounds for each man. The remainder of the company were armed with the long Enfield rifle. Nos. 1 and 2 Companies were the other skirmishers. They were armed with the long Enfield. The whole regiment had an average of forty rounds of ammunition per man.

Question—How long were they under fire when the right wing of the Thirteenth were advanced to their relief?

Answer—I could not form any idea as to the time. The men armed with the Spencer rifles were relieved by another company long before the Thirteenth Battalion went out to skirmish.

Question—Who gave the order to "Form square"?

Answer—Lieut.-Col. Booker gave the caution to "Look out for cavalry!" and I gave the command to "Form square."

Question—Can you state what portion of the Queen's Own were undrilled recruits?

Answer—They were, as a rule, partially drilled. some men undrilled. Recruits were joining every week, and all the available men. drilled and undrilled. were in the field.

Question—What proportion of the whole battalion had not been exercised with blank cartridge?

Answer—With the exception of one or two days in May, when the whole battalion were out skirmishing, I am satisfied that half of the men had never fired a shot.

Question—What proportion of the men had never practised with ball cartridge?

Answer—The proportion was about the same, about half.

Question—What proportion of the regiment was composed of lads under twenty years of age?

Answer—I should say more than half of the regiment.

Question—Did you observe any difference in the demeanor of the lads and the other soldiers going into action?

Answer—No. Each were equally cool. I particularly noticed the companies that morning as they marched out to the skirmish, and all were equally cool. I may state here that this was the first occasion on which the whole regiment had an opportunity to skirmish as a battalion. I also wish to state that I saw the right wing of the Thirteenth extend and advance in skirmishing order, and that nothing could exceed the steadiness and regularity with which they advanced.

EVIDENCE OF W. T. URQUHART.

The thirteenth witness called by Lieut.-Col. Booker was Wm. T. Urquhart, assistant editor of the Hamilton *Spectator*, who was a private in No. 4 Company, Thirteenth Battalion.

Question—Do you recollect seeing Lieut.-Col. Booker after the fight at Lime Ridge, and where?

Answer—I do. I saw him on the rising ground immediately in rear of where the action took place.

Question—Were you exposed to a heavy fire?

Answer—We were.

Question—Were you one of the retreating column?

Answer—In the rear.

Question by the Court—What was Lieut.-Col. Booker doing at the time you noticed him?

Answer—He was trying to restore order.

Question—Where were you when the right wing went out to skirmish? And did your skirmishers relieve those in front of you?

Answer—We were on the right. I was in the company forming the support of the skirmishers on the right, and the skirmishers of our company in front relieved those of the Rifles in front of them. The Rifles retired in good order to the reserves. I certainly saw two companies come in, but I cannot speak as to the whole line.

Question—From the time your skirmishers were posted until the retreat, how much time elapsed?

Answer—I should think about an hour.

Question—What caused the retreat, in your opinion, and what succeeded?

Answer—We retreated because the bugle sounded ''the retreat,'' and we were also ordered by Lieut. Routh, the officer in command of our company, who said shortly afterward that it was a mistake, as it should have been ''the advance,'' and ordered us to ''halt'' and ''front,'' and we did so accordingly. The skirmishers immediately came down upon us, who were all men of our battalion, and we all retreated together to the cross-road, near the place where we first deployed. Two or three companies of Rifles came down this cross-road from the right of the attack at this moment, and the whole became mingled together and the formation was immediately destroyed. Several attempts by officers of the Thirteenth and the Rifles were made to rally or re-form the men. I noticed Col. Booker and Adjutant Henery do this, and also Ensign Armstrong, who carried the colors. I saw Lieut. Arthurs endeavoring to stop the men, and also other Rifle officers whose names I am not acquainted with.

ADJUTANT HENERY RECALLED.

Question—State the names of the officers of the right wing of the Thirteenth Battalion who were present when that wing was ordered to skirmish?

Answer—Major Skinner, Capt. Grant, Lieut. Gibson, and Ensign McKenzie, of No. 1 Company; Capt. Watson and Lieut. Sewell, of No. 2 Company; and Lieut. Ferguson, of No. 3 Company.

Question—How long have you been connected with the regiment, and in what capacity?

Answer—As Drill Instructor and Adjutant, about four years.

Question—About what proportion of the Thirteenth Regiment was wholly undrilled at the time of the affair at Lime Ridge?

Answer—One man only, and the others were all drilled men.

Question—Had the whole battalion previously been exercised with blank cartridge?

Answer—Yes, but not frequently.

Question—Had they any practice with ball cartridge?

Answer—I think 180 men had previously had ball practice.

Question—Was a large proportion of the regiment composed of boys under twenty?

Answer—I think that about 150 were under twenty, and a large proportion of these were between the ages of 19 and 20 years of age.

Question—Did you observe any difference in the demeanor of the men when under fire?

Answer—No difference—all seemed equally steady.

Question—What number of rounds had the men of the Thirteenth when going into action?

Answer—Sixty rounds per man, with caps in proportion.

MAJOR SKINNER'S TESTIMONY.

Major Skinner, of the Thirteenth Battalion, was the next witness examined.

Question—Were you present at Lime Ridge on the 2nd of June last, when the right wing of the Thirteenth Battalion was sent out to skirmish?

Answer—Yes.

Question—State the orders given and by whom given for the movement, and what took place under your observation.

Answer—Col. Booker said to me at some distance (about ten yards): "Major Skinner, you will skirmish with the right wing." I then advanced with the skirmishers. We went over a fence and across a field and over another fence into an orchard on the right side of the road. We went through that orchard up to another fence, and there remained for some time. While approaching this fence the enemy's shots passed over our heads. After remaining some time at this fence we found their shot getting closer. We then crossed that fence and passed over a field to another fence, where we halted and remained for some time. I passed to the right of the skirmishers of our battalion. I went there because I saw a number of men in green uniform on our extreme right towards our front, and knowing they were some of our men, told my men not to fire upon them. I cannot say that I saw any of the enemy. They fired upon us from under cover. We met a few skirmishers in green in the orchard. We passed through them.

Question—Before you deployed, what was the position of your regiment as regards the Queen's Own?

Answer—The Queen's Own were all away in front, and the York Rifles also.

Question—How long after the first shot was fired by the enemy was it until the Thirteenth were ordered to skirmish?

Answer—About ten minutes elapsed from the time the first shot was fired until some men of the Queen's Own came in, and we were ordered to relieve the skirmishers. I heard a call for the surgeon to go to the front about seven minutes before we were ordered to skirmish. At the same time Ensign McEachren was carried to the rear. After going to the right of our skirmishers and cautioning the men not to fire upon the men in green on our right, I went back again to the centre of our men. We remained there at this fence about a quarter of an hour, and the enemy getting our range, it became so hot that we again advanced. We ran across a field this time. The whole of No. 3 Company must have been on the left of the road. I was on the right of the road. We found a brick house, with a wooden addition to it. It was locked up with a padlock, and one of our men opened it. We went in, and opening the front door, used the house for cover, firing through the door-way. We were about 150 yards from the woods occupied by the enemy. Some one on the left of the road called out, "Don't you hear the bugle?" I said, "No. What does it say?" The reply I got was, "Retreat." I then looked around to the rear for the first time since we came out, and I saw our men at the right running in. I then heard some one on my left say, "Why, they are preparing to receive cavalry." I looked around and said, "Where is the cavalry?" implying that I saw none. I then ran across the road to the left and saw that the men were all running as fast as they could to the rear. I ran for a barn and remained there a few moments to get breath, and then ran for another fence. I saw a few of our men behind me, and the enemy pursuing them. Two of our men were shot here—Stewart and Powell. I then made for the road where we had previously deployed, expecting to find the reserve there. I found none. Our skirmishers were then comprising men of all of our companies, mixed with those in green. I suppose there were about 150 red coats and about 30 or 40 in green. I then asked for the commanding officer, but got no answer. I then asked for Col. Booker, and one man in the crowd cried out, "He is off, three miles ahead." I do not know who it was that said so. I then called for Major Gillmor, and got no reply. I then thought that I should do something, and I ran to the front of the retreating men on the road and told them to halt. They paid no attention to me. I called upon an officer of our battalion, who was on the right of the men retreating, to draw his sword and see if we could not stop them. We then again went to the front of our men, retreating backwards for a few minutes, when we got them to halt. A couple of boys of our regiment had their bayonets fixed, endeavoring to stop them, and before I could do further a number of men in green rushed past on the left and one of the boys disappeared, and then commenced a further retreat of all present. No companies were formed for the retreat. I assisted to carry two boys who were wounded by getting doors and carrying them to Ridgeway. They were Rifles. When we reached Ridgeway there were about 150 of us, mixed red and green. We found no one of the force in Ridgeway when we arrived. It was half-past 10 o'clock when we reached Ridgeway. I remained there about three-quarters of an hour, the men continually leaving and going on towards Port Colborne. I left the village just as the Fenians were coming down the hill. I had about 50 men and officers with me. We took the road towards Port Colborne. At the turn of the road we halted and looked back, and saw a large column of about 400 of the enemy marching down the hill into Ridgeway. I wish to state that the whole regiment (Thirteenth) had sixty rounds each, and when the order to retreat was given we had not expended half of our ammunition.

Question—Is there anything of your own knowledge that you wish to state that it is important this Court should hear?

Answer—No.

ISAAC RYALL'S EVIDENCE.

Dr. Isaac Ryall, Surgeon of the Thirteenth Battalion, was the next witness examined.

Question—Were you present at Lime Ridge on the 2nd of June last, and in what capacity?

Answer—Yes, as Surgeon of the Thirteenth Battalion.

Question—State your position during the action, and what occurred under your observation.

Answer—I remained with my own battalion until the order was given by Col. Booker to skirmish and relieve the Queen's Own. The regiment at this time was standing on the road beyond the tavern. I followed the line of skirmishers behind No. 4 Company, which passed along the road to the schoolhouse and then advanced to a fence near an orchard. While here a man who was wounded came from the front. He was a rifleman, but I cannot say what corps he belonged to. I examined him and sent him to the rear. I then returned to

my post. A few moments afterwards No. 4 Company were
ordered to advance. and they went over the fence into the
orchard.   I then went down to the fence, with the orderlies
to assist, and then passed down the fence until coming near the
end of it, I cut across the angle to the main road. and there I
saw Col. Booker with his bugler and an orderly.   The Rifles
in reserve were behind Col. Booker, who was between them and
the line of skirmishers on the road.   Immediately on reaching
Col. Booker I heard an order or a cry (which was not from
Col. Booker) to ''Prepare for cavalry!''   I looked around and
could not see any cavalry.   I then walked to the rear.   I am
quite positive that the first order to ''Prepare for cavalry!'' was
not given by Col. Booker. because I was quite close to him at
the time. and the word came from the front.   An order was then
given by Col. Booker to ''Form square.'' which was done.   I
am not positive that this order was given by Col. Booker. but
I think so.   They did not seem to properly ''form square.'' and
in a few seconds they commenced retreating . The square I
have referred to was composed of Rifles and the color party of
the Thirteenth.   My orderly (Robert Maun) was with me at
this time.   I did not see any of the Thirteenth come up and
form in rear of the square.   I was going to the rear and saw
them commence running.   I walked down the road, and the men
passed me running.   About a quarter of a mile from where
the square was formed. I heard Col. Booker give an order,
which I repeated twice. for the men to go into a wood on the
left-hand side of the road.   The order did not seem to be
obeyed.   I spoke to one man of the Thirteenth, and asked him
why he did not obey the orders.   He said he would go in if the
others did. but he would not go in by himself.   Immediately
after I saw a man named Powell, of the Thirteenth, who had
been wounded and was being assisted by two men.   I examined
him and found there was no necessity for immediate action. and
then got him into a waggon and took him to a farmer's house
beyond Ridgeway.   I did not see Col. Booker again until I got
about a mile or more from the Ridgeway Station, on the road
south of the railway.   He had been giving some stimulants to
a sick soldier of the Thirteenth. who was mounted on his horse.
The man's name was Daniel Laker.   I went on with the men.

I saw the Rifles resting themselves by the roadside, and the Thirteenth passing them after leaving Ridgeway. When we arrived at the point where the railway track crossed the main road, some of the men took the railway track and some followed the road. Col. Booker and I both followed the track, and a train shortly afterwards came up, upon which a number of men got; as many as it would carry. Col. Booker walked on or remained behind. It was only an engine and a baggage car. There were no passenger cars.

LIEUT. FERGUSON'S EVIDENCE.

The next witness examined by the Court was Lieut. John William Ferguson, of No. 3 Company, Thirteenth Battalion.

Question—Did you command No. 3 Company of the Thirteenth Battalion at the battle of Lime Ridge on the 2nd of June last?

Answer—Yes.

Question—State what took place that day under your own observation.

Answer—About ten or fifteen minutes after the firing commenced, Major Gillmor came back to the rear and told Col. Booker that his men were tired and their ammunition nearly expended, and asked Col. Booker to send out the right wing of the Thirteenth to relieve his men. Col. Booker then gave the order to the right wing of the Thirteenth to deploy on No. 3 Company, and this being done, an order was given to extend from the left. We then advanced over a fence through a field, and in the middle of the field we were halted by bugle call. In a few minutes "the advance" was sounded, and we continued advancing until we came under fire. The Queen's Own were then retiring in good order. We then commenced firing and advanced across a field. My company had to cross the road to the left side. Here I changed my front a little to the right, and saw the enemy about 100 yards off. I heard a bugle sound "the retreat," and I gave the command to "retire." We retired about forty yards in line into the original position, firing as we fell back. While retiring I heard the bugle sound the "advance." I then ordered my company to advance, but

not to fire until they got where they were before, under cover.
I again heard a bugle call which I did not know, but on inquiry
was told it was "the alarm." I looked for the cavalry, but
could see none. I let my men remain where they were. I then
heard the bugle call "the assembly," followed by "the double."
I then ordered the men to make for the square the shortest way
they could, and they retired on the square. Three of them were
wounded while retiring at this time. When I saw the enemy
coming out of the woods I went after my men. I saw Major
Skinner and Adjutant Henery making for the same point, that
is, the square. When I reached where the reserve stood, scarcely
any men were there. On my way down I saw one of the Queen's
Own lying dead as I passed. Several ineffectual attempts were
made to form up the men. At Ridgeway I saw Col. Booker on
his horse forming up his battalion into column. They were
falling into column of companies, right in front, facing towards
Port Colborne, past Ridgeway. As soon as we had formed I
heard Col. Booker give the command, "Form fours—right. Left
wheel—quick march!" and the column moved off in the direction of Port Colborne. Col. Booker was in advance of the
column until we came near a wood, when he told us to keep a
sharp lookout for firing from the woods, and he passed back to
the rear and towards Ridgeway. The main body of the Rifles
was before us. I did not see Col. Booker again. I saw his horse
pass by with a body on his back in red clothing. This was about
four miles from Port Colborne.

CAPT. R. H. DAVIS' TESTIMONY.

Robert H. Davis, Captain of the York Rifles, was the next
witness called.

Question—Were you present at the engagement at Lime
Ridge on the 2nd of June last?

Answer—I was.

Question—State what position you held in the engagement,
and what you know, of your own knowledge, what occurred.

Answer—When the firing commenced I was in front of the
Thirteenth, in column of reserve. I was sent out with my company alone, as a company in support of the left skirmishing

company of the Queen's Own (that was Capt. Sherwood's company, Trinity College Rifles). I remained there until the skirmishers were called in, when I took my company to the rear in fours, and formed them up in rear of the reserve, which was then formed by the Queen's Own. After I had halted and fronted the company, I looked in front of the column and saw the Thirteenth were all out. I thought I was not in my right place, and I countermarched my company to the head of the column, taking, as I supposed, the ground I should have taken when I came in, namely, that held originally by the Thirteenth, to which I was attached. I had scarcely halted here when the order came for two more companies to extend, the leading company to take ground to the left. I went almost over the same ground from which I had just returned, and got to the left of the skirmishers already extended, when I extended my own company from the right, the company on my right being a Rifle company. When within about 500 yards of the enemy, we commenced firing and advancing. We crossed two fields on the other side of the cross-road called the Garrison Road. When I had formed my men by a fence to give them a direct fire into the enemy, I heard a bugle call which my sergeant said was "the retire." He said that it was a mistake, that it was "the advance" that was meant. In a few minutes "the advance" was sounded, and I took my company over the fence behind which they were lying and told them to get to the next one as soon as they could. When about half way across the field "the retire" was again sounded, followed by "the double." I looked along the line of skirmishers and saw them firing and retiring, and a good many running in. We retired, the men firing occasionally, until we reached the Garrison Road. I then closed the company on the centre and crossed the Garrison Road to the next field, then formed "fours right" and marched to where I had left the reserve. In the field on the Ridgeway side of the Garrison Road there was a small farm house on the hill close to the side of the Ridgeway road, and when I came up with the company to this house I saw a company of Rifles in close column of sections, kneeling to receive cavalry. I expressed my surprise at this, and moved my own company up the road. When I reached the fence alongside of the road I saw a good deal of confusion, and I asked generally what was the matter, and what they were going to do. Some officer told me that the order had been given to "Form square" on the leading company of the reserve. I did this with my company, and halted in rear of the column. The order was now passed from the front for the column to retire, and the attempt was made to retire, and in two minutes all was confusion.

Question—Have you any further information to give the Court respecting what occurred at the engagement at Lime Ridge?

Answer—I saw several officers of Rifles and infantry using all their exertions like good men to induce the men to rally and form up again, or to fight in any way. Among these officers were Major Skinner, Adjutant Henery, and Captain Gardner, of the Highland Company, Queen's Own. I had sixty rounds of ball cartridges on going into action, and the men expended between 15 and 20 rounds each.

CAPTAIN GARDNER EXAMINED.

The next witness called was Capt. John Gardner, of the Queen's Own.

Question—State the company you commanded at Lime Ridge on the 2nd of June last, and the particulars of the engagement which took place under your observation.

Answer—I commanded on that occasion No. 10 (or the Highland) Company of the Queen's Own. After leaving the cars at Ridgeway, the brigade was formed in quarter distance column, right in front, the Queen's Own leading, the York Rifles next, then the Thirteenth Battalion, with the Caledonia Rifles as the rear guard. After loading with ball cartridges, No. 5 Company of the Queen's Own (Capt. Edwards) was sent out as the advance guard. I believe that company was detailed for this duty because it was the only company that was armed with the Spencer rifle. I cannot say whether we were marching in column of companies or sub-divisions, but after the advance guard had got out a reasonable distance the column was moved on. After marching some distance we were halted, and then the skirmishers were thrown out. The whole brigade then ad-

vanced in this order, and halted once or twice to maintain their
proper distance. Upon seeing what they took to be the enemy
on the left, two additional companies were sent out. At this
time Col. Booker and Major Gillmor endeavored by the use of
their glasses to ascertain where the enemy were. Then the skirmishers on the left stopped for a moment, when the bugle
sounded "incline to the left," and some of them, I think, raised
their hats upon their rifles, but did not obey the call, probably
from not hearing the bugle call. A sergeant was sent out to
tell them to incline more to the left. He had just reached
them, when firing commenced by two or three shots being fired
on the left of the road, and almost immediately the enemy
opened upon us a regular volley from our front. Our men then
returned the fire, continually advancing until they occupied the
ground from which the Fenians first fired upon them. At this
time eight companies of the Queen's Own were out. Nos. 9 and
10 were with the reserve on the road. At this time No. 9 Company was sent out to the right of the skirmish line, and my
company as their support. I do not think I was two minutes
supporting them, when I was ordered to reinforce the line by
joining them. As soon as I did so, No. 9 Company moved into
the wood on my right. I remained fifteen or twenty minutes
in this open field, firing at the enemy who were under cover in
the woods, the bullets coming like hail. I was then relieved by
one of the companies of the Thirteenth Battalion, and I retired
to the reserve on the road. None of my men were injured. I
had just halted my company in rear of the column when Col.
Booker came up to Major Gillmor and told him he wanted a
company sent to our right, to prevent the Fenian left from
flanking us. The column at this time forming the reserve was
composed of companies in red and partly of companies in green.
Major Gillmor looked at the column, and said to me, "Captain
Gardner, take your company." At this time the column was
standing at the crossing of the Ridge Road with the Garrison
Road. I then faced my company to the right and marched
along the Garrison Road in file, all the time exposed to the fire
of the enemy, until we reached the wood on the right. I extended while marching towards the woods. I then ordered them
to enter the woods in skirmishing order. We had no support.

and so continued during the engagement. The enemy was in the
woods in front of us, and on our approach retreated. On reaching the other side of the bush they retired, and we found on
the ground they had been occupying several articles which I
believe are still forthcoming. We remained on the edge of this
field firing upon the enemy, who were in the bush opposite, and
kept up their fire upon us. The field between us and the enemy
was about 400 yards, varying in width. We continued here
engaged with the enemy for some time, until we heard some
cheering on our left front, along the enemy's line. I thought it
was our men cheering and making a dash on the enemy. I then
ordered my men to get over the fence and cross the field to the
left, in the direction from which the cheering came. As soon
as we came to the opening commanding a view of the field, we
perceived that it was the Fenians who had cheered, and were
advancing in large numbers towards our forces. Sergeant Bain,
from an elevated position, saw the enemy coming down on them
on a run, and cried out, "Retire, retire!" Then we made for
the head of the column of reserve on the road. In reaching this
point we had to pass through the fire of the advancing enemy
the whole time. At first the fire passed over our heads, but as
we neared the column it lowered, and bullets struck around us
everywhere. My left sub-division alone came in with me. The
right sub-division went with Ensign Gibson through the wood to
the rear and around to our reserve, but I cannot particularize
as to them. On crossing the fence next to the column I met
Capt. Davis, of the York Rifles, and saw the column in the road
standing in the form of three sides of a square, and a number
of men standing loosely around. Some of the men in the square
had their bayonets fixed and some had not. I here saw Major
Gillmor, Capt. Otter, Capt. Morrison, Lieut. Bennett, Lieut.
Beaven, Capt. Brown, Capt. Douglas, and perhaps others of the
Queen's Own. I also saw Capt. Henery, Adjutant of the Thirteenth Battalion. Other officers of that corps might have been
there, but I did not see them. Lieut. Ramsay came in with me,
and stayed to the very last. Capt. Davis and myself organized
a strong company of volunteers from this crowd, when Major
Gillmor came up to me and said there was no use in sacrificing
these men, as our main body was retreating towards Ridgeway.

These men who remained in the rear kept up an incessant fire upon the enemy all the time they were standing there. The fire from the enemy suddenly ceased, and it was then that Capt. Davis and I endeavored to form up the company composed of volunteers to make a stand. Major Gillmor having expressed his opinion that it was no use to sacrifice these men, we all deliberately retreated towards Ridgeway. As we proceeded a few stray shots were at one time fired at us, but no further attack was made upon us.

Question—Have you any further information to give this Court respecting the engagement at Lime Ridge which you think may be of public interest?

Answer—No.

ENSIGN MACLEAN'S TESTIMONY.

The next witness called by the Court was Thomas A. McLean, Ensign of No. 6 Company of the Queen's Own.

Question—Were you present at the engagement at Lime Ridge on the 2nd of June?

Answer—I was. Whilst the column was advancing on the road from Ridgeway to Stevensville, the advance guard gave the signal that the enemy was in sight. I saw on the left what I took to be a small party of our men running towards the woods, at a distance of about half a mile. A detail of several companies from the Queen's Own were now sent out to skirmish, and our company (No. 6) went out as the right flanking party, being posted at right angles with the line of skirmishers, in skirmishing order. We advanced through a wood on our right, feeling for the enemy. We saw no one and were recalled in about fifteen minutes and sent out as a support to a company on the right of the road and towards the right of the skirmishing line. As we were advancing in this order fire was suddenly opened from the enemy in front along our line, which the skirmishers immediately returned. As soon as the fire opened the skirmishers doubled up to cover, and we were advanced to a wheat field and were ordered to lie down. We again advanced, the enemy retreating. In about twenty-five minutes the order came to relieve skirmishers. We at once doubled up, extending

on the double, and relieved the company in front of us, who
retired, and I suppose formed our support. Our company, on
getting into the skirmish line, immediately fired and advanced
at the double over two fields. Then there was a check for a
short time, with a sharp fire on both sides. Then we advanced
again, inclining rather to the left, and drove the enemy out of
the orchard and from the barn and fences. We held the barn
and orchard for some time. A company of the Thirteenth came
up in extended order in our rear. They did not relieve us.
They were from 50 to 60 yards in rear of us. One or two officers and two or three men came up to the line of skirmishers,
and my men complained to me that those men of the Thirteenth
behind us would shoot them, as they were firing over the heads
of my company. I got up and asked them if they had come to
relieve skirmishers, but got no answer. I turned around to my
men and said, ''Boys, peg away. They are not going to help
us.'' They did not relieve us, but stayed at the fence in rear
of us, and some of them fired from that position over the heads
of my men, and some of them to the left. The firing continued
for a little while after this, and I saw the Fenians advancing
down the road. They were pushing forward their skirmishers
and were advancing, as I thought, in a heavy column of companies. They continued their advance, and we received an order
to retire. We then retired as skirmishers usually do in closing
in on their supports. We came out, but found no support to
close upon, and reached the open space where there was a large
body of men formed into square. After reaching this open
space I heard a cry of ''Cavalry,'' but saw none. I heard a
cheer from our square, and from some cause the rear of the
square seemed to turn and go down the road. The square now
seemed to dissolve, and the men formed a confused mixture of
red and green down the road to Ridgeway. Some men halted
in the rear and delivered their fire. Many of the officers used
their endeavors to stop the retreat. I left the main body because
I found that from the effect of a heavy fall I had just received
I could not keep up with the column, and I therefore went into
the woods on our right as we were retiring, and kept out of
reach of the enemy. I advanced in line with their skirmishers
as long as their fire lasted, from a half to three-quarters of a

mile. I then stopped and laid down to watch the main body of the enemy pass along the road. I had a good position to see from, at a distance of about 400 yards. I noticed that every time our men fired it checked the enemy, as their long line of skirmishers would halt. The main body advanced, as I thought, in column of fours. I counted a number of fours, and then as they passed I gauged another party, and so on until all passed, and allowing for their advanced skirmishers and rear guard, I think there were 1,500 men, if they were marching in fours, as I believe they were. After they had all passed I made for a farm house. Shortly afterward I left for Col. Peacocke's column, who I heard was a short distance away, at New Germany. I arrived there at half-past 1 o'clock and reported myself to Col. Peacocke, who ordered me to stay with his force.

Question—Have you any further information within your own knowledge, of public interest, to convey to the Court respecting the engagement at Lime Ridge?

Answer—No.

REV. MR. INGLIS EXAMINED.

The next witness called by the Court was Rev. David Inglis, a Presbyterian minister.

Question—Were you present at the engagement at Lime Ridge on the 2nd of June last?

Answer—I was.

Question—State your position on this occasion, and whatever part of the action or proceedings that came under your observation that may furnish any information to the Court.

Answer—I left Ridgeway in the ammunition waggon, and was behind the main body, among the rear guard. A little before the firing commenced the rear guard halted, and the waggon in which I rode was brought up to the rear of the main body. After the firing commenced the rear guard passed us, and the waggon was then halted. Rev. Mr. Burwash and myself left the waggon and hastened to the rear of the Thirteenth. A cry was raised that one of the Queen's Own was wounded. "Where is the doctor?" We hurried on and met Dr. May with several men of the Queen's Own bearing Ensign McEachren

from the field. They took him into a log house on the left side
of the road, and Dr. May desired me to inform him that his
wound was mortal. I told him so, and spent some time with
him in religious service. I then left him with Rev. Mr. Burwash, whose parishioner he had been for some time previously,
and went out to see if I could be useful elsewhere. I afterwards took up a position on a pile of stones on the road which
gave me a view of the position of the troops. I think it was
now about twenty minutes since the firing commenced that killed
Ensign McEachren up to the time of my getting upon the pile
of stones. At this time I observed a part of the Thirteenth out
as skirmishers, and other portions of the same regiment in more
compact bodies behind them. I think I saw a company of green
coats out on the right of those companies of the Thirteenth that
were skirmishing. At this time, on the main road near me, were
formed up a body of men in green coats, composed, I should
say, of three or four companies, and with these men were the
colors of the Thirteenth Regiment, surrounded by a few men of
that corps. The firing at this time from the enemy was very
rapid. I left this place and went back to the hospital, and
returned again in about half an hour. On my return I noticed
that the firing of the enemy on our left had very materially
slackened, but was kept up regularly, although not so rapidly
as on the right. A bugle sounded near the colors of the Thirteenth produced an obvious commotion among the men. They
were looking about them, very much as though they knew not
what to do. After a short interval another bugle call sounded
from near the centre of the reserve, where the colors were. The
men in the reserve by command formed a square after this
bugle sounded. It was not a perfect square. This was succeeded
by another bugle call and words of command. The result of
that was that these men who had "formed square" were getting back to their former positions. Then came a fourth bugle
call. The effect of this was that the whole line of skirmishers
and those in support of them, as well as those in the road near
me, made a motion to turn around. At this moment a small
number of men (about 25 or 30) broke from the ranks and ran
down the road, leaving the remainder standing mostly faced to
the rear. These men were all dressed in green. Immediately

behind those that were running away came from six to eight in
red coats, who ran after the others down the road. The skirmishers and supporters were all retiring. I then ran over to
the hospital and told Dr. May that our men were retiring. He
said he would take all the wounded men with him. Just afterwards I noticed a great rush of men to the rear. I had left
the hospital to see how matters were, and to see if our men were
still retiring, and had started to return, but the rush of men
was so great that I could not get across to the hospital. This
retreat continued, with the red and green mixed together. I
passed down and got up on the ammunition waggon, and found
that Dr. May was ahead of me with his patients. While on the
waggon I noticed in the rear of the retiring column a number
of men (between 100 and 200, I think), composed of red and
green, seeming to be drawn up across the road in pretty good
order. Down the road a short distance an attempt was made to
rally or re-form the men, which was to a good extent successful. Before we came to Ridgeway there was a halt. A man in
uniform came and took the horse which Col. Booker had been
using. Shortly after this I saw Col. Booker on the horse coming
towards Ridgeway. From all I saw and heard of the men, I
can bear testimony that with very few exceptions there was no
evidence of cowardice. They displayed good spirit, and were
all eager to meet the Fenians on the following morning.

This concluded the evidence taken by the Court of Inquiry
in regard to the matter under consideration. After due deliberation, and a careful sifting of all the testimony given, the
following was given as the result of the investigation, which
received the approval of the Militia authorities:—

OPINION.

The Court having duly considered the evidence brought
forward by Lieut.-Col. Booker, as well as such evidence as the
Court have considered necessary, with a view of the further
elucidation of the truth, are of opinion:—

First—That so far as the courage and character of Lieut.-
Col. Booker, with reference to his conduct in the command of
the force engaged with the enemy at Lime Ridge on Saturday,
the 2nd of June last, are affected, there is not the slightest

foundation for the unfavorable imputations cast upon him in the public prints, and most improperly circulated through that channel and otherwise. On the contrary, the Court desire to express the further opinion that Lieut.-Col. Booker having, as will appear, fallen into an error, promptly exerted himself in person to repair the effects of that error, in a manner which can leave no stain upon his personal courage and conduct, subsequently to the period of actual conflict with the force opposed, and also that the disposition of his forces, the manner in which, before an unseen enemy whose strength was unknown to him, he planned his attack, and the desire and anxiety which he showed to carry out these plans to the best of his ability at points where it was his duty to be, have in conjunction with the statements of officers and others in evidence before the Court, led the Court to believe that at no period of that day could want of personal coolness be imputed to Lieut.-Col. Booker.

With reference to the circumstances connected with the late engagement at Lime Ridge, this Court are further of opinion that the entire force under command of Lieut.-Col. Booker, from the formation of the expedition to the time it came out of action, was under disadvantages with which Her Majesty's regular forces have seldom or ever, it is submitted, had to contend—in the want of cavalry, artillery, commissariat arrangements, or even the requisite means of carrying with them cooked provisions, or supplying themselves with water in the country through which they were about to move, in a season when the heat rendered it especially needful that this last point should receive careful attention.

Further, that more than half of the two battalions forming the largest proportion of the whole force which left Port Colborne for Stevensville on the morning of the 2nd of June, was composed of youths not exceeding, and in many instances not having reached twenty years of age; that a large proportion of the force had been for a very short time accustomed to bear arms; that a somewhat less proportion had not even been exercised with blank cartridge, and that practice with ball cartridge was by very many of the rank and file of that force to be entered upon for the first time in their lives on that day.

That notwithstanding these disadvantages, the Court have, from the evidence produced, arrived at the conviction that no force could have commenced a march with the knowledge that they were advancing into a country occupied by an enemy whose numbers (exaggerated as they were afterwards known to be) were unknown to them, and whose position they might at any moment be called upon to attack, in finer spirits, or a more ready desire to show by obedience to command that they were deserving of the confidence which their employment on the occasion showed was reposed in their courage, and in this respect no difference was perceptible between the mere tyros and the more seasoned men of the expedition.

This the Court find was the state of facts up to the time (which will be referred to in a later part of this opinion) on the arrival of the force under Lieut.-Col. Booker at Ridgeway, on the line of the Buffalo and Lake Huron Railway, and its being formed in open column of companies. The Court find that the order in which it advanced to form a junction with the brigade under Col. Peacocke, of Her Majesty's 16th Regiment, at Stevensville, was as follows:—

The 2nd Battalion (or Queen's Own Rifles) in front, the York Rifles (attached to the Thirteenth Battalion, of which it formed the leading company), the Thirteenth Battalion next, and last the Caledonia Rifle Company, forming the rear guard, the advance guard of the force being No. 5 Company of the Queen's Own, having forty Spencer rifles as part of their armament; and the Court are of opinion that Lieut.-Col. Booker, in advancing, used every precaution by extending companies to skirmish to the right and left of the road by which he was moving his force, which military rule and the nature of the country demanded; and that in the forward movement from Ridgeway, the manner in which it was conducted by Lieut.-Col. Booker and the officers of the force under his orders, was regular, and in accordance with the well-understood rules by which such duties are governed; and here the Court think it their duty to point to the fact that in Lieut.-Col. Booker his force had a commanding officer who, for the first time in his experience, found himself in command of a larger body than one weak battalion on parade; and that this officer, being without the assistance of any staff, and not even accompanied by a mounted officer or orderly to transmit his instructions, was placed in a position of unusual difficulty in the event of coming into contact with the enemy.

The Court have further found, from the evidence adduced before them, that the column under Lieut.-Col. Booker was proceeding in this order and had reached a point on the way leading from Ridgeway to Stevensville, at about two miles from the former point, when the advanced guard became aware that the woods on the right and left fronts of the line of advance were occupied by the enemy; and are further of opinion, that the movements then directed by Lieut.-Col. Booker and the subsequent disposition of the force at his disposal (up to a time to be subsequently mentioned), were in strict accordance with laid down principles, and such as at least to hold an enemy not greatly superior in numbers in check, if not to drive them back —and that the manner in which the movements directed were executed, the advance of the companies of the Queen's Own sent out to strengthen the skirmishers on the left, the advance of the right wing of the Thirteenth Battalion extended on the right of the road, and No. 10 Company of the Queen's Own rather to the right, was highly creditable to the officers and men, particularly as during the whole of these movements the force was under fire from an unseen enemy under cover of the woods, our troops being in open ground and exposed to the effects of such a fire, which fortunately, though well sustained, was not very effective.

The Court is of opinion that to this point the direction of the attack and the position of the attacking force was well and skilfully managed, and the enemy had been forced back to a considerable distance from the position when first encountered.

The Court find that at this time, and when everything looked favorable for the attacking force, there occurred an alarm, of the truth of which a moment's reflection on the part of the men with whom it originated, and who appear to have been some of the advanced skirmishers, would have shown the impossibility. It was to the effect that a force of cavalry was advancing upon our force, and instantly the cry of "Cavalry" spread with electric rapidity from the front to where the Colonel stood in reserve, with which part of the force Lieut.-Col. Booker as commanding officer remained, and thus assuming the cry to have its origin in the fact that that officer gave the order "Look out for cavalry!" squares were formed instantly to meet cavalry, both by the column and by the skirmishers within hearing of that order—a mistake which, being as quickly discovered, Lieut.-Col. Booker endeavored to remedy by the order to "Re-form column."

The Court, with respect to this part of the affair, are of opinion that to adopt the idle rumor that the enemy's force was partly composed of cavalry in a country where such an arm could be of scarcely any value in attack, or to assume, even for a moment, that a mounted corps which he could not see was advancing at such a rate as to render it necessary to give the words of caution which he used, was ill-judged, and was the first act which gave rise to the disorganization of his force, which then followed.

This Court further find that at this moment, and when the officer commanding had, as before mentioned, given the order to "Re-form column," he perceived that the column was rapidly falling back. The attempt to re-form not having been successful, the men became mingled together, and that the effect of the mistake just referred to became so perceptible in the disorganization of the column at a moment when, in the opinion of this Court, to have given the order to advance would have had the best effect in the encouragement of the force, and in a very short period would have effected the rout of the enemy. The officer in command (apparently hesitating as to whether he should advance or retreat) unfortunately gave the order to retire, and the bugles having taken it up at the advanced posts of the attack, our force began to fall back; and notwithstanding the exertions of the officers, who in every case shown in the evidence before the Court behaved in a very steady and energetic manner to rally their broken ranks, the column had retreated too far in the direction of Ridgeway before the advanced parties had all came in to render this possible. This being the state of the force at the time, the officer in command (finding it impossible to rally) with the concurrence of the next senior officer, whom he consulted, decided upon falling back on Port Colborne by the road over which he had advanced.

And the Court lastly finds, that the whole of the wounded and sick were brought with the retreating column, and that it reached Port Colborne suffering much from fatigue and hunger, but without further casualties than those which are already known in the official reports of the affair.

G. T. DENISON,
Colonel, President.

J. SHANLY,
Lieut.-Colonel.

GEO. K. CHISHOLM,
Lieut.-Colonel.

Hamilton, 12th July, 1866.

THE FORT ERIE DISASTER.

REPORT OF PROCEEDINGS OF THE COURT OF INQUIRY APPOINTED TO INVESTIGATE THE CASE OF LIEUT.-COL. J. STOUGHTON DENNIS.

The appointment of a Court of Inquiry to investigate the charges made against Lieut.-Col. J. Stoughton Dennis was granted on the request of that officer himself. From the time that Lieut.-Col. Dennis hastily left his command battling with the Fenians on the streets of Fort Erie, the men of the Welland Canal Field Battery knew him no more, as he never came back. Therefore their relations were strained. Most of the men of the Battery and the Dunnville Naval Brigade were pronounced in their denunciation of his conduct during the fight, and freely expressed their minds in this respect.

When Capt. King's wounds permitted his return home to Port Robinson from the hospital at Buffalo, a large number of people assembled to give him a welcome. In replying to their greetings, Capt. King incidentally made mention of the experience of his Battery in the battle at Fort Erie, and during his remarks voiced the sentiments of his men by publicly accusing Lieut.-Col. Dennis of cowardice. This charge came to the ears of Lieut.-Col. Dennis and he demanded a Court of Inquiry to investigate the matter. In the meantime a formula of six separate charges was filed against Lieut.-Col. Dennis, and His Excellency the Commander-in-Chief appointed the following officers as a Court of Inquiry, viz.:—Col. Geo. T. Denison, President; Lieut.-Col. James Shanly, and Lieut.-Col. S. B. Fairbanks.

The Court assembled in the City Hotel at Fort Erie, on the 8th of November, 1866, for the purpose of taking testimony. Among those who were notified to appear as witnesses were a number of men who had been engaged in the fight as members of the Welland Canal Field Battery and the Dunnville Naval Brigade, besides several citizens.

For some reason four members of the Welland Canal Field Battery who had been summoned to testify were not called upon for their evidence, which they considered a very strange proceed-

ing as they were all present for that purpose, and had evidence
to offer which would tend to substantiate Capt. King's allega-
tions. Eight or ten witnesses were examined, when the Court
proceeded to sum up the evidence and consider the charges
seriatim. The result was that Lieut.-Col. Dennis was exonerated
by the Court, although Col. Geo. T. Denison (the President) dif-
fered from his colleagues on several important points stated in
the charges.

The following is the official report, published in General
Orders, which contains the charges made, the findings and the
remarks of His Excellency the Governor-General on the case:—

VOLUNTEER MILITIA.

HEADQUARTERS, OTTAWA, 14th December, 1866.

GENERAL ORDERS No. 1.

The Court of Inquiry lately assembled at Fort Erie on
application of Lieut.-Colonel Dennis, having presented its report,
the Commander-in-Chief directs that the several charges preferred against that officer, with the opinion of the Court of
Inquiry thereupon, be published for general information.

CHARGES.

1st Charge.—With having at Fort Erie on the afternoon of
the 2nd June last, after having received information that an
overwhelming force of the enemy was advancing on and was
within a very short distance of that place, evinced an utter
disregard for the lives and safety of the officers and men of the
Welland Canal Field Battery, and the safekeeping of a large
number of Fenian prisoners in charge of that corps and the
Dunnville Naval Brigade, in this: that he ordered billets to be
prepared for the Battery and told the officer commanding it
that he should leave it and the prisoners in Fort Erie and go
on himself to Port Colborne with the Dunnville Naval Brigade
with the steamer "Robb," then lying at a wharf in Fort Erie.

2nd Charge.—With having at Fort Erie on the afternoon
of the 2nd June last, after he had received information that a
large and overwhelming force of the enemy was within a very
short distance from his command, and that his command was
in danger of being destroyed or captured, and after having himself seen that force approaching, recklessly and uselessly landed

5 officers and 68 men of the Welland Canal Field Battery and Dunnville Naval Brigade from the steamer "Robb," marched them along an exposed road, and posted them in a most dangerous position, where they were exposed to a front and flanking fire from the enemy, which course on his part resulted in disaster to his command, the serious wounding and maiming (some of them for life) of an officer and five men, and the capture by the enemy of four officers and thirty-two men of that command.

3rd Charge.—With having at Fort Erie on the afternoon of the 2nd June last, after having placed his command in the dangerous position described in Charge No. 2, and when a force of the enemy greatly superior in numbers to his command was within a very short distance from and advancing upon his left flank, and another force of the enemy far stronger than the one first herein mentioned was within a very short distance of and advancing against his front and preparing to flank his right, the whole force of the enemy being overwhelming and numbering 500 or 600 men, while his command only numbered 5 officers and 68 men, neither ordering a retreat to the steamer "Robb," which there was ample time to effect, and whereby his whole command might have been saved, nor allowing a fire to be opened on the enemy, but on the contrary, neglecting to give orders for a retreat, and directing that no order to fire should be given.

4th Charge.—With having, at Fort Erie, on the afternoon of the 2nd June last, after he had placed his command in the dangerous and exposed position described in the preceding charges, and given the order not to fire as therein mentioned, disgracefully, in the face of the enemy, and in order to secure his personal safety, deserted his command and left it without orders of any kind.

5th Charge.—With having, on or about the 4th June last, in a certain report of his proceedings addressed to Colonel Lowry, commanding the Niagara frontier, untruly, and knowing it to be untrue, stated that, having advanced to meet the enemy at Fort Erie on the 2nd June last, he did, in order to save the prisoners then on board the tug "Robb" and prevent the enemy from obtaining possession of that vessel, order the Captain of that vessel to cast off and get into the stream, and ordered his (Colonel Dennis') men (meaning his command, landed as aforesaid) to retreat and do the best they could to get away, each man for himself, when in reality he did not give such orders, and had at the time of which he alleges he gave them, deserted his command.

6th Charge.—That he was guilty of misconduct at Fort Erie on the afternoon of the 2nd June last, in this, that having received information that an overwhelming body of the enemy was then within a very short distance of and advancing against Fort Erie, and in fact seen that body himself, he should and might, instead of placing his command then at Fort Erie in the dangerous position described in Charge No. 2, have embarked it in the steamer "Robb," so protected that vessel with materials at hand that she would have been proof against the fire and weapons of the enemy, and dropping into the stream, held the enemy in check without any casualty to his command, and prevented them from escaping to the United States before the arrival of a force sufficiently strong to capture them.

The Court having proceeded to the examination of the evidence brought forward against the accused, as well as what he has offered in exculpation, and having duly considered the same, are of—

OPINION.

As to the 1st Charge.—That the allegation that Lieut.-Colonel Dennis, after having received information of the near approach of an overwhelming force, made arrangements for billeting his men at Fort Erie, thereby raising the inference that in so acting he evinced disregard for the lives of the officers and men of the party under his command, is not sustained. And that of the part of this charge attributing to Lieut.-Colonel Dennis an expressed intention (with or without such information as he is alleged to have had) of leaving a part of his command at Fort Erie and taking the steamer and remainder of the force to Port Colborne, there is not any evidence whatever in support.

As to 2nd Charge.—That this charge, based on the assertion not only that the accused officer was in possession of certain information, but had actual personal knowledge of the approach of a large and overwhelming force of the enemy, is not sustained by the evidence before the Court. On the contrary, with reference to the alleged knowledge of that fact, the Court is of opinion that the rumors which immediately before his party was disembarked to repel any attack on the village of Fort Erie, were, in so far as regarded the strength of the enemy's force, so much at variance with previously received information of a definite nature, as to be disbelieved not only by Lieut.-Colonel Dennis, but to some extent by the officers who have preferred the charges against him. And it appears to the Court that it was only after he had got his men into position, and after they had come into actual contact with the enemy, that the great superiority in numbers of the attacking force became a matter of certainty.

As to the 3rd Charge.—That this charge, being also grounded upon certain knowledge alleged to have been in the possession of Lieut.-Colonel Dennis at a particular time with respect to the great superiority of the enemy's force, and that whilst possessing that knowledge, and there being time to avail himself of the line of retreat alleged to have been open to him, he neglected to do so, is not sustained by the evidence before the Court. And with reference to the remainder of this charge as to the aforesaid officer not allowing a fire to be opened upon the enemy, but on the contrary directing that no order to fire should be given, the Court are further of opinion that this part of the charge is not only not sustained, but is refuted by the evidence offered on behalf of Lieut.-Colonel Dennis.

As to the 4th Charge.—That with reference to the grave accusations contained in this charge, the Court are of opinion that throughout the whole of the affair, and up to the moment when he ascertained from personal observation that the enemy was on the point of cutting off his command by an overwhelming force, the dispositions of his party and the orders given by Lieut.-Colonel Dennis were carried out and given in a perfectly collected and regular manner, and that on the retreat of his force his position was not such as to warrant the use of the language in which this charge has been framed, nor did Lieut.-Colonel Dennis, as alleged, leave his force without orders, and that therefore not only is this charge not sustained, but this

Court are further of opinion that the imputation contained herein against Lieut.-Colonel Dennis is by no means supported by the evidence.

As to the 5th Charge.—That as to this charge nothing which has transpired in the evidence offered before this Court having varied the report made by Lieut.-Colonel Dennis to Colonel Lowry, the officer commanding on the Niagara frontier, as published in the Gazette of the 23rd of June last, and finding that the statements therein contained are fully supported by evidence before the Court, this Court are further of opinion that this charge is not sustained.

As to the 6th Charge.—That with reference to the allegation of misconduct on the part of Lieut.-Colonel Dennis contained in this charge, the officers preferring it, having based that assertion on an opinion which they appear to have formed as to the course which ought to have been, but was not adopted by Lieut.-Colonel Dennis with the force at his disposal, the Court are of opinion that although subsequent events and results may have properly led to the conclusion that such a course might have resulted in the manner alleged in the charge, no charge of misconduct in not adopting such a course is sustained, first, because it does not appear from the evidence that at the time when it is alleged that this course might have been successfully adopted, the officer in command had foreseen occasion for it. And also because it is by no means clear to the Court that there was time after he became aware of the vicinity of the enemy to have taken the steps suggested in this charge.

(Signed) GEO. T. DENISON,
Colonel, President.

J. SHANLY,
Lieut.-Colonel.

S. B. FAIRBANKS,
Lieut.-Colonel.

Fort Erie, 8th November, 1866.

———

Colonel Denison, the President, having been overruled by the majority of the Court, has signed the proceedings as its

President. and now desires to express his dissent from the finding of the majority for the following reasons:—

Second Charge.—That as to the first allegation, "that he had received information that a large and overwhelming force of the enemy was within a very short distance from his command, and that his command was in danger of being captured," it appears to be proved by the evidence that this fact is established. The evidence of Drill Instructor McCracken, Lieutenant McDonald. Henry Cole, Thomas Carlisle, Lieutenant Nimmo, and of Lewis Palmer, show clearly that messenger after messenger arrived with this information, that most of the officers and men were aware of it, and that the remonstrances of Capt. King and Capt. McCallum show not only their appreciation of the danger. but also afford the strongest presumption that Lieut.-Colonel Dennis must have been aware of it before he marched his command off the dock. This is also further established by the admission of Lieut.-Colonel Dennis in his "Statement of Facts" submitted to the Court, that he himself, after hearing the report. saw at least one hundred and fifty of the enemy before landing his men. and his further statement of his having sent word to the "Robb" to secure the boat and prisoners in case he was overpowered. and his having withdrawn his men from Ramsford's Corner to a position near the "Robb." all prove the evidence of doubts in his mind as to whether he had sufficient strength in his command to successfully resist the force which he was informed was about to attack him. And as to the remainder of the second charge the evidence proves it conclusively.

Third Charge.—Colonel Denison also dissents from the finding of the Court upon the third charge. as he is of opinion that the third charge is proved. with the exception that the allegation that Lieut.-Colonel Dennis did not allow a fire to be opened on the enemy. On this point there is a certain amount of rebutting evidence. although the weight of evidence seems to support the charge.

(Signed) GEO. T. DENISON.

Colonel. President.

Fort Erie. 8th November. 1866.

With respect to the foregoing charges and opinion, and to the evidence generally taken by the Court of Inquiry, His Excellency directs the publication of the following remarks:

1. Although the order for the assembly of the Court was general in its terms, the special memorandum of instructions furnished for the guidance of the President and members, stated that the Court was assembled to give Lieut.-Col. Dennis an opportunity of refuting charges which had been "made against his personal conduct on the 2nd June, at Fort Erie," and directed the reception of any evidence which might tend to elucidate the truth.

2. The only one of the above six charges which, strictly speaking, the Court was required to consider, was the 4th, which imputed disgraceful and cowardly conduct to the accused officer.

3. His Excellency approves of the opinion of the Court with respect to the 1st, 3rd, 4th, 5th and 6th charges.

4. With respect to the second charge, His Excellency is of opinion that Lieut.-Col. Dennis committed an error in judgment in removing the small force under his command, from the means of secure retreat afforded by the steamer, before he had ascertained with some degree of certainty the probable force of the enemy, of whose near approach he was informed; but if the accusation made against Lieut.-Col. Dennis in this charge be correct, that he did so remove his force from the shelter of the steamer for the purpose of attacking an enemy, whose numbers he knew to be overwhelming—the proceeding savours rather of rashness than of timidity. Had Lieut.-Col. Dennis been the coward which his accusers would have the public believe, he would in such a case have eagerly availed himself of the remonstrances which it is stated were made to him, to return with the men under his command to the deck of the steamer.

5. The first charge being one of imputed intention only, the fulfilment of which it was not attempted to establish, was not a proper charge for investigation by any Court.

6. The sixth charge is also an improper charge to have preferred or investigated. No Commanding Officer would be safe

if his subordinates could be allowed to frame a charge of misconduct against him for not having adopted a particular course, which, judging deliberately after the event, his accusers might think to have been advisable. There is no pretence that the course which Lieut.-Col. Dennis is accused of misconduct for not adopting, was suggested to him and rejected.